"*Walk, Eat, Repeat* is both a glorious guide to the joys and hardships of the legendary trail, and a moving personal memoir. It also reminds us of the importance of putting one foot in front of the other, whether on the trail or in life."

    —DON GILLMOR, author of *To the River: Losing My Brother*

"There are few activities as foundational as walking, eating, and connecting with others around the table. Lindy Mechefske brings us along on a delicious adventure, sharing recipes inspired by the people and places we meet along the way."

    —JULIE VAN ROSENDAAL, author of *Out of the Orchard: Recipes for Fresh Fruit from the Sunny Okanagan*

Also by Lindy Mechefske

Ontario Picnics: A Century of Dining Outdoors

Out of Old Ontario Kitchens

Sir John's Table: The Culinary Life and Times
of Canada's First Prime Minister

A Taste of Wintergreen

Walk, Eat, Repeat

Culinary Adventures
on the Camino de Santiago

LINDY MECHEFSKE

Edited by Simon Thibault.
Copy edited by Naomi K. Lewis and Jess Shulman.
Cover and page design by Julie Scriver.
Cover image by Lindy Mechefske.
Map by Nicola Ross, nicolaross.ca.
Printed in Canada by Marquis.
10 9 8 7 6 5 4 3 2 1

Goose Lane Editions acknowledges the generous
support of the Government of Canada, the Canada
Council for the Arts, and the Government of New
Brunswick.

Goose Lane Editions is located on the unceded
territory of the Wəlastəkwiyik whose ancestors
along with the Mi'kmaq and Peskotomuhkati
Nations signed Peace and Friendship Treaties
with the British Crown in the 1700s.

Goose Lane Editions
500 Beaverbrook Court, Suite 330
Fredericton, New Brunswick
CANADA E3B 5X4
gooselane.com

Library and Archives Canada Cataloguing
in Publication

Title: Walk, eat, repeat : culinary adventures on the
Camino de Santiago / Lindy Mechefske.
Names: Mechefske, Lindy, author.
Description: Includes bibliographical references
and index.
Identifiers: Canadiana (print) 20230582656 | Canadiana
(ebook) 20230582893 | ISBN 9781773103280 (softcover) |
ISBN 9781773103297 (EPUB)
Subjects: LCSH: Mechefske, Lindy—Travel—Spain—
Camino Francés. | LCSH: Spain, Northern—Description
and travel. | LCSH: Christian pilgrims and pilgrimages—
Spain—Santiago de Compostela. | LCSH: Camino
Francés (Spain) | LCSH: Cooking, Spanish. | LCGFT:
Travel writing. | LCGFT: Cookbooks.
Classification: LCC DP285 .M43 2024 | DDC 914.6/
10484—dc23

The author and the publisher have made every effort
to ensure that the information contained in this guide
is as accurate as possible. Neither the author nor the
publisher accept any liability, implied or otherwise,
for accident, loss, injury, inconvenience, or any other
damage that may be sustained by anyone using the
information contained in this book. Those who rely on
the information contained herein do so at their own risk.

MIX
Paper from
responsible sources
FSC
www.fsc.org   FSC® C103567

For Chris, Laura, and Elly, with endless love and gratitude

Contents

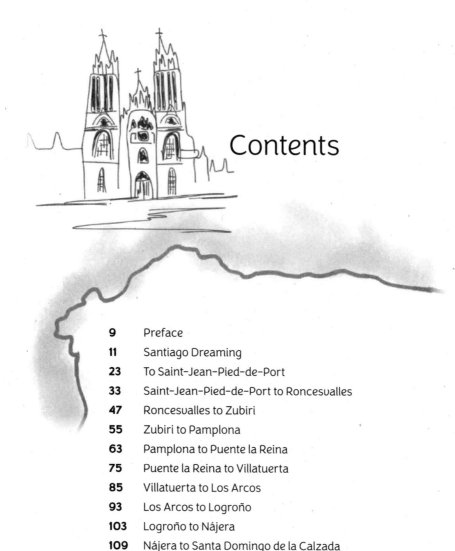

9   Preface

11   Santiago Dreaming

23   To Saint-Jean-Pied-de-Port

33   Saint-Jean-Pied-de-Port to Roncesvalles

47   Roncesvalles to Zubiri

55   Zubiri to Pamplona

63   Pamplona to Puente la Reina

75   Puente la Reina to Villatuerta

85   Villatuerta to Los Arcos

93   Los Arcos to Logroño

103 Logroño to Nájera

109 Nájera to Santa Domingo de la Calzada

117 Santa Domingo de la Calzada to Belorado

125 Belorado to Agés

133 Agés to Burgos to Hornillos del Camino

147 Hornillos del Camino to Itero de la Vega

155 Itero de la Vega to Carrión de los Condes

163 Carrión de los Condes to Terradillos de
     los Templarios

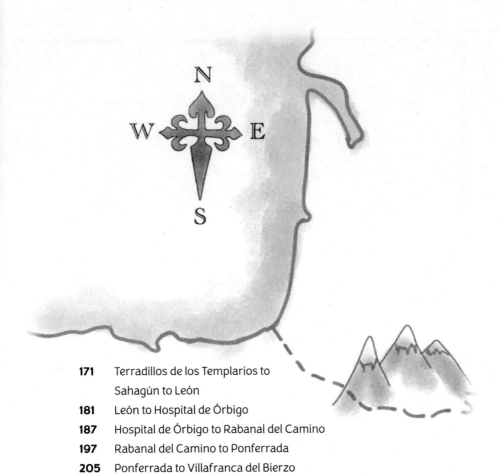

171   Terradillos de los Templarios to
          Sahagún to León
181   León to Hospital de Órbigo
187   Hospital de Órbigo to Rabanal del Camino
197   Rabanal del Camino to Ponferrada
205   Ponferrada to Villafranca del Bierzo
213   Villafranca del Bierzo to O Cebreiro
223   O Cebreiro to Samos
233   Samos to Ferreiros
243   Ferreiros to Palas de Rei
249   Palas de Rei to Arzúa
255   Arzúa to O Pedrouzo
261   O Pedrouzo to Santiago de Compostela
267   Homeward Bound

275   Acknowledgements
277   Packing List
279   A Short Glossary of Spanish Food and Beverage Terms
281   Notes
283   Index of Recipes

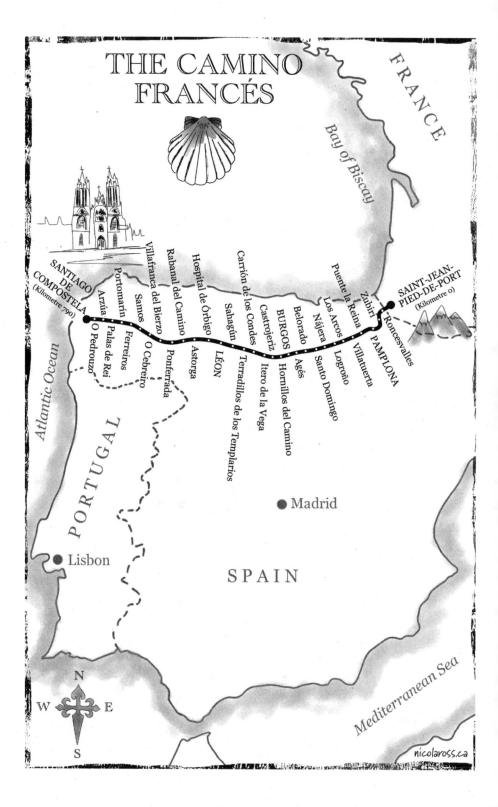

THE CAMINO FRANCÉS

FRANCE

Bay of Biscay

SANTIAGO DE COMPOSTELA
(Kilometre 790)

SAINT-JEAN-PIED-DE-PORT
(Kilometre 0)

Villafranca del Bierzo
Portomarín
Rabanal del Camino
Arzúa
Hospital de Órbigo
Samos
O Cebreiro
Carrión de los Condes
Ferreiros
O Pedrouzo
Palas de Rei
Ponferrada
Astorga
Sahagún
Castrojeriz
Puente la Reina
Zubiri
Roncesvalles
Terradillos de los Templarios
LÉON
Itero de la Vega
BURGOS
Belorado
Los Arcos
Nájera
Villatuerta
PAMPLONA
Hornillos del Camino
Agés
Logroño
Santo Domingo

Atlantic Ocean

PORTUGAL

Madrid

Lisbon

SPAIN

Mediterranean Sea

N
W   E
S

nicolaross.ca

Preface

For at least six million years, we human beings have been bipedal. The ability to stand upright and walk on two feet was the first major morphological change that separated humans from our primate ancestors. Walking upright is a defining characteristic of humans. It's fundamental to our existence. We stood up on two feet and walked everywhere. We walked upright so that we could more effectively gather food in our arms. In a sense, this is who we are as a species: we walk, eat, sleep, repeat.

Between five and seven million years ago, our earliest human ancestors took to their feet and became nomads.[1] Then, around twelve thousand years ago, came the first origins of agriculture, and with that came domesticated animals. Until a mere two hundred or so years ago, walking was the main means of transportation for most of the global population. It's only since the Industrial Revolution that we have largely stopped walking as a primary means of transport and propel ourselves mechanically instead.

We lose something by not walking.

We lose a simple, fundamental, and organic connection to the Earth itself. Having our feet on the ground is the simplest definition of what it means to feel grounded. We find this connection when we start walking again. And along with that, we find so much more.

What I found on the Camino—the collective name for all the various pilgrimage routes leading to Santiago de Compostela in Spain—walking, as I was, on layers of history, was a return to basic human needs. My life was reduced to little more than walking and eating.

We are the only species that consistently walks upright and cooks its food, and these two uniquely human activities[2] are so primal, so fundamental, that it seems their stories belong together. I began to think about how these two intensely elemental actions are wrapped up in each other, how they feed each other, linking us to places both geographic and spiritual.

Along the ancient trail, I broke bread and shared wine with people whose language was not my own. I drank coffee with complete strangers, joined people I didn't know at dinner, and plucked figs from trees along the path. I pulled chunks of chorizo, Manchego cheese, and rustic breads from my backpack. Snacked on huge green manzanilla olives and the sweetest oranges, on classic Spanish tortilla de patatas, on empanadas layered with cured meats, sundried tomatoes, and olive tapenade encased in beautiful, buttery pastry. I ate chocolate daily and shared it with anyone near at hand and quenched my thirst with water from centuries-old fountains and drank red wine almost nightly. I found a huge sense of healing, intense feelings of well-being, gratitude, joy.

Walking is propulsion. It is freedom. It is a commanding deceleration. By its very nature, walking is slow, deliberate, and grounding; it invites thinking. We walk for the sheer physicality. For exercise. We walk to get from one place to another. The further and longer we walk, the more we realize we walk to reconnect with the Earth, with the natural world, with our history, with our species, with our own bodies. We walk for enlightenment, for knowledge, for the powerful spiritual, medicinal, and meditative aspects. For the clarifying effects. We walk to give our lives meaning. We walk because it is purposeful. We walk to experience nature's transcendent beauty. We walk to find courage.

We walk because it is who we are.

CHAPTER ONE

Santiago Dreaming

"Midway on my journey through life, I woke to find myself alone
in a dark wood."—Dante Alighieri, *Inferno* Canto 1

Spain beckons. I am studying maps, making checklists, and endlessly researching the most appropriate hiking equipment. For years, I have been thinking
about walking the Camino de Santiago. I have read several books about the
long walk across Spain. Some, twice. One of them, three times over. I make
notes with each book, compile whatever invaluable, critical information I can
find, and on a photocopied trail map, in tiny print, I painstakingly note all the
recommended places to stay and those to avoid.

I am obsessed with the transformative power of walking, drawn to the path,
the trail, the walk, the hike, the trek. But more than anything, I am hooked on
the idea of the physical journey as a mechanism for sorting out an inner journey, of walking as a path to sanity, to clarity, and the idea of both following and
making trails in my own life. I am fixated on the profound relationship between
walking and thinking. I need this long walk to find my way again.

I am in a state of transition, having spent decades moving between countries
and continents, leaving great chunks of myself behind with every move. I have
started from scratch over and over, never feeling that I truly belonged anywhere.
My life spent working in various writing and editing jobs at universities has
amounted to mere fragments of a career, that seem barely threaded together.
My long marriage has fallen apart. My father, the intrepid mountaineer and

long-distance walker, has fallen to cancer. My mother has been diagnosed with Parkinson's disease and is disappearing in increments. And my children have grown up and left home.

For as long as I have known about El Camino de Santiago de Compostela—which loosely translated means, The Way of Saint James of the Field of Stars[3]—I've been besotted with the idea of this ancient trail that follows beneath the path of the Milky Way, a trail lit at night by a band of starlight thought to contain one hundred billion planets and as many as four hundred billion stars.

Known by the short forms El Camino, The Way, or simply the Camino, there are many routes to Santiago, all of them legitimate pilgrimages, and all of them converging at the magnificent Cathedral of Santiago de Compostela, where it is widely believed the remains of Spain's patron saint, Saint James the Apostle, are buried. St. James was one of Christ's twelve disciples and is thought to have been Christ's cousin. He was beheaded in Jerusalem in 44 CE, before his remains were spirited away to Spain. For over a thousand years, pilgrims have walked this route to pay homage to St. James the patron saint of Spain, who was thought to have once defended the nation against the invading Islamic Moors.

But well before Christ, and long, long before Christians claimed the route, the Celtic Druids of Iberia are thought to have forged this path under the stars towards Finisterre—the rocky, rugged peninsula plunging into the sea—then believed to be a pagan sun altar and the end of the world. The varying theories about the earliest history of the Camino trail suggest it may have been a path of initiation for the Druids, who made their way past rivers, through forests, and over mountains, creating a trail by using their maps of the heavens. Druids were the highest-ranking members of Celtic society—the religious, medical, legal, and political authorities of their era. But because the Celts did not use the written word, they left no account of themselves. Without scholars like Pliny the Elder, 23–79 CE, who wrote about the Celtic Druids in Iberia, there would be little record of the Druids at all.[4]

Pliny was a diligent documenter, churning out thirty-seven encyclopedic volumes of information of varying accuracy about the natural world. He was the first-century equivalent of the internet—the source of all knowledge, right and wrong. Amongst a vast array of topics, Pliny wrote about God (fifty-seven times); onions (thirty-one times); vomiting (thirty-one times); carbuncles (thirteen times); quince (seven times); mushrooms and toadstools; a perfume made of hair of the hare; avoiding drunkenness; hydrophobia; adders, earth- quakes; and Pythagoras (thirty-one times).[5] Pythagoras, Pliny said, had written an entire volume about onions and their medicinal virtues and properties, which Pliny himself meant, "to deliver upon in the next booke."[6]

But it is not the pathway of the Celtic Druids, nor the Romans that followed; nor Pliny or the remains of Saint James; nor a desire to shore up my floundering faith that calls me to walk the ancient trail. What I am drawn to is the idea of a long, hard, slow walk.

I think of walking as medicine—the cure for all that ails us. I am drawn by the compelling lure of travelling so far on foot, of being part of a community that stretches backwards and forwards in time across hundreds and hundreds of miles and hundreds if not thousands of years through layers of civilization and antiquity. I am intrigued with Goethe's idea that Europe grew up along the pilgrimage roads that led to Santiago. Enticed by the fact that the Camino is living human history. What I want is the distillation of self, the focus on nothing more than forward movement and the momentum of self. I am curious to learn more about a trail so imbued with spiritual power and meaning, and illuminated at night by the Milky Way.

It is the Camino Frances that I am drawn to—the oldest known path to Santiago, a route first described in the twelfth-century manuscript known as the *Codex Calixtinus*, a work intended as an early guide to pilgrims following the Way of St. James. The trail begins in the small village of Saint-Jean-Pied- de-Port, France (hence the name Camino Frances), and then meanders west across mountains and plains for nearly eight hundred kilometres, ending in Santiago de Compostela, Spain. The Camino Frances is also the most heavily travelled route to Santiago and so offers more in the way of facilities and com- pany—both of which strike me as important, especially as a female who is likely to be travelling much of the long trail alone.

I picture days spent crossing mountain ranges and big open fields and nights spent sitting in cafés drinking silky-smooth Spanish wine, eating tapas and rustic Spanish stews. And of mornings drinking cortados or café con leche and eating croissants a la plancha.

I go to Camino information sessions and take Spanish language lessons at night school, repeating after Carola, our instructor, a grad student from Peru: mi esposo—my husband. Mi esposa—my wife. Mi amiga—my friend. Un vecino—a neighbour. We conjugate verbs and speak awkward formal sentences badly to each other. Me llamo Lindy. ¿Como te llamas? My name is Lindy. What is your name? Su esposa es pediatra. His wife is a pediatrician.

At night, I sit up in bed, peering at the Duolingo app on my cellphone. Spanish is much easier when no one is listening. "Los gatos beben leche. Los perros beben agua." The cats drink milk. The dogs drink water. I repeat the words aloud, over and over, perfecting my lousy Spanish accent. If I need to talk about the drinking habits of cats and dogs while I am in Spain, I am ready.

If ever there was a good time to take a long walk, this is it.

I come, after all, from a long line of roamers and trampers and mad keen hikers. For as far back as I can trace, very likely dating back to the Viking invasion of the north of England in 793 CE, my ancestors lived and roamed in the rugged Yorkshire moors. A beautiful, wild, desolate place of heather clad rolling hills, dissected by deep green valleys. A landscape perfectly suited to long days of solitary tramping.

A memory: I was barely five years old and newly transplanted to North America. My father, an engineer by week and mountaineer by weekend, was luring me up Mount Marcy in the Adirondack Mountains of New York State. I was kitted out with hiking boots, a small khaki green canvas knapsack containing an aluminum water flask, a raincoat, and a tiny pearl-handled penknife, and a child-sized walking stick that my father had whittled from a fallen branch. When I began to flag, he doled out peppermints, mini Mars Bars, and small red boxes of Sun-Maid raisins. He alternated between praising me, coaxing me, and sternly ordering me onwards.

"Soldier on," he said when I whined, which was often. So, I soldiered. But there were times when I shed tears. My frail five-year-old legs quaky, my heart thumping and hammering in my chest.

We made it to the summit, though failure had never been an option. Afterwards, we set up camp in a lean-to and ate a dinner of packaged Knorr oxtail soup cooked on a tiny portable backpacking stove, along with rye bread and big hunks of cheese that my father cut with his jackknife. I fell asleep before dark, while my father lit a fire and reassured me that the fire would keep the bears away during the night.

I learned early that physical exertion brings rewards, even when I was far too young to understand them: what it means to feel grounded, to be connected to the earth, to revel in the strength of my own body or to feel the curative powers of walking.

Every time I go to book my trip to Spain, my heart lurches and hammers and pounds. I hesitate, and snap my laptop closed. I'm not ready to walk that path. I will know when the time is right, I tell myself.

I will go in spring, I say, because spring is when everything comes alive, with forests and fields full of exquisite tender new growth in various hues of green. But once again spring passes, and I tell my friends I will go in the autumn, because the weather is apt to be more stable, and the trail will be less busy. Come autumn, I am hunkered down at my desk, meeting a book deadline. Next spring, I say once again. But when spring comes, I am working on another book and attending a writing retreat.

It is dangerously easy to procrastinate, and there are so many reasons to do so. I push my departure date back. Several times, in fact, over a couple of years. Each time, I legitimize my decision. It is because of very real work and family commitments. Because of my frail, elderly mother. Because of my big shaggy, needy dog. My daughters' university graduations or birthdays. Because the trail will be too busy. Because the weather might be too hot. Or too cold. Or too wet. Because I haven't done enough research. Or preparation. Because I don't have all my equipment.

On what seems to me like a mere whim, a friend suddenly announces she is going to walk the Camino. She leaves in mid-July—the absolute hottest and busiest time on the trail. I wonder if she is well enough prepared. She acquires much of her equipment in a mass buying spree. I worry that her equipment will be all wrong. That once she is on the Camino, she won't find beds for the night because of the sheer staggering volume of people on the trail. I fear that she will melt in the intense heat of the Spanish summer. That she has not properly broken in her boots. I shake my head. No good can come of this, I think to myself while nodding affirmatively as she tells me her plans. I am worried about her. Or possibly I'm just prone to overthinking everything and maybe even envy her courage and free-spirited nature.

She is undaunted by the travels, by the long walk, the heat, the lack of planning. She posts stunningly beautiful photographs of her travels on social media.

She returns glowing, triumphant, joyful. She has had the most wonderful, informative, clarifying, and powerful time of her life.

Still, I waver, alternating between desperately wanting to go and not wanting to go yet. The employees at my local hiking store are starting to recognize me. I've already bought and returned three pairs of boots after test-walking them around inside my house. I've sat at my computer writing in hiking boots, I've cooked dinner and done laundry in hiking boots. I reject them all—they are too tight, or too loose, or too stiff, or just don't feel right. I am determined to find the perfect boots, because more than anything else, I believe that the right boots are critical. I've done enough long-distance walking to know that boots alone can make or break the journey. I finally settle on an expensive but sporty pair of lightweight purple hiking boots and then pick up a fantastic ultra-stylish purple Swedish-made backpack that I am smitten with. The boots are a perfect fit, the most comfortable pair yet, and an exact colour match to the backpack. The cashier who rings in my purchases asks me, with what sounds like a note of disdain, if I made my choices based on the colour. I refrain from mentioning that they are the fourth pair of boots I have purchased. And that they are the first purple pair. The pack is one I have been eyeing for some time. Not only is it a perfect match for my boots, but it has also just been reduced in price. I am committed to this pack, these boots—they will not be returned. It seems that I, myself, have perhaps finally reached a turning point.

I already have a packable down jacket, a microfibre towel, and a compact, lightweight sleeping bag. After an inordinate amount of time spent studying the pros and cons of ponchos versus rain jackets and pants, I finally decide on buying the latter—a decision I end up regretting on the trail, primarily because of the weight. I will come to learn that almost everyone along the way seems to regret their choice of raingear. Those with ponchos liked them until they had to walk in the wind, when they said their ponchos were either full-time slapping them in the face or lifting up like a parachute in the wind. Others said that their flapping nylon ponchos made such a racket in the rain and wind that they couldn't hear themselves think. Or that they were as wet or wetter under their ponchos as they might have been if they just walked naked through the rain. The descriptions made me laugh out loud. The truth is, there's no perfect solution, and walking in the pouring rain and wind is far from ideal, no matter what gear you've got. Best to buy whatever you like and hope for sunshine and good weather.

I sort the one set of clothes I will wear, along with one spare quick-dry T-shirt and a spare pair of ultra-light hiking pants that also zip off into shorts. I have three pairs of fast-drying underwear and three pairs of wool socks. The right socks, like the right boots, are critical for avoiding blisters and other foot problems that plague long-distance walkers. I have flip-flops to wear in the shower. My passport and a pilgrim passport known as a Credencial del Peregrino—the small, folded booklet that will enable me to stay in hostels, known as either refugios or, more recently, as albergues, along the way. I have a thin Moleskine notebook and a couple of pens. My guidebook. A compact medical kit. A pillowcase. A small bag of toiletries, laundry detergent, a folding brush, hand wipes, lipstick, mascara, toothbrush, a few clothes pegs, safety pins, and earplugs. Sunglasses, of course. An eye mask for sleeping. Phone and charger and super compact Canon camera. A battered paperback copy of Hemingway's *The Sun Also Rises*. A pair of cotton leggings that will double as both pyjamas and emergency pants. Half a dozen granola bars. One large chocolate bar—dark chocolate, fondant-filled. Two empty five hundred millilitre water bottles. A large stylish lightweight scarf for wearing over my sweater to go out at night. A polar fleece hat. A pair of micro gloves.[7]

When I try to pack my rucksack, it quickly becomes obvious that I have far too much gear, and it weighs more than the recommended ten percent of my body weight. I spend hours pre-emptively packing and repacking my rucksack. There is seemingly nothing left to remove, and still it feels too heavy.

One by one I take things out and weigh the pack again between each extraction. Even two hundred grams can make a difference. First goes the chocolate. Which I promptly eat. Then the leggings, the book (farewell, Hemingway), the shampoo, the small, overpriced packages of laundry detergent, lipstick, mascara, flip-flops, and large scarf. I have two scales going. My regular one on which I weigh myself (now with my pack on) and my tiny kitchen weigh scale. On the kitchen scale, I check the weight of individual items, balancing things like pairs of pants and flip-flops on the small platform. Finally, my pack is down to seven kilograms, and I can swing it about with ease. By the time I add water and food each day, it will weigh at least another five hundred grams. There is nothing further that I can shed.

I am set to go. I have used every excuse I can think of to not go. Except the real one. I know full well what is stopping me. I am terrified of flying.

The irony is that I've spent my life flying. I was born on an overseas business trip and have crossed oceans and continents my entire life. My fears were intensified by a series of horrible incidents on planes: a fire on an airplane over the vast South Pacific hundreds of miles from landfall; forced emergency landings; violent passengers. A miscarriage en route from Australia to Fiji. I was the one miscarrying, folded over in the tiny toilet cubicle, my body shuddering, gripped by pain and fear and sorrow, and managing to blame myself for flying pregnant. I decide once again against going.

I don't need to walk the Camino. There are plenty of walks much closer to home. I start listing them in my head to remind myself of everything that doesn't require a flight path. The Bruce Trail in Ontario is practically on my doorstep, and I've already walked most of it, so finishing it should be a breeze. The Rideau Trail is even closer, and I could embark on becoming an Adirondack 46er, climbing the forty-six highest peaks in the range. The Trans Canada Trail. The Appalachian Trail. The Pacific Crest Trail. Then, remembering Cheryl Strayed's *Wild*, I quickly rule out the Pacific Crest Trail. Way too hard. With bears.

And then I catch myself. I have everything I need to do this trip: two feet, a heartbeat, and a well-organized pack. I am letting my full-on, brutal, stomach-churning fear stand in the way of my dreams. The very thing I've preached relentlessly to my children never to do.

"When in doubt, eat," I can hear my late father say. I head to the kitchen and churn out traditional Spanish dishes instead. A classic lemon and olive oil cake; tortilla de patatas; caldo Gallego—the traditional Galician soup made with hardy greens, pork, beans, and potatoes; empanadas washed down with Spanish wine; gambas a la plancha—pan-grilled shrimp with olive oil, lemon, and salt; and a dreamy slow-cooked Catalan beef stew rich with tomatoes and olives.

When I exhaust my Spanish culinary repertoire, I borrow every Spanish cookbook from the library and continue exploring the cuisine of Spain, a country whose history is rich, fraught, and complex. Whose remarkable culinary history includes layer upon layer of civilizations, cultures, and faiths from the Stone Age hunters to the Druids to the Greeks, Romans, and Visigoths to the Berbers of North Africa, the Moors of Morocco and the Phoenicians, the Muslims, Jews, and Arabs of the Middle East, and Christians including Roman Catholics and the Knights Templar. All have left their culinary mark. Even General Francisco Franco, the military dictator who ruled over Spain from 1939 to 1975, left a lasting impact on Spanish cuisine, when he required by law that all Spanish restaurants offer a low-cost menu del dia: a three-course meal served with wine and water. The law stands to this day. The menu del dia guarantees that dining and drinking in Spain is a remarkably affordable prospect.

I knew it would be hard to visit Spain without falling in love with Spanish cuisine. The Spanish take eating seriously and value food immensely, and as a result, Spain is one of the world's truly great food cultures. Spain is also one of the world's most accessible, affordable food democracies. It is a place settled as many as thirty-five thousand years ago by the pre-Roman Iron Age cultures that controlled most of Iberia: the Iberians, Celtiberians, Tartessians, Lusitanians, and Vascones. They were joined by the Phoenicians, Carthaginians, and Greeks of the Mediterranean coast, plus the Basques, and the Moors and Visigoths, and various other Europeans including Jews and Christians. All brought their foods and set about growing, gathering, and cultivating more.

Spain is the world's biggest producer of olive oil[8] and the world's third largest producer of wine.[9] It produces almost all its own livestock, dairy, and produce and is also the largest producer of frozen seafood in the European Union. Most of Spain lives on the Mediterranean diet—a diet based on fruits, vegetables, plenty of legumes, fish and seafood, liberal amounts of heart-healthy olive oil, small quantities of meat, whole grains, red wine, and very little processed food. The Spanish love affair with tapas means that they are accustomed to eating sensibly small servings of remarkably delicious, healthy, flavourful food. Though fast food does exist in Spain, it is neither prevalent nor particularly popular. One could walk for days without seeing any kind of fast-food outlet or chain restaurant.

With its myriad of influences from the Ancient Greeks and Romans to the Phoenicians, North African Moors, and early Jewish communities dating as far back as 70 CE, Spanish cuisine may well be the earliest fusion food culture. Spain's remarkable history and diverse geography show up over and over in the wonderful variety of flavours found in its foods and abundance of restaurants, including the world's oldest continually operating restaurant, Sobrino de Botín, established in Madrid in 1725. Neither the Spanish Flu epidemic of 1918 nor the Spanish Civil War of 1936 to 1939 saw the restaurant cease operations. The only time the restaurant closed in its nearly three hundred years of operation was in Spain's mandatory nationwide shutdowns during the global COVID-19 pandemic.

Quite simply, Spain is a global food powerhouse.

In my kitchen, laden with books and armed with recipes, I cook my way through Spanish history and Spanish geography. I am immersed in a world of Basques and Catalonians, Andalusians and Galicians, the Islamic Moors who ruled Spain for nearly eight hundred years, Kings and Queens and dictators.

And then I stumble upon the words of Spanish journalist and author Josep Pla, who said of Spanish cooking that it is "merely the landscape in the saucepan."[10] I read the words over and over again. I am besotted by the idea of the landscape in a saucepan. I imagine peering into my pan and seeing a whole nation contained within it. No wonder Ernest Hemingway loved this country so much.

Suddenly, just like that, I am all in. I need to get myself to Spain and see for myself this nation where the cuisine is the landscape in a saucepan. No more procrastination. In celebration, I head straight to the kitchen and make a pitcher of white Sangría with fresh ripe summer peaches. After a large glass, I call my friend Celine, a busy doctor, and ask her if she'll come with me for the first week of the Camino. She seizes the moment, immediately books the flights, and purposefully refuses cancellation insurance.

"Send me a packing list," she says.

And with that, we're on.

A SHORT HISTORY OF SANGRÍA

Spain is one of the world's biggest and most important wine cultures, with more acres of vineyard than any other country on earth. Wild grapes have grown in Spain since the Pliocene period, before the existence of Homo sapiens. In other words, grapes predate humans, and therefore predate civilization and cultivation. Archaeologists believe that grapes were first cultivated in Spain sometime between 4000 and 3000 BCE.[11] By 200 BCE, vineyards planted by the Romans covered large tracts of the country.

As early as 1000 BCE, a drink known as hippocras was made by the early Greeks and Romans. Hippocras, a precursor to sangría, was made by mixing wine with sugar and spices such as cinnamon. Hippocras was drunk both warm and at room temperature and was thought to have both medicinal and aphrodisiac properties.

Alcohol largely disappeared in Spain in 711 CE, when the Islamic Moors crossed the Strait of Gibraltar from Northern Africa and invaded the Iberian Peninsula. For eight hundred years the Moors ruled Spain, making many advances, especially in terms of agriculture, scientific techniques, literature, and education. They brought with them rice and new spices including cumin, caraway, nutmeg, sesame, coriander, aniseed, mint, and cinnamon, and introduced crops including oranges, lemons, peaches, apricots, figs, dates, pomegranates, sugar cane, and saffron—all of which have had a lasting impact on the cuisine of Spain.

In 1492, the fall of Granada marked the end of Muslim rule in Spain, and with it came the return of alcohol, including a new interpretation of hippocras, known as sangría. Spain is a drinking culture, but not a drunk culture. Alcohol is treated with reverence. It is often served well diluted, as is the case with sangría. Traditionally, sangría is made with Spanish Tempranillo or similar young fruity red wines, typically from Rioja, along with citrus fruit (usually orange slices and sometimes lemon slices), brandy, orange juice, soda, sugar to taste, and ice. Mix everything except the soda water and ice the night before or at least several hours ahead of serving and add the ice and soda immediately before serving.

Sangría is sweet, fruity, and modestly alcoholic. Contemporary sangría can be made with red, white, rosé, or sparkling wine, with sliced oranges, lemons, and other citrus fruits. Additions often include a small amount of sugar, liqueurs such as peach brandy, Limoncello, Triple Sec, brandy, or cognac, soda or sparkling water, and ice.

Tinto de Verano, a simple sangría, is incredibly popular in Spain. It is both less expensive than sangría, and less likely to mark you as a tourist. It is made from a simple combination of red wine and a sweetened, lemon flavoured fizzy drink, plus a slice of lemon, over ice. Unlike sangría, it does not generally contain other fruits or the addition of any liqueur and does not need to be made in advance.

Tinto de Verano

Serves 4–6

750 mL (3 cups) of red wine (vino tinto)

2 × 355 mL (approx. 3 cups) cans of any lemon-flavoured
  soda (or ginger ale as a substitute if you prefer)

1 lemon, washed and sliced

Combine the ingredients in a pitcher, stir, and serve over ice.

CHAPTER TWO

To Saint-Jean-Pied-de-Port

October 7-8

"The beginning is the most important part of the work."
— Plato, *Republic*

As if by miracle, the seat beside me in the otherwise completely full airplane is empty. Celine is beside me, on my other side. We are flying from Toronto to Paris on the Friday before the Canadian Thanksgiving weekend. Just as we were leaving for the airport, the entire rest of the nation was going home to join family, practise gratitude, and eat a Thanksgiving feast. We spent most of the day getting to Toronto, as the roads were choked, the buses packed, and the trains sold out.

Up in the air, Celine and I are drinking French wine and leafing through the in-flight magazines. After dinner, she falls asleep, awkwardly slumped over in her seat. I watch movies, half-awake, half-asleep, until well into the middle of the night. I finally doze off, only to be jolted fully awake almost immediately, with the plane buffeting about horizontally and vertically, things thumping in the overhead bins. The seatbelt signs are lit up, and the intercom crackles to life with the pilot's deep, calm, authoritative, voice telling us to stay in our seats and reassuring us that the turbulence will only be temporary. I clutch my bottle of Ativan in my hand but am wary of taking any, lest I need to be alert. Celine stirs from her sleep briefly, opens her eyes and looks vaguely alarmed, but promptly shuts her eyes and resumes sleeping. I slump down as best I can, pull the blanket over my head. The plane pitches, my stomach lurches. Breathe, I tell myself, as I concentrate on remembering to draw in air slowly, hold, and then exhale fully. Hours into the flight, I eventually peek out from under the blanket, and just as I do, France makes its first appearance on a map on the seatback screen. Its appearance in the middle of all the quaking and jostling is so heartening that I finally manage what feels like a few minutes' sleep. I wake just as breakfast is served, and the little white airplane on the onscreen map appears mere centimetres from Paris. I calculate that I've had forty-five minutes of sleep, possibly less. It's not quite three o'clock in the morning Toronto time, and yet here we are all merrily drinking coffee and eating croissants. Vive la France!

In theory, we have two hours to find the train station and purchase tickets. In practice, our airplane lands twenty minutes late, and by the time we make it through customs and navigate the airport, we have little time left. We are racing through Charles de Gaulle airport in hiking boots, packs on our backs, trying to find the train station to purchase tickets. We find the ticket office with minutes to go, stand in line and manage to get tickets for the only train of the day with connections. The train leaves the station at 10:10 a.m. We have ten minutes to find the track and board the train.

After all the rushing around, the train feels strangely slow. It shuffles off through tunnels and under ribbons of crisscrossed overhead wires. It is gray and grim as we head through the Paris suburbs. I've never seen this side of Paris before. It bears so little resemblance to the famous city with its tree-lined streets, colourful awnings, legendary buildings, and impeccable, impossibly beautiful, formal gardens. Here, it's all graffiti-covered building backsides, broken down fences and walls, and ditches full of litter. It's hard to tell where the suburbs end and the industrial outskirts begin.

Eventually we emerge into the French countryside, and soon we arrive in Bordeaux. The Gare de Bordeaux-Saint-Jean, the city's elegant train station, has been in operation since 1898. In the station café we order cappuccinos and a jambon-beurre, the traditional French baguette filled with butter and ham, and use the free wi-fi to touch base briefly with home. With time before our connecting train, we wander around the vicinity of the station, admiring the architecture, the wine shops, and the signs advertising *Vin Blanc Nouveau*, €2.50/*litre*, which we regard with more than a little envy.

A second train takes us to Bayonne, where we disembark and wait again. We leave the train station with the intention of taking a short walk, but bleary eyed and too tired to navigate, we promptly return and sit leaning up against our packs, struggling to stay awake. We do not want to miss our final train connection. When it eventually arrives, the third train of the day is old and short—only a couple of carriages. The few of us waiting climb on board and then, like the little engine that could, the elderly train sets off on a slow steady incline, huffing and puffing its way past smaller and smaller villages, into the Pyrenees mountains.

The Basque village of Saint-Jean-Pied-de-Port is our destination for the day. It's the second-most popular starting point of the Camino Frances or French Way, so called because of its starting point in France. The most popular, for the record, is Sarria, in Spain, one hundred kilometres from Santiago.

Dusk is descending when we disembark. After two full days in transit, during which I calculate that I've slept for a total of about two hours, possibly three, we are both dishevelled and disoriented. And we are already late for dinner at the hostel.

Inside the door of the hostel, there's a long line of boots and walking sticks and a great heap of backpacks. Our smiling host appears. "Leave your boots and walking sticks with the others, and leave your pack here," he says, pointing to the heap. "We will show you to your beds after dinner." Dinner begins with baskets of bread, jugs of red wine, and a large tureen of vegetable soup. We are asked to introduce ourselves and say where we are from. The host then translates so that everything is said in French, Spanish, and English. I am so tired that I can hardly follow. I drift off a little and am jolted fully awake when the main course is finally served—a large green salad and tortilla Española, the classic Spanish omelette made with eggs, potatoes, sometimes onions, and plenty of olive oil. When one tortilla Española disappears, another arrives, along with more bread and more red wine.

Between courses, we are asked to play a game in which we are required to call out a name of one of our fellow diners and toss an imaginary ball at that person. Addled by lack of sleep, the only names I can remember are Phillip from Brazil, Pierre from France, and Uda, an older woman from Germany. Pierre stands out in part because he is good-looking in the surliest, darkest sort of way. Like me, he is scarcely interacting and seems defensively aloof. Although I wonder if I am just overwhelmed by fatigue and red wine, or perhaps projecting a condition that I understand all too well.

When we are asked to answer why we are walking the Camino, Pierre answers gruffly, "I will know why I am walking the Camino when I have walked the Camino." To me, this makes perfect sense: how would one begin to explain to perfect strangers, most of whom do not share a common language, the millions of reasons we are here about to embark on this particular walk? The evening goes on and on. Eventually dessert is served—Natillas, a classic Spanish custard. Maybe it is the lack of sleep making me slightly unreasonable, but serving an egg-based dessert, right after an egg-based main dish, seems quite odd to me. Nonetheless, I eat up every last spoonful and thoroughly enjoy it. Moments later our relentlessly cheerful host brings us each a small glass of port. We raise our glasses together and toast each other's journeys.

Finally, at long, long last, we are shown to our rooms for the night.

The large bunkroom on the main floor appears to be full of men. Uda, Celine, and I are led up a narrow staircase to a series of closed doors and are shown to a room towards the back of the building. Our small, surprisingly cheerful room has three single beds with bright red covers, one overhead light, one electric outlet for charging cell phones, and three hooks on the wall—one for each of us. It is perfect. I cannot wait to lay my body on my skinny little bed and close my eyes.

I find my way to the single bathroom on our floor. When I come back, Uda has somehow managed to wash all of her undergarments and is merrily hanging her underpants, bra, and socks on the three hooks. I climb into bed as Uda turns off the light and plunges us into darkness. Within seconds, I am oblivious to the world.

What feels like minutes later, I am jolted awake by the sound of choirs of what I think are heavenly angels singing loudly enough for all the heavens to hear. It is pitch black, and at first I have no idea where I am. My eyes begin to focus. For some reason Uda is up and gathering her undergarments and packing her bag like a seasoned pro. She looks over at me. "You were asleep the second your head hit your pillow," she says.

I am too dazed to respond. Surely, I have only just fallen asleep. What is this music, and where is it coming from? Why is she up? It's pitch-black outside, the middle of the night. She looks at me and recognizes my confusion. "It is six o'clock in the morning," she says. "Time to get up and get on the Camino!" She opens the door to the hallway, and the hall light and piped in music floods the room. "Breakfast time," she calls out gleefully. It takes me a moment to remember: I am in France, about to embark on what may well be the greatest walk of my life.

I stagger from my bed and make my way to my backpack. I stuff it clumsily and then head to the main floor for breakfast. There, at the same table we ate at last night, is a huge flask of coffee, a jar of hot chocolate powder, a large jar of muesli, baskets of sliced baguette, jam, and foil-wrapped triangles of cream cheese. Pierre from France is making a large bowl of hot chocolate and dunking his bread in it. He is just as surly this morning, and yet I find this strangely comforting and enormously appealing. He is genuine in his gruffness despite being amongst a sea of idealistic peregrinos looking for answers. He lights up when I ask him about his walking stick. When he finally smiles, surly Pierre is devastatingly handsome. "Je l'ai trouvé dans la forêt," (I found it in the forest) he says. "Maintenant, c'est mon ami." (Now it is my friend.) It really is a beauty, a staff more than a walking stick, really—a tall, weathered, gnarled, and knotted piece of wood that has been polished with wear. Pierre is walking the long route from Le Puy all the way to Santiago, 1,550-plus kilometres. A god among walkers.

It is still dark out when I leave the hostel, even though I am one of the last to leave. Celine is finishing breakfast and needs to organize her gear, so we plan to meet at the Pilgrims' Information Office when she is ready. I stand alone on the narrow cobblestone road outside the hostel, listening to roosters crowing and looking up at the stars above, watching the first glimmers of dawn in the sky. Down the hill below me, the village is coming to life, one small, yellow, lamplight at a time. A trail of pilgrims is already heading off, disappearing into the dark, their walking sticks clickety-clacking on the cobbles as they go.

I am thinking of my mother and remembering my last visit to her in the nursing home shortly before I left for France. She lives a six or seven-hour drive from where I live in Eastern Ontario. A trip I make about every six weeks, weather permitting. It is never often enough nor long enough.

On this particular visit, I remember feeding my mother, holding the cup to her lips. Lifting the fork to her mouth. Each time, she opened her mouth before the fork reached it, forming a small o with her lips. Her pale blue eyes were locked on me.

The role reversal felt simultaneously tragic and tender. I feigned a false bravado, leaned in towards my mother, encouraging her to eat her dinner. I wiped her chin just as she must have done for me when I was too young to remember. Always small, my mother is now a tiny wisp of a woman.

"I could pick you up, put you in my pocket, and take you home," I told her.

"I wish you would," she said softly, longingly. Everything about her is diminished, her voice scarcely more than a whisper. Most of the time, though, she makes reasonable and appropriate answers even though she has Parkinson's, crippling arthritis, and lapses in and out of lucidity. She is completely immobile and needs two people to lift her in and out of bed.

Outside the nursing home window, the leaves had begun to turn colour. I told my mother that I was leaving for Spain and that by the time I came home it would be well into November and that the leaves would have fallen. I told her that I would be gone for almost six weeks, that I was going to walk the Camino de Santiago. That I would come to see her as soon as possible, after I return home.

"Will you start in that small French village?" she asked. "What is its name?" She was searching for something. Some memory. "Saint-Jean-Pied-de-Port," I said, haltingly. I could not believe my mother knew anything of the Camino, let alone that it started in a small French village, whose name was escaping her.

"That's it!" she said. "Saint-Jean-Pied-de-Port." She looked alert and triumphant. It was her turn to lean in towards me. She told me that she and my father were there sometime in the 1990s while touring France and walked the first day of the Camino, while I was off living in Australia. It is true that my parents went to France many times, and that they were always walking and hiking and exploring the various regions. My father lived for the mountains.

"We walked all that day," she said. "We stopped along the way and had a glass of wine and lunch at a little place with a patio cantilevered over the mountain valley. It was just magnificent, breathtakingly beautiful. I've never forgotten that day. We always wanted to return and walk the whole long trail."

This was more than she had said to me in many visits. She stopped and was lost again, searching through her memories. But I remembered what followed that trip. Not long after, my father was diagnosed with cancer for the third time in his life. He died in a great hurry, leaving my mother to plummet alone into depression and old age.

A minute or two passed. We were both thinking, remembering. "I expect that you're walking it for us," my mother said clearly, brightly, and with purpose. She took the fork that I had put down into her own hand and guided it shakily towards her mouth. I added this to the long list of reasons for walking the Camino. For the bloodline of hale and hearty walkers.

I am still thinking of my mother as I look down the hill at Saint-Jean-Pied-de-Port below me. I can imagine her standing here, right where I am standing. I can see her clearly—her wooden walking stick, a small rucksack on her back, a floppy hat on her head, secured by strings below her chin. Quiet and determined. She loved France. She would have adored this historic village. She would have spoken French to everyone, inquired about all the local dishes, and collected all the tourism information brochures—she was an inveterate collector of pamphlets and booklets. She would have simply loved Pierre, his handsome exterior, his prickly interior. "Un vrai français," she would have called him.

I reach inside my pocket for the stone I am carrying for my mother. The small, black, smooth, round stone I picked up from the waterfront in front of her home on the shores of Georgian Bay. In accordance with Camino tradition, I will leave the stone along the trail for my parents, so that they might have a place here, on this path for eternity.

Standing here at the start of this path, the path; I have visualized this moment for so long. I have seen myself, here, in Saint-Jean-Pied-de-Port. In my mind, this walled village on the Nive river has near mythical status. I pictured myself here, sitting in a café near the river, my backpack at my side, maps spread in front of me on the table. I would be brimming with anticipation and without a worry in the world. The sun would be shining. I would be eating a generous slice of Gâteau Basque—the legendary local flan filled with black cherries and pastry cream, or perhaps a wedge of Basque burnt cheesecake. I would be fuelled by enthusiasm and strong black French coffee.

And yet here, now, it is cold and dark, I have barely slept, and my bag already feels heavy. I never once imagined setting off in the cold and the dark, filled equally with excitement and trepidation. I think back to my mother in her nursing home half a world away. I am tearing up a little and blowing my nose and watching a steady stream of walkers disappearing into the dark, early morning. I hold the stone in my hand and soothe myself with its smooth edges. My mother will have a place here. My father, too. This stone will have a place here.

I hold my breath, still my heart, wipe the tears from my face. I am here, and it seems that I have brought my parents along with me.

THE BASQUE COUNTRY AND CUISINE

The Basque Country spills across the border of Southern France into Northern Spain, extending from the Bay of Biscay to the western Pyrenees mountains. The region includes the French cities of Bayonne, Biarritz, and Saint-Jean-Pied-de-Port, and the cities of Pamplona, Vitoria-Gasteiz, Bilbao, and San Sebastian in Spain.

A genetically and linguistically unique population, the Basque people are believed to have been the earliest human inhabitants of Europe, and there is compelling evidence that they have lived in the area now known as the Basque Country for thirty-five to fifty-five hundred years. Many Basques still speak the traditional Basque language, Euskara.[12]

The Basque Country is famous for its distinctive culture, cuisine, and plethora of Michelin starred restaurants. Basque cuisine is central to the Basque identity and forms the heart of Basque culture. Txokos—private gastronomical societies—are a fundamental part of the Basque culinary scene, allowing people to come together regularly to cook, talk, eat, sing, and drink. Txokos have played an important role in holding onto and building Basque culinary traditions. Until the late 1900s, txokos were mostly for men, with females and children only allowed by special invitation. The rules are slowly changing, and since the 1990s, txokos have invited more women and children to participate in the festivities.

Typical Basque dishes include a fantastic variety of pintxos (Basque for tapas), grilled meat and seafood, sheep's milk cheese, and a variety of hearty stews and bean dishes. Tomatoes, paprikas, and red peppers (both sweet and hot) are important local ingredients used in many main dishes. Standard desserts include Gâteau Basque, Goxua (similar to trifle), and Basque burnt cheesecake. Fermented cider and txakoli—a low alcohol, sparkling white wine—are traditional Basque drinks. Kalimotxo (half red wine, half cola served with plenty of ice) is another popular Basque drink.

Basque Burnt Cheesecake

The original Basque burnt cheesecake (circa 1990) came from La Viña restaurant in San Sebastian. Recipes for Basque burnt cheesecakes—essentially a simple, crustless, cheesecake with a deeply caramelized top—abound. In fact, all cheesecake recipes, including this one (adapted from my mother's cheesecake recipe) are merely a variation on a very similar theme. Caramelize the top to your own taste by adjusting the time you leave the cake in the oven at the final higher temperature. The darker it is, the more flavour it will have. Be adventuresome! Do not be afraid to get it good and browned. This cheesecake is best made a day ahead.

Serves 6
454 g (1 lb) cream cheese, at room temperature
133 g (2/3 cup) white sugar
½ tsp fine salt
17 g (approx. 2 tbsp) flour
1 tbsp vanilla extract
3 large eggs, at room temperature
150 mL (2/3 cup) whipping (or heavy) cream

Preheat the oven to 200°C (400°F)

Generously butter a 20 cm (8 inch) springform pan. Line the buttered pan using a couple of pieces of parchment, overlapping. This does not need to be perfect, but trim away any excess parchment that spills over the edge of the pan, so that it doesn't burn.

Combine the softened cream cheese, sugar, salt, and flour, stirring well. Using electric beaters, beat in the vanilla and the eggs, one at a time, beating well between each egg. Pour in the heavy cream and stir to blend. Pour the batter into the prepared pan, and tap the pan gently on the counter to release any bubbles.

Place the cheesecake in the middle of the oven and cook until puffed, about 45 minutes. Then increase the oven temperature to 220°C (425°F), checking carefully from about 6 to 7 minutes on. By the 10-minute mark the top should be very dark brown; if not, leave the cheesecake for a minute or two longer. You are aiming for a very dark brown, well caramelized top, not a blackened top.

When the top is sufficiently dark, remove the cake from the oven and set aside to cool fully, at least 4 to 5 hours, on the counter. Once fully cooled, refrigerate the cake. It is best made a day ahead.

Serve it as it is or dress it up with fresh berries or a spoonful of any tart, full-flavoured jam, such as strawberry-rhubarb or black or red currant, and whipped cream.

CHAPTER THREE

Saint-Jean-Pied-de-Port to Roncesvalles

October 9

"Let yourself be silently drawn by the strange pull of what you really love. It will not lead you astray." —Rumi[13]

I am sitting in the dark, alone, on the stone step outside the Pilgrims' Office, waiting for it to open so that I can get my credencial (the required pilgrim passport) stamped with my official Camino starting point. Pilgrims are pouring out of buildings and onto the narrow cobblestone street that leads down the steep hill through the village of Saint-Jean-Pied-de-Port. Moments later Celine appears, and with the requisite stamp taken care of, we're off, taking our first tentative steps towards the trail, adjusting our packs as we go.

Back at my desk in Canada, long before we would arrive in France, I planned to take things easy to start off. There are two routes from Saint-Jean-Pied-de-Port to the Spanish village of Roncesvalles, which lies across the Pyrenees. Both are long and notoriously difficult. The Route de Napoléon climbs uphill sharply for twenty kilometres, until reaching Col de Lepoeder, a 1,450-metre mountain pass, whereupon the trail begins a precipitously sharp five-kilometre descent to Roncesvalles. The other route, Via Valcarlos, is recommended in bad weather, when taking the high mountain pass can be seriously dangerous. However, at least half of the Via Valcarlos route is either on or immediately adjacent to busy roads. Either way, the walk from Saint-Jean-Pied-de-Port to Roncesvalles is said to be one of the toughest days on the entire Camino.

Imagining that we would be jetlagged and exhausted after our travelling, I suggested to Celine well before we started on this trip that we cut the long first day short by reserving beds in the refuge at Orisson, on the French side of the Pyrenees, the only stopping point on the first day. Our walk for the day is only about nine kilometres. If we were driving, it would take about sixteen minutes. The walk, I calculate, will take an absolute maximum of three hours, allowing for the fact that it is a steep ascent the entire way. Celine and I deliberately take our time, stopping to admire shop windows in the village, ambling along like tourists, even backtracking at one point to look for an open grocery store for supplies for the day. Nothing is open. I entirely neglected the fact that we were starting our journey on a Sunday in a largely Catholic country, and that stores might be closed or not open until much later in the day. With the sun climbing higher in the sky, we decide to forego supplies and tackle the trail in earnest. By eleven o'clock, we are well ahead of schedule and have arrived in Orisson. Feeling rather pleased with ourselves, we are sitting in the sunshine on a cantilevered patio. There is no village, nothing else in sight. Simply a building perched on the edge of a mountain. It is exactly as my mother described it to me.

Celine and I drink beer and eat a crusty baguette stuffed with shaved ham. I've never had nor wanted a beer this early in the day before, but I am thirsty and jetlagged enough that the hour on the clock seems meaningless. Orisson, as far as I can see, consists only of this one building with its grand view into the belly of the deep green valley below, while the magnificent rocky Pyrenees frame the horizon all around us.

As beautiful as the patio is, by noon I realize it does not make sense to spend the entire day here, only to wait to stay the night. Despite the fact that we've pre-booked and prepaid for our dinner, accommodations, and tomorrow's breakfast, we decide to leave Orisson and attempt to negotiate a refund—a request that is soundly and abruptly rebuffed, even when we find another pilgrim who would like to take at least one of our places. The options are to stay all afternoon on the patio and wait until night or forfeit the money and hike on. We have nothing to do for hours except sit on the patio and wait. We don't even have books to read. I flash back to discarding my copy of *The Sun Also Rises* and start to wonder if I was being too frugal about the weight of things.

Given the perfect weather and the lack of options for things to do if we stay, we settle on forfeiting our money. We head onwards, upwards, onto the trail that will take us over the fourteen-hundred-and-fifty-metre Roncesvalles Pass. So much for starting slowly. "Onwards!" I yell, enthusiastically. To hell with the lost Euros. We're on a mission.

We start off together, but before long we are walking separately, each at our own pace. The climb is long, hard, unyielding. Now and then I pause to gather my breath and watch the raptors circling overhead and in the deep valleys below. Clouds float below as the mountains fall away to steep, vividly green valleys dotted with sheep. I can hear the bells ringing on the livestock in pastures far off. Closer by, the fittest looking, most compact pigs I have ever seen gather beneath stands of trees, roaming free, keeping to the shade. None of the animals appear to be fenced. Several times I look up ahead and see what appear to be wild horses standing high on mountain ridges, silhouetted by the sun behind them. It all seems orchestrated, too majestic to be real.

After walking almost straight uphill for a couple of hours, we turn a corner to find a van perched on the side of the narrow trail. Parked on a grassy knoll with a few pilgrims gathered around, the man in the van is apparently selling cheese. Celine, a full-blooded Quebecoise, cannot resist a van full of cheese and diverts to investigate. I press on, tired and saving my energy for the relentless climb.

The trail wends upwards, higher and higher, until it appears to be parallel with the mountain tops in the distance. There are several false disorienting and disappointing summits when it seems I must surely have reached the top, only to turn a corner or climb over a hill and see the path still winding upwards beyond. The crowds we started with this morning have thinned out now, and I am walking more or less alone save for the odd person who passes and those whom I pass. When someone greets me, I return their "¡Buen Camino!" even if the Spanish still feels foreign in my mouth. The walk is slow, mostly silent, except for the sound of my breathing and the odd greeting. The ascent is over twelve hundred metres, which sounds easy enough until you imagine climbing a ladder looking straight up into the sky for over a kilometre. On I go, continuing endlessly uphill.

Dazed by lack of sleep, I come to realize that if only Celine and I had half an ounce of foresight earlier, we could have stayed at Orrison and used the afternoon to catch up on some much-needed sleep. But back then, only a few hours ago, we were still raring to go. Now, punch drunk with could-haves and should-haves, I keep walking towards Roncesvalles.

Roncesvalles, population thirty-four, is a place made famous by men fighting. Spanish for "valley of thorns," it was here that the great armies of Charlemagne, the medieval emperor who ruled much of Western Europe from 768 CE to 814 CE, fought, and where his nephew Roland, commander of Charlemagne's rearguard, was defeated by the Basques in the 778 Battle of the Roncevaux Pass. Roland died after the battle, his brains leaking from his skull, still desperately attempting to break his own sword so that it could not be used against him. He was heralded as a hero for his bravery, and later became a role model for the knights of the Middle Ages. Roland's memory is still celebrated in these parts, immortalized by the epic eleventh-century poem "La Chanson de Roland," thought to be the oldest surviving major work of French literature. Almost a thousand years later, in 1813, Roncesvalles was the site of another famous battle, of more men fighting. This time it was the Battle of Roncesvalles, part of the Peninsular War between the French and the Anglo-Portuguese. Stories of the wars still persist in these parts, a reminder of how conflict defined history, shaped borders, and moulded countries.

Suddenly and quite unexpectedly, on a downward slope flanked by forest on one side, we come across a trickling water fountain identified with a plaque as the fountain of Roland. Celine and I, who have just found each other again, cross over a cattle grid and into Spain. According to the map in my guidebook, the water fountain is in France, and the cattle grid is in Spain. If there was a sign welcoming us to Spain, we missed it. We set off, taking our first steps in the Autonomous Region of Navarre, a medieval Basque Kingdom. Roncesvalles is still nearly ten kilometres off. Navarre is one of Spain's seventeen autonomous administrative regions, known in Spain as comunidades autónomas (autonomous communities) that are somewhat akin to provinces or states elsewhere in the world.

Five kilometres further along the trail, we arrive at a sign: *HELPoint Lepoeder.* Here in the absolute middle of nowhere, high atop this mountain pass, at 1,450 metres altitude, is an SOS radio call button, along with free wi-fi with multilingual instructions for its use. Celine sets off. Unable to resist the idea of accessing wi-fi high atop a mountain pass, I stop to send my daughters a quick message:

I am here. Middle of nowhere on a high mountain pass. Climbed out of France, into Spain. Have walked all day thru scenes straight out of Heidi. Miles from any-where & free wi-fi! Love, mum, xoxo.

I hit send and rejoin Celine. Downwards we head, still walking west, face to the sun. The precipitous descent is just as intense as the ascent was earlier. My toes ram into the fronts of my boots, and the only solution is to step sideways, requiring focus. I lift and place my feet carefully. One slip and I could be on my backside sliding down the hill or hurtling down an embankment. One foot. The other foot. Down, down, down.

At times Celine is ahead of me, and at times she is behind me. Even when we catch up to each other, we are silent. There is no energy left for talking. It feels like hours since we've seen anyone else.

It is only when I pause that I realize I am walking through the most beautiful alpine forests of ancient beech trees, growing on nearly vertical hillsides. As tired as I am, I am also thrilled. I'm in Spain. I'm really here. Walking the Camino.

Had we known we were going to do the whole walk today—thirty-two kilometres (adjusted for the cumulative fourteen-hundred-metre plus climb), we would have left briskly in the morning and paced ourselves accordingly. I would not have stopped and lingered in the Pilgrim Office or spent time peer-ing in shop windows in Saint-Jean-Pied-de-Port, nor spent an hour on the patio having a beer and sandwich at Orisson.

At times, I wonder if I am safe. I'm starting to feel slightly wobbly, and I don't know if it's because I am a little dehydrated, if I am exhausted from the flights and the jetlag, or if it's because I just undertook a serious and rigorous climb. Sometimes I look around and think I might even be lost. But then I catch sight of Celine either ahead of or behind me, and we traipse on together—safety in numbers, even if it is just the two of us. Just when it seems we really cannot go another step, we round the corner and see the monastery that is to be our home for the night.

But even more importantly, I also see a cinderblock toilet building, scruffy looking and slightly overgrown. It's the first bathroom I've seen since Orisson, twenty-odd kilometres and half a long day ago. It's staggering how quickly life is reduced to the basic necessities on the Camino: food, water, sanitation, shel-ter, sleep. I trudge over to the building and head inside. It is filthy. Riddled with graffiti. Dirty toilet paper strewn everywhere. Stinking. Putrid. I retreat as fast as I can, holding my breath before I can see or smell any more. I am back outside within seconds, gasping. Celine simply nods, and we head off, slogging on silently towards the monastery.

The Real Collegiata de Santa Maria is a massively sprawling Gothic monastery complex, run by Augustinian monks. The building dates to the early 1200s, possibly earlier. Once inside, we remove our muddy boots as instructed and leave them in the hallway and join the long line of other bootless pilgrims, all of us waiting to be admitted to what appears to be the registration office. We are all tired, dirty, and hungry. The line doesn't seem to be moving, so we take turns, one pilgrim at a time, using the monastery's bathroom, while the rest of us hold the place in the line that creeps along slowly. Others trickle in and fall in line behind us. I have yet to hear anyone speaking English. I look back, and the line continues to grow and grow. Apparently, we are far from the last to arrive.

Eventually we are permitted through a set of glass doors and into another shorter line, where we watch the proceedings in front of us. The rapid-fire Spanish is new to my ears, difficult to make out. It appears that we will all be assigned bed numbers and may or may not be able to make dinner reservations.

The Augustinian Monks who have run this place for centuries were once famous for their acts of charity, and their care of pilgrims walking the Camino. They would bathe pilgrims' feet, tend to their wounds, feed and house weary walkers. Since the twelfth century, the monks have welcomed "all pilgrims...sick and well, Catholics, Jews, pagans, heretics, and vagabonds."[4] Apparently things have changed a little since the twelfth century, as at the front of the line there is a commotion. There are no monks to be found, but rather a young woman behind the counter arguing with two Israeli men who do not have their credenciales—the all-important pilgrim passports. Voices are raised. The Israeli men are not walking the Camino, they are biking it, and backwards apparently, or so it seems from what they are shouting loudly in English. It seems that they have biked the entire Camino *from* Santiago de Compostela and never had a problem until now, their last night. They just want a bed for the night. The monastery staff do not relent. The Israeli men are ushered out—disappointed and angry, still arguing, still shouting. Men fighting, I think to myself. How apt in this place, where men have fought for centuries. An ominous silence falls over the room; it feels wrong, heretical almost, to raise one's voice in a place like this.

We are next in line, so we front up to the counter and hand over our passports and credenciales. No one says anything. My bed number is quietly assigned, and then I am pointed towards the next person behind the counter.

This young woman appears to be the person who takes the money and also makes dinner assignments. I wait my turn, and then ask her in English about dinner. "No cena," the woman says. I stand there looking crestfallen. Stunned. "¿No cena?" I repeat, seemingly unable to imagine how there could be no dinner. Then I try again. "Can I have dinner? Dinner? Please. Somewhere? ¿Por favor. La cena, por favor?" My English has quickly become as broken as my Spanish.

By now Celine has joined me, and she tries in French. The Spanish woman raises her voice, answers again in lengthy, rapid-fire Spanish. We don't understand a word, only that the response seems hostile, and getting what we need seems unlikely. Then she turns around and heads to another desk to take a phone call while we stand there, not knowing what to do. The line is not moving. First it was the Israelis. Now it's us. The dinner request appears to have been the final straw.

Finally, the woman returns and starts another loud monologue directed at us. We stand there dumbfounded, uncomprehending. Finally, exasperated, she has an inexplicable change of heart, and it seems we are being allowed to have dinner. She says we can eat at eight o'clock. It is half past five. We are already ravenous.

"Can we eat earlier?" I ask, stupidly. She shakes her head. I may have gone too far. But then, abruptly, yet another change of heart. She grabs the dinner docket out of our hands and leaves again. There is another wait. La señora returns with a different docket, across which she has scrawled in large letters, 6:30. We pay immediately, thank the woman profusely in English, Spanish, and French, and get out quickly before she can change her mind.

An older man, presumably a volunteer, takes us to our dorm. Along the way, he tells us things in Spanish. I let the words wash over me. Spanish may be an expressive language, but my command of it in this moment suddenly seems abysmal. Celine, who is bilingual in French and English, understands a bit more. I have stopped trying to understand and am just enjoying the cadence and rhythm of the language when I hear a phrase that lifts my spirits more than I ever thought possible: lavadora y secadora. "¡Si, lavadora y secadora!" I cry out. "¡Comprendo!" (Washer and dryer. I understand!) I learned these words in Spanish class. I am jubilant. I know something after all! Our guide laughs out loud, smiling and repeating, "¡Si, si, buena, lavadora y secadora!"

We learn about the laundry facilities, the elevator, and the common room, where there is free wi-fi. And then finally, the guide takes us to our dorm. The place is huge, sprawling—almost a village unto itself. There are two wings, possibly more, and three floors devoted to beds for pilgrims. We are in the furthest wing on the top floor, under a massive ancient soaring ceiling. He walks us through the room, shows us the doors to the bathrooms, "Los baños," (the bathrooms) he says, and looks directly at me. "¡Si, señor, los baños! Comprendo!" I say triumphantly and with confidence. He seems thrilled with my incredibly juvenile and limited comprehension of Spanish and is still grinning when he stops and points out "las camas" (the beds), and then he departs immediately.

There are sixty-four beds on our floor, separated into pairs by very short partial walls. Standing, I am able to see the entire room, the people at either ends of the room, the couple with the beds next to us, the people heading to the bathrooms. We are smack in the middle. A guy in the adjacent space is stark naked and rummaging through his massive backpack. His companion is calmly setting up her sleeping bag.

I look around in despair. To say it is utilitarian would be a compliment. It reminds me of scenes from *Orange is the New Black*, only with men—lots of them. I look at Celine. "It's like a jail," I say, while at the exact same moment she says, "This is so nice." She is being completely sincere. She genuinely thinks it is lovely. The big open space. All the people together. The cavernous ceiling above. There isn't much that Celine can't face. She's tough, feisty, and relentlessly game for whatever life presents—a constant education for me.

All I can think of is all the bodies packed into this space. Four toilets and four showers, two of each for the females, two of each for the men. All the snoring and other bodily noises that are bound to follow come nightfall. The acoustical properties of the very tall cathedral ceiling should be spectacular—a concert of human sounds.

I lie down on my assigned bed and attempt to get my bearings, to centre myself. When I look directly across the dorm, there sitting on a bed, calmly sewing, is Uda, our roommate from the previous night. It is so comforting to see her. Uda already seems like an old friend. Here in this place with its multiple dorm rooms and space for hundreds of pilgrims, how remarkable that the three of us should be together again. I cross the dorm and greet her enthusiastically.

Uda also has a story about the reception desk. "That woman," she says, in her thick German accent. Turns out that Uda was given a docket for dinner at eight o'clock, despite her protests (and the fact that she arrived a good hour before us). We tell her to join us. The worst thing they can do is throw her out and make her come back later. Uda, who I am guessing is well into her seventies, and who has presumably walked all day over the mountain pass, does not appear to be any the worse for wear. She agrees and keeps on sewing.

By the time we clean up, unpack, and set up our sleeping bags, Uda has disappeared. We head off to find our dinner and ask someone, who appears to be a staff member, where the dining room is. The instructions come in a great jumble of Spanish—the only thing I understand is "a la derecha, a la izquierda" (to the right, to the left). So we go right and then left and then ask someone else, who points us up a flight of stairs. When we finally arrive at an empty dining room and manage to find a staff person, they check our dockets and send us somewhere else. We repeat this procedure two more times, finding different empty rooms, and are losing hope of making it to dinner in time.

Twenty minutes and at least another kilometre later, we finally find someone who actually knows where the dining room is. We are the last to arrive and are ushered in quickly and assigned to a table. Uda is nowhere to be seen. We join our tablemates, thankful to have finally found our way to dinner. There are three older men at one end of the table, and at the other end a middle-aged British couple who live in France, and a young Korean man.

What follows is the Camino tradition we encountered at our first meal in France—the exchange of names and details of everyone at the table. David and Camilla are the lovely English pair. Because they have limited time due to their work, they are walking from Saint-Jean-Pied-de-Port to Burgos, about halfway to Santiago. The young Korean man is called Sung Kim. The three older men, who are at our end of the table, are old friends. One lives in Andalusia, one in Catalonia, the other in Andorra. They are speaking French, but they call themselves Spaniards. They are tanned, well-padded, don't appear to be exceptionally fit, yet seem immensely pleased with themselves. I'm dubious of them, as it is not at all clear that they are actually walking the Camino. To me, they look rather suspiciously as if they have just stepped off a luxury yacht, and not at all like they have just hiked a significant mountain pass. They are dressed in natty attire and dress shoes, not hiking boots and walking clothes like the rest of us. Nonetheless, when the wine arrives, we all partake and raise our glasses to drink to the journey. "¡Salud! ¡Buen Camino!" we say to each other, clinking glasses.

The wine is a local Navarra Tempranillo. Tempranillo grapes, a black grape varietal, are known as noble grapes, because they produce such high-quality wines and retain their character almost wherever the grapes are planted and harvested. This Tempranillo is bold and full of flavour, but surprisingly smooth and easy to drink. With table introductions made and our first glasses of wine gone, we are all feeling relaxed and happy. The first and possibly hardest day of the Camino is behind us, and we are already seduced by the scenery, by the walk, and, no doubt, by the wine.

Outside the monastery, night falls over Roncesvalles. The dining room lights are slowly coming on, their reflections twinkling in the plate-glass windows. Our waiter brings us more wine and more bread and drops off the first course of vegetable soup along with a communal bowl of plain pasta. He takes our orders for the second course—trout or chicken. I choose the trout. This part of Navarra, located on the French border, is world renowned for its excellent trout fishing in the cold clear rivers that run down from the Pyrenees. I'm reminded that this was once Hemingway's favourite trout fishing territory, and it seems right to eat trout here. After I have ordered, one of the three Spanish men tells me the trout likely comes from China. Whether that's true or not, the fish is good, and I am hungry. We eat everything that is put in front of us and drink yet more wine.

Towards the end, still trying to ascertain if the three older Spanish men are truly walking the Camino, I ask them where they are staying in the dormitory. I am curious because having seen the two Israeli men turned away, I wonder if these men have pilgrim passports and if they are really pilgrims or if they are staying in some separate quarters within the grounds. "Où sont vos lits?" (Where are your beds?), I ask.

They erupt into gales of laughter. As it turns out, they think I am propositioning them. "Mon Dieu! Vraiment. Absolument pas. Quelle horreur!" I say, somewhat embarrassed, but mostly aghast at the hubris of these men. But they will have none of it. They are convinced that I am after them, and they are in absolute stitches. Celine and I quickly take our leave. "What on earth do I want with three fat old men?" I whisper to her as we exit the restaurant. We are practically staggering from laughing so hard.

This is so far from what I expected when I set out on this journey. I somehow imagined great insights and stimulating intellectual discussion with people from all over the world. I thought we would be discussing the demise of religion and the simultaneous uptick of pilgrimages, the value of faith, the quest for meaning and transcendence. Wasn't that what we were all here for—transcendence?

No, here we are reduced to sentence fragments and only the vaguest of abilities to communicate.

Tired, tipsy, and full, Celine and I head out into the cold starry night and walk quietly across the cloister, back towards our beds in the monastery dormitory. Celine is asleep the moment she hits her bed. Meanwhile, I find myself listening intently to all the various sounds through my earplugs. I toss and turn inside my sleeping bag, the wadded foam in my ears doing nothing to silence the sounds of people returning to the dorm, bathroom doors opening and closing, toilets flushing, showers running, people rummaging in their packs, some already snoring.

A group of pilgrims arrives back from the late sitting of dinner, clearly under the influence of alcohol. They are laughing and talking much too loudly in a foreign language. Somebody roars at them to be quiet. The room falls temporarily silent. A few moments later, the clock strikes ten and the volunteer hospitalero appears. He walks up and down the dormitory looking into each bed and calling out, "¡Buenas noches!" There is a little blessing spoken quietly in Spanish before he turns off the lights and plunges the entire room into darkness.

Moments later, the snoring begins anew.

For three hours, I toss and turn, sleepless. A man keeps walking up and down the dormitory, peering into the beds along the way. He does not appear to be staff. In my still jetlagged state, I consider why he might be doing this. It would be foolhardy to attempt to rob or assault somebody in a room with so many people as witnesses. Perhaps he is restless and cannot sleep, like me. But it is more than a bit unnerving that he is peering into each bed as he goes past. He walks by again, and my eyes, now accustomed to the darkness, watch as he clearly pauses and looks into our little partitioned area. I make deliberate eye contact with him, half sitting up inside my sleeping bag, staring him down. My super compact sleeping bag has a polyester exterior, and every time I move, it rustles noisily. If he hasn't seen me, hopefully he has heard me.

If I am alarmed by the roaming man, perhaps Celine should be alarmed, too? I start to unzip my sleeping bag. The racket seems deafening. I stay put. Celine sleeps on. The man seems to have disappeared. I check my phone. It is one o'clock in the morning. I have been up since six o'clock on what is now the previous day and have walked endless kilometres across the Pyrenees. My body no longer has any idea what time it is. Finally, in complete frustration and exhaustion, I take half a sleeping pill and fall asleep.

THE FOOD AND WINE OF NAVARRE

Navarre is one of Spain's seventeen comunidades autónomas (autonomous communities), created in accordance with the Spanish Constitution of 1978. Somewhat like provinces or states elsewhere in the world, the regions are autonomous in that they have their own executive, legislative, and judicial powers.

The autonomous community of Navarre (as it is known in English) lies nestled at the very top of Northern Spain along the French border. The region is known as Navarra in Spanish, and Nafarroa in Basque. It is renowned for its beautiful lush green landscapes, dramatic mountains, and rushing rivers full of trout. The trout brings eager anglers and fly fisherman from around the world. Navarre is also famous for the San Fermín Festival, otherwise known as the running of the bulls, which happens in Pamplona, the capital of Navarre, every July.

The Navarrese are fiercely proud both of their gastronomy and their wine culture. Wine has been made in Navarre since the Ancient Romans' conquest of Iberia beginning in 218 BCE, though wild grapes are believed to have thrived in the region since before the Ancient Romans arrived. The region is a prolific producer of high-quality red wines, typically made from Tempranillo, Cabernet Sauvignon, and Merlot grape varieties. The introduction of grapes such as Pinot Noir, Garnacha, Syrah, Chardonnay, and Sauvignon Blanc has resulted in an expanding variety of wines including whites and rosés.

Navarre is also celebrated for its locally produced cheeses, lamb, beef, fish (especially trout), and pintxos (tapas), as well as some specific regional dishes, including Ajoarriero, a famous cod stew made with garlic, potatoes, peppers, olive oil, and parsley. There is a Canadian connection to cod and this region, as many a Basque and Spaniard fished what are now known as Canada's Grand Banks in the 1500s, and possibly earlier. There are still places in Newfoundland with names that harken back to this time, such as Port-Au-Basques. European fishermen arrived in droves, and widespread overfishing of the waters off the coast of Newfoundland continued until the eventual collapse of the cod fishery in 1992.

Trucha a la Navarra

Years before Ernest Hemingway published his first hugely successful novel, *The Sun Also Rises*, he was a reporter for the *Toronto Daily Star*. On June 26, 1920, he published a dispatch entitled "Camping Out: When You Camp Out, Do It Right—Tips for bugs, bedding, and baking," in which he explained how to cook a trout in the wild. His method included coal, several cans of Crisco or Cotosuet (a lard or butter substitute made from hog fat and cotton oil), bacon, and cornmeal. Hemingway, who was, by all accounts an extremely enthusiastic eater, raved about the dish.[15]

In 1923, Ernest Hemingway and his wife, Hadley, travelled to Spain, where they attended the Festival of San Fermín in Pamplona, to witness the running of the bulls. While they were in Spain, the Hemingways spent time in the Basque village of Burguete, where they stayed at the Hostal Burguete, and Ernest fished in the local Irati River. It was in Burguete that Hemingway discovered that his bacon-wrapped trout was remarkably similar to a local dish known as trucha a la Navarra—a pan-fried whole trout stuffed with jamón serrano—Spanish ham (from white pigs), dry-cured in sea salt and hung from the rafter to cure for a year to eighteen months.

This is my own version of trucha a la Navarra, adapted to use ingredients available in North America.

Serves 2
2 fresh trout (or frozen and thawed in the refrigerator) about
    20 cm (8 inches) long when whole or 15 cm (6 inches)
    when cleaned and gutted)
Salt and pepper
4 thick slices of high-quality ham such as jamón serrano,
    or any good, cured ham such as prosciutto, speck, or
    pancetta
4 thick slices of bacon
A couple of teaspoons of flour or enough to coat the trout
    lightly
30 mL (2 tbsp) olive oil
2 cloves of garlic, cut in fine slices

Pat the cleaned trout dry with a paper towel. Season inside and out with a little salt and pepper, then stuff each cavity with two slices of the jamón serrano, prosciutto, speck, or pancetta.

Sprinkle the flour on a large plate and gently toss the trout in the flour (adding a little more flour if necessary) to lightly dust the skin. Using wooden toothpicks, skewer the trout to hold the cavities closed. Set aside.

Warm the olive oil in a skillet, add the bacon and fry until it is lightly browned but not crispy. Remove the bacon to the plate holding the trout, and add the garlic to the olive oil and bacon fat in the pan. Remove the garlic slices when golden and set aside with the bacon.

Add the trout to the olive oil and bacon fat in the pan and turn to medium-high heat. Cook for a couple of minutes on each side, turning over gently to make sure both sides are nicely browned.

Remove the partially cooked trout from the pan and place on a plate or board. Remove the wooden toothpick or skewer, rinse, and set aside. Wrap the cooked bacon around the trout, using a fork to flip the trout to avoid handling the hot fish with your hands. Once the bacon is wrapped around the fish, secure the bacon using the toothpick or wooden skewer and return the trout to the pan. Turn the heat down and continue cooking the trout gently until the internal temperature reaches 62°C (145°F) at its thickest part. In the absence of a meat thermometer, the flesh should be fully opaque and flake easily.

Place the trout on warmed plates and finish by pouring on the pan drippings, including the fried garlic. Serve immediately.

CHAPTER FOUR

Roncesvalles to Zubiri

October 10

"Methinks that the moment my legs begin to move, my thoughts begin to flow." —Henry David Thoreau, *Thoreau's Journal*, "19 Aug, 1851"

It is half past six when I awaken. All the lights are on in the dormitory. Everyone is up and moving. Celine is sitting on the edge of her bed, dressed, and stuffing her sleeping bag into its sack. "Wakey, wakey, sleepyhead," she says, apparently oblivious to all the danger we were in only hours earlier.

We step out of the monastery into the cold of the morning. The stars are still shining brightly overhead. The air is so frigid that our breath forms white clouds that hang in the air. Both Celine and I are wearing every single item of clothing we brought with us: sweaters, pants, boots, heavy socks, gloves, hats, our packable down jackets zipped up to our chins, and our rain jackets over top of everything else. We tuck our faces down into our jackets to stay warm, thinking of warm breakfasts to come. But first there's a three-kilometre walk to Burguete, the next point on the Camino.

The trail to Burguete heads off across the road and into a forest so dark that we can scarcely see the ground below us. The darkness is disorienting. We use the flashlights on our cellphones to navigate the terrain, wary of the stones and tree roots and the undulations of the dirt path along the forest floor while simultaneously trying to watch for yellow trail-markers that mark the way. There is almost nobody about. Perhaps everyone is at breakfast or not yet up.

Eventually a couple of much younger walkers pass us, silently. It feels too early to talk yet. Here in the forest, in the dark, I stay close to Celine. We are quiet, too. Slowly the darkness begins to soften, and before long we turn off our flashlights and put our phones away. The cold is easing too. In the light, we step up our pace. It is just over three kilometres from Roncesvalles to Burguete, where we hope to find coffee and breakfast.

Ernest Hemingway made the tiny Basque hamlet of Burguete famous when he stayed there in the 1920s, using the village as a base for trout fishing excursions on the Irati River. He wrote about Burguete in *The Sun Also Rises*, where the narrator, Jake Barnes, and his friend Bill Gorton stayed in an old mountain inn and played the piano to keep warm. Their dinner, all washed down with plenty of wine, consisted of vegetable soup, followed by fried trout, and for dessert, a bowl of wild strawberries. It was a meal that sounded much like my dinner of the previous night, minus the strawberries, now long out of season.

We reach the tiny village nestled in the heart of Spanish trout fishing territory, just as the sun rises. It does not appear that much has altered since Hemingway immortalized the picturesque village nearly a hundred years earlier. The traditional Basque architecture lives on in the old buildings with their white stucco facades, red tile roofs, painted red wooden shutters, and window boxes. Even the old Hostal Burguete where Hemingway and his companions stayed seems largely unchanged, including the piano with his signature on it, and the menu made famous, at least in part, for its soup, immortalized by Hemingway. We're not interested in Hemingway this morning, though. We're in dire need of coffee. We turn in at the Bar Frontón, where I head straight to the counter to order, determined to practise my Spanish.

"Buenos dias! Dos cafés con leche. Dos croissants. Por favor," I say carefully, speaking like a child, enunciating one word at a time. The lovely Spanish woman behind the counter serves the croissants to me plain, untoasted, no butter, no jam. I only remember afterwards that I should have ordered the croissants a la plancha—grilled croissants slathered in butter.

"¿Mantequilla, por favor?" I ask hesitantly. She hands me a couple of pats of butter. I try asking for jam, but I cannot think of the word. "Jam," I repeat several times, motioning as if spreading jam on a croissant. The woman looks at me with curiosity but absolutely no comprehension. "Jam, JAM," I say, speaking more loudly. Finally, I look to Celine, who is sitting at a table by the window behind me. "¿Confitura?" she says, uncertainly, trying a Spanish version of the

French word confiture. "¡Si, la confitura!" says the woman, and hands over a few packages of jam.

I'd forgotten how frustrating it is to not be able to communicate fully, clearly. Getting jam is one thing. Dealing with an emergency, being lost, or worse yet sick or injured, would be another thing entirely. It feels so inadequate to have such limited ability. Walking over to Celine with our croissants, I recognize that I have mere days to get more familiar with speaking Spanish before she returns home, when I will be on my own. I must learn everything possible now, while I can. Every new encounter requires planning. And each time there will some new unforeseen hurdle to get past.

I want to tell this woman, who serves us, that she is kind and patient, and that I am grateful, but I lack the vocabulary, so I tell her gracias three times over, and grin at her. "De nada," she says, grinning back.

The little café is quiet and clean, and the freshly baked, flaky, buttery croissants and strong coffee are excellent. As new as we are to the Camino, to Spain, Celine and I are already beginning to sense a pattern to the days. We have stepped out of one world and into another. In this world, we are sitting by a sheet glass window in the Spanish sunshine, drinking coffee, watching fellow pilgrims coming down the street, and looking out upon a courtyard where Hemingway once sat. We order more coffee, this time slightly more confidently. Suddenly the place is full of pilgrims, and there are no seats left. We drain our coffee cups. Time to take our leave and make room for others.

Today is a kinder, gentler walk, which is fortunate for Celine, as she is already suffering with serious blisters on her feet. It's strange, because my feet tend to blister easily and at every opportunity. Before leaving, I researched footwear and socks extensively, not wanting to suffer with blisters or sore feet. My feet are fine. So far, my wool hiking socks and my jaunty purple boots seem to be doing the trick.

By the halfway point of the day—about a dozen kilometres down the trail from Ronscesvalles, we stop so that Celine can bathe her feet in the Erro river. There is a long tradition of bathing feet in the rivers along the Camino, and many believe that the rivers have special healing properties. I hope so, as I'm raring to go, but Celine is definitely suffering. She needs bandages but didn't pack any, so I haul out my medical kit and hand her bandages. She looks up at me and asks if I have any food. So I haul out my granola bars, and watch pilgrims pass by. The whole time I'm just itching to get back to the trail.

With her feet bathed and bandaged, we hit the path again. The trail travels up and down, mostly along gravel paths, passing through woodlands and fields, farms and small hamlets. It is neither as remote nor anything near as difficult as the mountain pass that we climbed yesterday.

By early afternoon, we are headed sharply downhill towards Zubiri, population four hundred, our destination for the day. A medieval bridge, the Puente de la Rabia, once believed to cure rabies, leads us across the Rio Arga and directly into the old village of Zubiri, where we make a snap decision to avoid the albergue and find a hostal for the night instead. Spanish hostals, distinct from hostels and albergues, are more like small residential hotels and offer private rooms, usually with private bathrooms. For thirty-five euros, we have a long narrow room with twin beds placed end to end, a private bathroom, and the use of both the lounge and the kitchen upstairs. The place is tiny and immaculate, the owner helpful and accommodating. After unpacking our gear, we head straight back to the river so that Celine can soak her feet again. She has left her boots in the room and is running around in her spare shoes, a pair of faux fur-lined Crocs. I sit on the bank reading my Camino guidebook.

Afterwards we find a patio and sit in the sunshine drinking wine and beer. Celine strikes up a conversation with Shell, a tall, long-legged, friendly Swedish man, who plans on walking forty kilometres or more a day. He complains bitterly about the demise of Sweden, and the perils of socialism. "Sweden," he says, "is not all ABBA, IKEA, and pickled herring." Shell likes to talk. Celine is happy to listen. They order more beer, and I leave the two of them to commiserate about the ineptitude and horrors of Swedish bureaucracy while I head back to the room to wash my clothes in the bathroom sink and hang my wet laundry on a rack on the patio.

Soon Celine reappears, and we head out to find a grocery store to get something to cook for dinner. We made an agreement beforehand: if we stay in an albergue, we'll go out to find a decent meal. If we stay in a private room, we'll offset the cost by making our own dinners. In theory, it seems like a good balance.

The mini-supermercado is tiny, completely foreign, and all so unfamiliar. We attempt to navigate the small space. We have no seasonings, no olive oil, and no real idea what's back in the kitchen at our hostal. There is an impressive meat counter for such a little store, but it is all behind glass, and we have no idea what any of it is called. How would we order pork chops for example? Or the dried sausage, or ground beef? Or jamón? We are too intimidated to know where to start with all the different varieties of Spanish ham.

This is a country that takes its pork products seriously. There's jamón Iberico, jamón Iberico de Bellota, jamón serrano, jamón de la pata negra. And even a whole film about jamón with Penelope Cruz and Antonio Banderas. Too complicated, we decide. Fruits and vegetables are safely out of reach on the back wall, behind a man standing at the counter like an old apothecary. Apparently, we will need to speak Spanish if we want to order meat or fruit. We turn to the accessible shelves, pick out some nice-looking chocolate with almonds and a bottle of local rosé. Hunger and fatigue are setting in. Our priorities are to eat something and then get some sleep. We are unable to figure out what to cook for dinner, too new in the country to know what to look for, too uncertain how to ask for help. We settle on a boxed pizza from a glass fronted freezer compartment. This is not what we planned or hoped for, but for tonight at least, it will have to do.

The picture on the package shows a pizza with a perfect golden-brown crust, loaded enticingly with all kinds of melted cheese. "4 Quesos," the box says. "Emmental, mozzarella, grana, cheddar." My mouth waters as I read the names of the cheeses, and I realize how famished I am. Emboldened by our choices, I ask the man at the counter for two oranges. "Dos naranjas, por favor," I say, practising saying the Spanish words out loud.

Back in our quarters, we head upstairs to make our dinner. I turn to Celine, standing for a moment in the kitchen looking around, perplexed. "There's no oven," I say.

"Wait, what do you mean there's no oven?"

"Well, just that. There's no oven. At least not one I can find."

Even though it seems ridiculous, we go on a small hunt in case the oven is tucked away somewhere, or perhaps disguised as something else. We open all the cupboard doors, check the living room, the hallway, a large closet. Sure enough, there's no oven.

There is, however, a countertop electric unit with two small coil elements, a microwave, a sink, a kettle, and a small kitchen table with two chairs. I open the few mostly empty cupboards trying to find some sort of pizza pan. The only thing I can find is a rectangular metal tray which I place the pizza on, then set the pan on the elements and turn them both on medium. I rinse mismatched wine glasses, dry them, and pour wine. Celine is sitting at the table, head in her hands, slumped over in exhaustion.

Within a few minutes there is foul, acrid smell. Apparently, the pan is made of plastic, and merely has a metallic coating. We spend the next ten minutes trying to scrape the melted plastic off the element before anyone catches us. For a few moments, we consider abandoning the pizza and going out into the dark night to find dinner. But we are both hungry and bone tired, and Celine's feet are absolutely raw with blisters. She cannot even contemplate putting anything on her feet. I don't like the idea of going out alone in the dark, in this unfamiliar village, with my rudimentary grasp of the Spanish language, trying to figure out what else we might have for dinner.

For a moment we consider trying to use the microwave to cook our now very soggy, very white looking pizza, but agree that would just create an even bigger lumpier, soggy, white mess. I find a small fry pan and attempt to fry the pizza, cut into slices. There is no olive oil, no butter, nothing at all to assist with the task of frying the frozen pizza, but I persist anyway.

We pour more wine, and the evening begins to improve. We sit together in the ill-equipped kitchen, eating the doughy fried pizza. It's not so bad. At this point, it's no longer a pizza, but rather fried dough with a load of melted cheese. All four cheeses, which had excited us with their promise of deliciousness when we bought the pizza, taste exactly the same. We wash it down with the last of the bottle of wine, which thankfully is absolutely excellent.

We finish off with impossibly sweet oranges and chocolate. Not that bad, really. And this, after all, is not meant to be a gastronomical pilgrimage. Many a pilgrim has survived on far less for thousands of years. Soldier on, I can hear my late father say.

Sitting up on our twin beds, I reinforce the hems of my pants, which are too long for my boots, while Celine rifles through her gear. Moments later, we turn the lights out, and Celine begins snoring. I lie in bed, reminiscing about our sweet breakfast in Burguete, and thinking about Hemingway, who loved this part of Spain. I think about Hemingway soup, about the joy he took in trout fishing and the pleasure he derived from eating even the humblest of foods. Despite dinner, I am so hungry that my stomach is audibly rumbling. Celine stirs in her bed and for half a second, then resumes snoring. It is only then that I remember it is Thanksgiving Day in Canada. A sacred day of feasting and glorious food and gratitude.

Hemingway Soup

In 1924, while he was visiting the small village of Burguete, Ernest Hemingway stayed at the Hostal Burguete and began his dinner with a bowl of Sopa de Navarra a la Burguete. Later, he wrote about it in *The Sun Also Rises*. The Hostal Burguete is still open and largely unchanged and continues to serve a version of this hearty soup, which became known as "Hemingway Soup," following the 1997 publication of a version of the recipe in the *New York Times*, with the title "Savouring the Soup of Hemingway Country." This recipe is from *The Hemingway Cookbook*, and is used with permission.[16]

Serves 4

30 mL (2 tbsp) olive oil

5 cloves garlic, crushed

1 onion, finely chopped

2 leeks, white part only, thinly sliced

454 g (1 lb) cured ham such as serrano or prosciutto, preferably in one piece

180 g (1 cup) dry white beans (such as Navy, Cannellini or Great Northern beans)

1.5–2 L (6–8 cups) water, as required

90 g (1 cup) thinly sliced green cabbage

100 g (1 cup) green beans, trimmed and halved

140 g (1 cup) frozen peas

Salt and pepper to taste

In a large saucepan, combine the olive oil, garlic, onion, and leeks. Sauté on medium-low heat until the onion has softened, about 10 minutes. Add the ham, white beans, salt, and pepper. Add the water, enough to cover everything.

Simmer, covered, for about 2 hours, or until the white beans are tender, adding more water as required. Once the white beans are tender, add the cabbage and green beans. Cook and simmer for another 20 minutes. Add the peas and cook a further 5 minutes.

Remove the ham* and serve the soup.

*Some of the ham may be chopped up and added back into the soup, and any remainders may be reserved for other uses.

CHAPTER FIVE

Zubiri to Pamplona

October 11

"If I couldn't walk fast and far, I should just explode and perish."
—A letter from Charles Dickens to John Forster, written in September 1854;
included in the *Life of Charles Dickens*, by Sir Frank T. Marzials

The days are taking on a definite rhythm: wake early, pack bags, tumble out the door into the dark, start walking. From the moment I first wake and am still in my sleeping bag, I'm reaching around gathering things—phone, charger, guidebook, pen, notebook, earplugs, socks, clean undies. I am both half packed and half dressed by the time I emerge from my sleeping bag, which now takes me about two minutes to stuff and compress.

It's so cold in the morning that we leave wearing all our layers, including our packable down jackets, which are proving indispensable. The last thing I do is sling my pack on, along with the small flat cross-body bag that contains my passport, pen, pilgrim credencial, and a flat, zippered pouch that contains my credit card and bank card, and a couple of days' worth of euros.

The first order of operations is to find coffee and breakfast. After last night's fried pizza travesty, we decide to try to find a decent breakfast before leaving. Uncertain if anything will be open so early, we head into Zubiri's tiny main square to find signs of life at the Bar Valentin. Inside, the place is hopping with locals and pilgrims. Celine and I grab a pair of seats at the end of one of the long communal tables and park our packs against the wall. At the counter, I order from the scrawled Spanish menu over the bar. "Dos cafés con leche" (espresso with steamed milk) "y un bocadillo con jamón y queso, por favor," I say, enunciating carefully—still experimenting with speaking Spanish aloud. The bocadillo is a Spanish version of a ham and cheese breakfast sandwich, served hot on half a large baguette. It is more than big enough for both of us. We share it and down our coffees. The coffee is so good that we promptly order more. The bill for our four barista coffees and the substantial grilled ham and cheese baguette is just a little over the equivalent of ten Canadian dollars— the coffees alone in Canada would have cost us more.

I look around the Bar Valentin, breathe in deeply, and commit it to memory. The cigarette vending machine in the corner; the old Coca-Cola advertisements tacked to the wall; a group of handsome silver-haired men in the corner, drinking coffee and talking Spanish animatedly. Beside us, a long table of pilgrims are having a vigorous conversation in German.

The place is packed, and yet somehow pilgrims and locals still seem to be piling in. Some are venturing into the adjoining store—the same store we shopped at last night. In the background a Spanish radio station plays on. The air is thick with the scent of strong coffee and of sizzling meat. The place is absolutely humming with life, even though the sun is not yet up.

I take our empty cups to the counter and lay down a tip. "Gracias, señor, muy bien," I tell the man behind the counter, who grins and blows me an air kiss—a clear, simple statement with no words. This sweet little moment, I think to myself, this is Spain!

As we leave the café, the sun is just beginning to edge the horizon, the dark easing into the soft light of early morning. We cross back over the magnificent old stone bridge out of Zubiri and turn west onto the trail. This, too, is fast becoming a routine—dark mornings, leaving before the sun has risen, finding the trail, and then heading west towards Santiago, the sun rising at our backs.

It feels good to be back on the trail, to be back outside, to stretch out my legs. Good to spot the markers on the path, the ones that tell us the number of kilometres to Santiago. To see those numbers begin to drop, little by little.

I don't remember when I last spent so much time out of doors. There is an unexpected joy for me in long days under the Spanish sky, the earth under my feet, the sun rising at my back and setting on my face. I stride out to meet it, all of it, already feeling stronger.

The trail today is a little easier. It is gently rolling, rather than fiercely up and down. Once again, the trail is adjacent to a major road, but for the most part we are unaware of its presence. Walking alongside the banks of the Rio Arga, the trees and the river become the company we keep for most of the day. At regular intervals we pass through small villages and streets lined with old stone buildings. It is another perfect Spanish day.

Before long, we run into Shell, the amiable, opinionated Swede. He wants to know where we spent the night. "It was absolute hell in the albergue last night," he announces. Apparently, there were a couple of very serious, unrelenting snorers, "...so noisy that no one slept." I am belatedly thankful for the quiet of our small room. Shell's boots were not working out for him either, so he bought new ones in the little hiking shop in Zubiri. The new boots are already causing him grief, and he seems unlikely to be walking forty kilometres a day at this rate. Despite this, he seems undeterred, if not impressively cheerful, even while complaining about everything. We walk on and leave Shell behind to find some coffee.

By early afternoon we are on the outskirts of Pamplona and begin the trek through the city's suburbs. Pamplona is the first city of any size along the route. Although it only has a population of just under two hundred thousand, its reputation precedes it. Everyone we run into is excited about visiting this city that owes so much of its notoriety to the famous running of the bulls during the San Fermín festival. There's more talk of Hemingway too. His name seems so deeply etched on the place that North Americans, at least, can scarcely speak of Pamplona without the mention of it. I was never that interested in him before I decided to go on this trip, when suddenly his presence felt weighty, tangible.

Celine and I head into the old city, crossing the Rio Arga on the magnificent twelfth-century stone pilgrim bridge, El Puente de la Magdalena. As soon as we cross the river, we turn left along the riverbank in search of the hostel where we hope to spend the night. It's a small place with just twenty-six beds, right on the riverbank, just a little way off the Camino. We're anxious to get booked in, because even in October, many of the hostels and albergues fill up at night and finding another place in Pamplona might be challenging.

Thankfully we arrive in time to book in for both bed and breakfast. We hand over our passports, our pilgrim papers, and our euros. A volunteer shows us up a narrow staircase to our room, where we are happy to find just two bunk beds. At most, there will be four of us. We shed our backpacks, take turns showering, and then set up our sleeping bags for the night. Our plan is to have a quick siesta before heading back out to explore Pamplona.

Just as we climb into our bunks, we get a new roommate, an elderly German woman. She climbs with great difficulty onto the top bunk, then proceeds to spend thirty minutes frantically and noisily rifling through every single item in her very large backpack. She needs some acetaminophen, which it turns out she doesn't have. Once again, I haul out my medical kit and dispense tablets, and she promptly lies down and goes to sleep. However, Celine and I are now wide awake due to our roommate's rummaging, so we skip the nap and set off to explore the city.

Back along the riverbank, we head through a park and soon get our first views of the original medieval walled city of Pamplona, looming above us. A path leads us to an impressive drawbridge, where we pass through the remains of an old city gate built in 1553. Pilgrims have been entering Pamplona through this gate, the Portal de Francia, for nearly five centuries.

Once inside the city walls, we walk along narrow cobblestone laneways packed with ancient taverns, endless small shops, restaurants, and patios. We pass tall and narrow brightly painted buildings, the magnificent medieval San Saturnino church, and the fifteenth century Cathedral of Santa María la Real. Everywhere we look we see wrought iron fretwork, elegantly disintegrating stone and brick walls, clay pots of red and pink geraniums, balconies strung with fairy lights. Pamplona is a storybook town—deeply and seductively gorgeous.

We wander on admiring the architecture, the gardens, the stylish stores. I'm afraid to go into the shops—afraid to have to speak Spanish. I've already lost my sunglasses and need to replace them. But how would I even begin to ask?

Frustratingly, all my high school French comes flooding back, somewhat uselessly. "Je voudrais acheter des lunettes de soleil, s'il vous plaît," I think to myself. My high school French teacher, Mademoiselle Paraschuk, would be proud of my adult competence en français, but it's Spanish words I need. Spanish words have come and gone through my head all day long, but just as I need them, they seem to evaporate. If I have to speak Spanish, I can live without sunglasses for a bit longer. I can wait. Even though the sun is still surprisingly intense this late in October.

We walk the narrow streets of the old city until hunger forces us to make our way back towards a café we spotted earlier. By luck, we manage to get one of the two outdoor tables. We order a Garnacha, the local rosé or rosado, as it is known in Spanish, and the house special—hamburguesas topped with Seville orange whiskey marmalade. Beef seems like a likely bet in this city so famous for bulls. Plus, tonight we're not pilgrims, we're tourists, hence the hamburgers. No humble pilgrim menu tonight.

We sit back and watch the world pass by—the well-dressed locals, the tourists and visitors, and the pilgrims who, like us, are obvious due to their walking gear. Soon our waitress is back with two of most glorious burgers either of us have ever eaten in our lives. We sit grinning at each other, ordering more wine, impossibly happy.

After dinner we wander the streets heading to the famous fourteenth century Plaza de Castillo. Along the route, we stop to buy some chocolate for dessert. In a confectionary store, we choose a block of creamy, soft turrón de chocolate. Turrón's origins can be traced back to the Moorish conquest of Spain in the Middle Ages. Originally a hard nougat, new versions have evolved, and turrón in all its forms is now a quintessential Spanish sweet.

Sitting on a bench on the edge of the plaza we take in the old buildings, the balconies with their ornate railings and pots of cascading ivy and trailing roses, the small twinkling lights everywhere, and a million stars in the dark sky above. We are surrounded by centuries of history. It was here where markets were held, where the military marched, where bullfights once took place, and where Hemingway hung out drinking and womanizing. It is so hard to tear ourselves away that we temporarily forget we need to get back to our hostel before the doors are locked tight at ten o'clock. It is well past nine o'clock when we come to our senses and take off in haste, making our way backwards through the old city and towards the river. Going back though, nothing seems quite familiar.

"It's this way, right?" we say to each other, each hoping for confirmation. But the old city looks so different in the dark heading back to the hostel in the reverse direction. Neither of us acquired a European data plan for our cellphones, and without wi-fi, we're stuck. We pause to ask a couple of people for directions, but apparently nobody has heard of our hostel, nor are we sure if they can understand our mangled Spanish. Eventually we realize that we left the old city on a street that appears to be parallel to the one we came in on, but quickly diverged, and now we have twice as much territory to cover. We sprint through a rather grim, dark, industrial-looking part of town that appears to be full of parking lots, back entryways, and people lurking in the shadows. We keep checking our phones and watching the time, all while trying to figure out where we are. With time closing in on us, we end up running the last kilometre through the pitch black until we can finally see our hostel up ahead and make our curfew by less than five minutes.

Turrón de Chocolate Blando

Turrón is traditionally a Christmas treat in Spain, Portugal, Italy, and much of Latin America, though it is now widely available year-round throughout Spain. This nougat confection can be either soft and fudge-like (turrón blando) or hard and crunchy (turrón duro), which needs to be broken or smashed into smaller pieces.

The origins of turrón can be traced back to the Moorish conquest of Spain in the early Middle Ages. The earliest version of turrón—turrón duro—was essentially a hard nougat made from eggs, honey, sugar, and nuts. Turrón duro is usually made with Marcona almonds, which are grown almost exclusively in Spain and have a distinctive buttery taste.

Turrón blando, with its more fudge-like consistency, became immensely popular after the Spanish landed in Mexico and brought chocolate back to Spain. The introduction of chocolate to Spanish confectioners brought about a new turrón—turrón de chocolate, of which there are many varieties in Spain.

Dozens of varieties of turrón blando are sold in Spain, and include ingredients such as marzipan, coconut, nuts, caramel, dried or candied fruits, candies, and sprinkles, as well as puffed rice and other cereals.

Makes 16 small pieces

80 g (1/3 cup) butter, preferably salted

500 g (18 oz) chocolate (I used half milk chocolate and half dark chocolate)

32 g (2 tbsp) honey

Additions:

100 g (3 ½ oz) roasted almonds, skin on, loosely chopped

65 g (½ cup) or more of dried cranberries or whatever other additions you prefer (see list of additions below)

Small pinch of cayenne pepper (optional)

Possible alternate additions: Chopped walnuts, pumpkin and sunflower seeds, goji berries, chopped dried apricots, dried blueberries, raisins, pistachios, cookie bits, candied orange, candied ginger, and crispy rice cereal (very popular in Spain).

Butter, or line with parchment paper, a 20 × 20 cm (8 × 8 inch) glass baking dish.

In a heavy saucepan, melt the butter over low heat. Once the butter is melted, add the chocolate. Keep the heat on low and stir frequently until the chocolate is completely melted and glossy. Do not attempt to speed the process up by turning the heat up, or you will scorch your chocolate.

Once the chocolate is melted, remove the pan from the heat, and stir in the honey, incorporating it fully. The mixture should be shiny and glossy.

Add the nuts and cranberries, and cayenne pepper if using, along with any other additions.

Using a spatula, scrape the chocolate into the prepared baking dish.

Set the dish in the freezer for thirty minutes or in the refrigerator for an hour or two.

Remove the turrón and cut into sixteen small squares; store in an airtight container.

¡Disfruta! (Enjoy!)

CHAPTER SIX

Pamplona to Puente la Reina

October 12

"Susurrus: a whystering, or soft murmuring, or such noise as trees do make
with the wind, or a river when it runneth, or birds when they chatter."
—Thomas Eliot, *The Dictionary of Syr Thomas Eliot, Knyght*

Once again, Celine and I wake up with just enough time for breakfast in the
hostel, to be followed by our now usual hasty departure.

The breakfast room feels small and is awkwardly silent. After the spirited
Spanish cafés and bars that we've encountered, this hostel feels all wrong.
The tables are too close together, and everyone seems slightly on edge, as if
everyone's space has been infringed upon. There is no music, no chatter, no
percussive hustle or bustle. The quiet seems unnatural.

I am no sooner in my seat than the woman serving tables approaches me.
"Are you sneaking in?" she says, accusingly, standing over me. "No," I say, con-
founded, "I am definitely not sneaking in."

"Did you pay for breakfast? Or are you sneaking in?" she asks again, scru-
tinizing me from head to toe. She has a heavy German accent, and, perhaps to
make herself understood, she is talking embarrassingly loudly.

"Ja und nein!" I reply, equally loudly. I start thinking of what else I could
possibly tell her in German. But for some reason at this moment, I can only
think of insults in French. I tell her again, in English, that YES, I did pay,
and offer her my name so that she can check the records. Celine, as under-
caffeinated as me, verifies this with her. "Yes, we arrived together, and we both

paid at the same time. JUST GO CHECK THE LOGBOOK!" she says, dismissing the matter firmly, as if this will obviously resolve the situation. I wonder what Celine might yell at her in German, if she spoke it.

Celine is used to being heard, to being in control. She's strong and forthright and confident. But even she is not enough to deter this woman. Breakfast is instant coffee and white bread toasted, so even if someone hasn't paid, it hardly seems a serious crime. When I ask for a second piece of toast, the woman eyes me up again before acquiescing. She keeps staring at me, still regarding me with suspicion. I feign disinterest, ignore the entire situation. I dare not ask for more coffee, but I hold my ground and continue to drink the instant coffee and eat my toast, knowing full well that I paid for this breakfast—such as it is.

Eventually the server moves to another table and accuses someone else. It seems that perhaps there is one more person in the breakfast room than the records indicate, though this is just a guess. She keeps doing a head count, pointing her finger at each of us as she adds up the number. This shouldn't be complicated, as there are fewer than ten of us. The other guests staying in the hostel seem to have decided wisely to find their breakfast somewhere else. But still, our server counts us all several times. Eventually she asks a third person if they paid, and by now all of us in the room are exchanging looks and grinning. It seems rude to laugh out loud, but it is hard to contain ourselves.

When she announces that she is going to check the logbook again and leaves the room, one of the other breakfast guests calls out to the room at large, "Well, well, well, what a mystery! A real whodunnit! I'm on the edge of my seat wondering who the next suspect will be." "Careful," someone else says, "it could be you!" At this point it's almost like a party game, each person commenting and riffing on the previous jab. We part as a group, all of us in high spirits, united by a common foe.

The Camino leaves Pamplona via the old city, and we stop once again to buy supplies at the market. Because of our breakfast in the hostel, we left later than usual, so by the time we arrive in the old city, the mechanized street sweepers are out in full force. They are a common sight in every Spanish city of any significant size, machines sweeping and washing the streets, making things beautiful again. The general cleanliness of Spain surprises me over and over.

Celine heads off to buy fruit and bread, while I shop for sparkling water, our daily chocolate ration, and a wedge of cheese. "Un poco de Manchego por favor," I say to the stall holder in the market as I hold up my thumb and finger to show her what size wedge. "¡Si, perfecto!" she says in acknowledgment. She cuts me a wedge, weighs it, wraps it, then cuts me a separate sliver to eat on the spot. It's buttery and nutty and salty-sweet, and the flavour that lingers on my tongue is like a creamy, melting, salted caramel. The Manchego that I buy at my local supermarket in Canada is delicious enough, but this Pamplona version is in an entirely different class. I could eat this cheese every day for the rest of my life and never tire of it. I am as thrilled with the cheese as I am with my successful attempt to obtain it. My confidence in speaking Spanish is slowly expanding, word by solitary word.

Purchases made, I find Celine, and we set off in earnest, walking the now-immaculate streets of the old city. Buoyed up by my success at the market, I stop at a small store selling glasses and, in my new enthusiasm for doing business in Spanish, manage to buy myself a pair of overly expensive sunglasses.

Maybe it's because the city feels so appealing, so full of things to stop and admire, or maybe it's just us not wanting to leave, but the trail markers are much harder to spot in Pamplona. Celine and I find ourselves double checking to make sure that we are actually still on the Camino. When we cannot find a trail marker, we watch for people sporting backpacks and walking sticks to follow them. At one point, we spy Phillip from Brazil, who we met at the hostel in Saint-Jean-Pied-de-Port on our first night. His legs are long and lean, loping along the path. We've seen him ahead of us on the trail on previous days. His gait is unmistakable, even from behind and a couple of hundred metres away. When everything is new and different and distracting, a walk as clearly and reassuringly identifiable as his is like an ambulatory compass point.

For the first five kilometres, the Camino follows the tree-lined city streets and wends through the western suburbs of Pamplona, past an immaculate university campus. Everything is well cared for and looked after. It isn't until we pass through the suburb of Cizur Menor that we leave the urban landscape behind and find ourselves surrounded by immense wheatfields. The wheat has recently been harvested, and only the remnants of the golden stalks remain blowing softly in the wind, whispering to us, susurring gently as we pass by.

It seems premature and disappointing to leave Pamplona so soon. The constant walking away from something while walking towards something is a given on the Camino. But as sad as I am to leave Pamplona behind, I am just as happy to be back in the wide-open Spanish countryside again, feeling the sun warm my back, as it has done every morning so far.

Thankfully, out here in the open country, the path and the way markers are almost impossible to miss. We walk by crumbling monasteries and through windswept golden fields with bales of hay stacked as big and as tall as fortresses, into the foothills of the Sierra del Perdón. To our left in the southeast, there is a long high ridge, topped by a dramatic and impressive single-file row of massive, white, modern wind turbines slowly turning, their white blades slicing through a cornflower blue sky.

In the little village of Zariquiegui, we pause long enough to find a cup of good strong Spanish coffee before tackling the two-and-a-half-kilometre ascent to the summit of the Alto del Perdón (the Mount of Forgiveness). This is a place made famous by *The Way*, a 2010 film about the Camino that featured the iconic metal sculpture of pilgrims that straddles the summit of the now renowned site. Had I read my guidebook properly, I might have anticipated both the steepness of the ascent and the fact that we were closing in on the famous sculpture, but I've largely abandoned reading the guidebook and use it almost solely as a rough guide for telling me more or less where I'm meant to be. I discovered only after I arrived in Saint-Jean-Pied-de-Port that I could have bought a much slimmer, lighter, less expensive, and maps-only version of the same book. I had a moment of guidebook envy when I saw it—who knew such envy exists?—but that was before I remembered that I have an astoundingly lousy sense of direction and am almost useless at reading maps. That said, I think best on my feet and have an uncanny ability to sniff out and follow a trail.

The weather is turning cold and overcast, and the wind picking up speed as we begin the climb to the summit. The trail is busy, yet wide enough only for one pilgrim at a time here. We are walking single file, a long procession of pilgrims zigzagging our way along a series of narrow switchbacks that crisscross the entire steep face of the mountain.

We are packed so closely together that we can hear the conversations and sometimes even the breathing of the people ahead of and behind us. Despite the lovely scenery, this is not my idea of an idyllic walk. The path is so narrow ahead that the crowd clumps up, and the only choices are either to find a place to step off the path and wait it out or simply keep pace. Given the long line of walkers behind us and the lack of places to move off the trail, we decide to keep pace. It is only while walking that I remember that Pamplona is a common starting point along the Camino for many pilgrims, so the number of walkers is growing.

Directly in front of us are three Englishmen, at least a decade or two younger than us. The one in the rear is overweight and apparently not the most fit of the trio. He is pushing on valiantly enough, though gasping and wheezing at the pace. A member of his trio, the one out front, is boasting loudly about everything including his own fitness level. "This is a bloody joke," he yells aggressively to no one in particular. "I thought this was supposed to be challenging. I could do this blindfolded, backwards, and drunk. I could run up here, me. I could." Everyone on the trail can hear him, and he clearly has no intention of slowing down to help his friend.

"Fuck off," I say under my breath. Then I say it again and add a whole chain of other expletives. Letting off steam into the wind. "You say something?" asks Celine. "Not me," I say. "That ass up ahead is talking enough for everyone."

"Yeah, we can all hear him all right. Hey, do you know the number for emergency services in Spain?" she asks me. She nods towards the poor guy bringing up the rear who is struggling so badly it looks as though he might just end up having a heart attack. I don't have the number. And I realize that in all the information I've ever seen about the Camino, I've never seen a number for emergency services. If it's in my guidebook, it's certainly too buried to find in an actual emergency.[17] "Don't worry," I tell her, "I'm sure some of the Europeans on the trail will know the number and be able to communicate the issue."

It starts to rain, and someone stops on the path ahead to get out their raingear, yielding a chain reaction of everyone else stopping to get out their ponchos, raingear, and pack covers. Ours already on, we manage to plod on ahead, leaving the three Englishmen to follow. Even when ahead of them, we can still hear them, and when we pause at the switchbacks, we see that the poor guy in the rear is still struggling on. Yet he is gamely making progress. For some reason, I feel quite attached to him. He is such a quiet, persevering contrast to his friend the lout. Someone else is behind the lads now, and with a bit of luck, nobody will need rescuing.

It is a tough but far-from-impossible slog. The worst part is not the angle of the path, but rather walking headlong into driving wind and intermittent rain. The summit, at a mere seven hundred and ninety metres, is hardly high enough to warrant mention, save for the remarkable and almost vertical drop-off to the plains below, along with the surprising beauty of the famous pilgrim monument—a wrought iron depiction of pilgrims from the Middle Ages to the present, on foot and on horseback, in the form of a long procession. The monument bears the poetic words, "Donde se cruza el camino del viento con el de las estrellas" (Where the path of the wind crosses that of the stars). The unrelenting winds at the Alto del Perdón are said to carry away the burdens, regrets, and heavy hearts of the pilgrims who pass by this place. Fittingly, the wind is blowing ceaselessly.

The rain abates, and so Celine and I head to the large stone summit marker to sit behind it. Sheltered from the worst of the wind and huddled together, we eat our picnic lunch of cheese and bread and fruit, along with the leftover turrón from Pamplona. We eat slowly, not just to savour our meals and the scenery, but to extend our break. We want to make sure the struggling Englishman arrives safely. He does. And when I give him the two thumbs up, he returns the gesture and gives me the loveliest smile. Meanwhile, his loud, obnoxious companion is still bellowing at full volume. Luckily the wind is so high that his words are carried away, and we can all ignore him entirely.

With our lunch over, Celine and I begin our descent towards Puente la Reina, passing along the way through the small towns of Uterga, Muruzabal, and Obanos. I like the names, how they sound, and how they anchor me here, in Spain. I am thinking about how many pilgrims have passed through these small towns for century after century, about walking, about how much this journey means to me, and about the long history of the Camino. The path is wider again now, and we are no longer walking in a long line of pilgrims. It seems that all of us, all the pilgrims, have fallen into contemplative silence. A welcome contrast to this morning's noisy ascent.

The approach to Puente la Reina is via busy roadways, so Celine and I are walking on sidewalks and along the sides of the road. Once again we find ourselves back in another long line of pilgrims who have converged on the town, all trying to find accommodation for the night. The sky is dark and broody, and it is raining intermittently again. In the dark and damp, Puente la Reina seems a bit of a shock after elegant Pamplona and so many pretty, old Spanish villages.

The first place Celine and I try to find was recommended to us earlier in the day by Sandra, a German woman whom we keep running into. Sandra pre-booked all her accommodations before leaving Germany, using recommendations from her German guidebook, which lists entirely different places than mine. Her hostel for the night offers private rooms. We pass all manner of albergues and small hotels and finally find Sandra's hostel, only to be told there are no beds available. As we exit the hostel, it starts to pour. We walk dejectedly back through the darkening streets, attempting to find a place to stay. Celine remembers having seen a large municipal hostel, so we trek back to find it—the Albergue Padres Reparadores. When we get there, we join a large crowd of pilgrims all seeking beds.

When it comes to our turn, we hand over our passports, our credenciales, and in return, with no words whatsoever spoken, we are given a scrap of paper bearing our room and bed numbers. We find the door to our room and walk in. It is an austere, cold space filled with a sea of seemingly ancient iron bunk beds with equally old, bare mattresses. The bunk beds are cheek by jowl. The room is lit by bare fluorescent overhead lights. It all seems chilly, unwelcoming, and depressing. Institutional, perhaps even penal. Several people are sitting on their beds, swabbing their weeping, oozing blisters and dressing their various wounds. One person is pulling a needle and thread through someone else's blisters for them. My stomach turns. My heart sinks. And my old nemesis, agoraphobia, takes hold, and I just want to flee and find someplace where I can be by myself.

If I manage to sleep here, it may just be the single worst place I will ever have slept, I tell myself. I am on the verge of tears. I think of my father—of all his walks and expeditions, and of him telling me, "What doesn't kill you makes you stronger." And of him telling me over and over to "soldier on." If I were alone right now, I know that I would turn around and keep walking, even in the rain, even if doing so made no sense at all. But I am not alone, it is getting late in the day, and Celine's feet are sore. We both need to eat, shower, and sleep.

I walk the length of the room, passing bunk after bunk, looking for my bed. Suddenly I see David and Camilla from the first night. My shoulders soften. And there is beautiful Constance from Melbourne, whom we also met briefly along the route. I stand a little straighter. They are together, in a clump of bunks at the far end of the room. By miracle, our bunks are amongst theirs. It is such a sweet little moment of reunion and happiness, and the room doesn't seem so big and empty and cold anymore.

When I find my bed, though, I realize I have been assigned an upper bunk, and I am terrified of sleeping on it. It is ridiculously, crazily high and has no guardrail (at least none that I can see), and I am afraid I will roll right off in the night. I have never heard of an upper bunk without a guardrail. It is insane.

It is then that I notice that all these rusty old iron beds look to be older than me. So unsafe. So tightly stacked together. There are only a couple of feet between each set of bunks. My shoulders slump. My face crumples. I don't sleep well at the best of times, and I cannot imagine sleeping a wink in this over-crowded room, in this horrible bed. It's been a long day, and this is the last straw. I can no longer hold back the tears. I don't care who sees me crying.

Camilla, who has the bunk under David, sees me and offers me her bunk, the last bed in the room, up against the far wall. "But how will you sleep up there, with no guardrail?" I ask her. She waves me to her bed, dismissing my perfectly reasonable query. "Take it. I will be just fine," she says. "Look, I want you to take it." She takes her gear, which is already set up, and moves it to my bunk. Then she gives me a pair of wax earplugs. "Here, try these," she says, smiling, "I think they will help." When I ask her later how she could sacrifice her lower bunk, tucked so neatly in the far corner of the room, the bed under her husband, she says, "It's nothing—a small, simple act. The Christian thing to do." At this moment, to me, it is not a small thing at all, it is remarkably generous. I am not sure how I am ever going to repay her. I thank her profusely, but she just smiles and waves me off. "Return a favour to someone else, sometime," she says quietly.

Anxiety abated, hunger leads Celine and me into a dodgy-looking restaurant, where we find a table and take a seat. I look at the grubby menu and at the litter laying on the floor. I can't stand it. Why is there rubbish on the floor? I have the urge to find a broom and clean the place up. If this is the dining room, what on earth does the back kitchen look like? "There's no way I can eat here, Celine," I say, and then, because she looks exasperated, I add, "Look, it's filthy. Please let's try to find something cleaner."

I seem to be having a complete meltdown. Or perhaps I'm just looking after myself. I don't want to sleep in an unsafe upper bunk, and I don't want to eat in a filthy restaurant. It isn't like me to make unnecessary demands. I'll eat almost anything. And so long as I have some earplugs, I can usually sleep almost anywhere.

Celine agrees, reluctantly, to look for dinner elsewhere. Just down the road, we locate a small bar serving food. It looks at least slightly better from the outside than our last stop, but when we get inside it is surprisingly appealing and very busy. There is a glass case filled with spectacular looking pastries and cakes and a lineup of people waiting for a table. I take all this as a very good sign. While we are in the line waiting, we notice David and Camilla sitting at a table having a glass of wine. Camilla waves us over. "Let's see if you can join us," she says, motioning to the server. Then Constance appears, and despite the crowd in the restaurant, the staff manage to drag a table over to join David and Camilla's table and seat us all together. I think of this morning's hostility versus this evening's hospitality. We order wine and food, and just like that our dismal night has turned into a little party. For the second time in one day, I have been rescued by Camilla, whose graciousness knows no limits, and for whom my gratitude is enormous.

My ensalada verde con limones is absolute perfection, and the langoustines are one of the most memorable seafood dishes I've ever eaten, anywhere. The langoustines, from Spain's rugged North Atlantic Galician coast, are tender and sweet; the lemon sauce a creamy counterpoint to the sweetness of the flesh. I am suddenly acutely happy. My earlier breakdown seems a very distant memory now that I am sitting here, eating, being with others. It is such a joy to be sitting at this table, sharing food and wine with fellow pilgrims after a long day of walking. I know I won't soon forget this evening. This dinner. This beautiful group of people.

On the way back to the hostel, the whole group of us decides to stop and attend evening mass at the Iglesia del Crucifijo, a twelfth-century stone church originally founded by the Knights Templar. The service is entirely in Spanish, so I sit in my pew trying to pick out Spanish words that I recognize. Eventually I stop trying to think, trying to decipher what is being said, and simply let the experience wash over me. I start noticing everything else that surrounds me. The spectacular acoustics, the better to hear the priest (for those who do understand him). The medieval octagonal stone pillars support the multitude of interior stone arches, which in turn, support the roof. I look up, and down, and marvel. I may not understand Spanish, and I may not be Catholic by faith, but I am familiar with the ritual of the mass. The stand, the sit, and the genuflect. I say little silent prayers to any god who will listen. Prayers for my family and friends back home, for tolerance and strength, for the world, for finding my way on the Camino and in life in general. Prayers of gratitude for the people I've met along my Camino. I feel my heart shift as though the prayers and the gratitude are changing me.

I am lost in thought when a group of tourists bursts into the church, completely oblivious to what is happening around them. They begin wandering about taking photographs, laughing, and chatting amongst themselves. The priest has apparently seen this happen before, as he continues on with barely an eyebrow or a voice raised. Eventually the curate who has been assisting the priest gets up and whispers something to the interlopers. They continue a few minutes longer, taking more photographs. One of the female tourists leans up against a sculpture of Christ on the cross and poses suggestively, seductively, before the group finally takes its leave. The priest takes it all in stride, never misses a single beat. The service continues. This extraordinary little interlude was all just part of an ordinary day in his life.

After the service, we depart and shake hands with the priest, thanking him quietly, reverently. I may not have come on a religious pilgrimage, but apparently I am not a complete disbeliever either. The priest hands each of the women in attendance a necklace with a stylized square cross pendant—the cross of the Knights Templar. The gift feels special, almost protective. Perhaps I haven't stopped hoping that there might be a benevolent power looking after the universe. Celine, who hasn't been inside a church for quite some time, says she's just thankful she did not spontaneously combust.

Back in the dorm, everything seems calm. Many of the pilgrims are lying in their beds. Those who aren't sleeping are being respectfully quiet. Even I, after this long day of highs and lows, find myself incredibly calmed by the day's events. I climb into my bottom bunk, tucked up against the wall, along with my new cross. A few moments later the hospitalero enters the room and shuts off the overhead lights. The entire room settles, like children in a dormitory. The quiet is agreeable, appreciated, and in my case, protected and ensured by the gift of new wax earplugs. I thank Camilla in my head, lie quietly still in the dark, and fall asleep counting my blessings.

Ensalada Verde con Limones

Find preserved lemons in the Middle Eastern section of most major grocery stores, your favourite delicatessen, or in many specialty food stores. Recipes for preserved lemons can also be found online. Ingredients usually include lemons, kosher or sea salt (the iodine in regular salt can discolour the lemons), bay leaves or other simple seasonings, and water. Just be sure to follow the guidelines for proper storage.

Serves 4 as an appetizer or side salad

Approx. 360 g (approx. 6 cups) of mixed robust organic leafy greens (any mixture of arugula, romaine, Boston, bibb, radicchio, leaf lettuce, baby kale, baby chard, spinach, etc.)

Fresh chives, to taste

A handful of fresh, young mint leaves

1 preserved lemon

120 g (4 oz) chèvre, crumbled

Dressing:

125 mL (½ cup) extra virgin olive oil

30 mL (2 tbsp) lemon juice

2 tsp white sugar

¼ tsp salt

Wash and dry the greens and tear into desired-size pieces. Snip the chives and mint leaves and add to the greens.

Cut a preserved lemon into slivers and add to the above.

Mix the dressing ingredients together in a bottle with a lid. Just before serving, shake the dressing and pour over salad. Toss gently.

Sprinkle with chèvre and serve immediately.

CHAPTER SEVEN

Puente la Reina to Villatuerta

October 13

"Our greatest glory is not in never falling, but in rising every time we fall."
—Oliver Goldsmith, *The Citizen of the World: or, Letters from a Chinese Philosopher, Residing in London, to His Friends in the East*

Our massive bunkroom is mercifully quiet all night long. There is no snoring, no yelling, no misbehaviour of any kind. Nor anyone falling from their bed. I wake up refreshed, surprised that it is morning already. It is the first night since leaving Saint-Jean-Pied-de-Port that I have slept all the way through. My new wax earplugs are nothing short of a miracle, ten times as effective as the foam ones I came with.

Within minutes of my waking, the dorm lights are turned on. The entire dorm awakens, with everyone emerging from beds, clambering down from top bunks, rolling up sleeping bags, and packing their rucksacks. Doors open and close all the way down the hallway. There is a stampede for the bathrooms. Somehow, though, we all manage, and Celine and I are out quickly and back on the road. We head straight back towards the restaurant where we ate the night before, this time in search of coffee and pastries.

We leave town via the Puente de los Peregrinos, the magnificent Romanesque bridge from which the town of Puente la Reina (Bridge of the Queen) takes its name. The bridge was built almost a thousand years ago, at the request of Muniadona of Castile (circa 995–1066), who was the Queen of Pamplona from 1011 to 1035. She had the massive, six-arched, 360-foot-long bridge—a spectacular early feat of engineering—built over the river Arga specifically to allow pilgrims safe passage across the river on their way to Santiago.

Standing atop the bridge and looking down at the expanse of moving water, I find myself thinking about those early pilgrims who crossed the Arga River, here at its widest point, for nearly two hundred years before the bridge was built. I imagine them wading and swimming through the river in their sturdy shoes and broad brimmed hats. I think about the animals they might have brought along with them, their satchels, and their scallop shells—the iconic symbol of the Camino de Santiago, the lines on the shell representing all the many different routes leading to the tomb of Saint James in Santiago de Compostela. I think about the dangers and difficulties those pilgrims must have faced. There are moments like this along the Camino when I feel the full weight of time, of history, of all those who have walked the path for centuries and centuries before me. It puts everything into perspective.

Looking back towards Puente la Reina, I am sad that I didn't appreciate the town more. Now bathed in morning sunlight, Puente la Reina looks so much prettier, so much more appealing than it did yesterday, when we arrived in the rain, walking on modern roadways under ominous skies.

Walking along with Celine, leaving the city behind us, I recognize that I am also leaving behind a lot of preconceived notions and fears, including many that kept me from being here, walking this path. I have lived for so long with an intense fear of being stuck in a crowded space with a lot of strangers that I thought my reticence completely normal. I've lived a good part of my life avoiding restaurants, concerts, movie theatres, and basically all forms of public transportation. It's why I had a meltdown in the hostel in Puente la Reina. Why I'm phobic about flying—why I feel trapped long before I enter an airport or step into an airplane. For weeks in advance of every airplane trip, I wake in a cold sweat, certain I will die if I board the plane. When I was a student at university, I always picked the seat closest to an exit door in every lecture hall. I didn't even know I was doing it until I realized that if all the seats near the doors were occupied, I simply skipped the lecture. Now, here, on the Camino, I am sleeping in crowded rooms stacked with strangers. For me, this has long been the stuff of nightmares. It's why I do so much research before any travels, why I wear earplugs to drown out noises that could trigger me, why I am so cautious and nervous, and why it took me so long to make this trip that I dreamed of for years.

I don't know for sure where and when all this began, but it's been with me since I can first remember, probably since before I even went to school. I was only formally diagnosed after I asked my therapist to help me deal with my morbid fear of flying. The rest came tumbling out.

My therapist sat listening, then said, "This is classic agoraphobia."

This clinical diagnosis shocked me. "Doesn't everyone feel this way?" I asked the therapist. "Doesn't everyone dread flying? And hate being in enclosed spaces with strangers? Isn't this completely normal?" I couldn't imagine anything else. Who would want to sit in a tin can flying through the sky rammed full of strangers? Anything could happen. I knew that all too well.

She shook her head, "No."

"What's the cure?" I asked.

"Exposure, exposure, and more exposure," she answered frankly.

Well fuck! I thought but didn't say out loud. I was pretty sure too much exposure to too many crazy experiences on airplanes and all manner of other public transport and in public spaces was why I became agoraphobic in the first place.

The more I thought about it, the more my trip to Spain seemed like one massive experiment in exposure therapy. And it seemed as though it might, at least tentatively, be working.

Once we leave the city behind, we walk through what is fast becoming familiar Navarrese terrain: farms, vineyards, olive groves, fig trees, the odd almond tree, wildflowers, and quaint old villages perched atop hills, all largely untouched by time. Some are beautiful and others look a little beaten down—the kind of places where I imagine wild dogs might lunge forth at any moment.

The skies are overcast and threatening rain. But by lunchtime, the sun is shining, and Celine and I are in the medieval, walled, hilltop village of Cirauqui, (Basque for "nest of vipers"), population four hundred and fifty. With its steeply winding narrow streets, stone buildings and arches, and ornate balconies, Cirauqui is an extraordinary treasure, a gem of a place. Our lunch today is a picnic of rustic bread and great wedges of Roncal, a local sheep's milk cheese made in Navarre's Roncal Valley. Our dining room is the picturesque, gated garden of the parish church of San Román, built around 1200. We leave the village travelling on a two-thousand-year-old Roman road flanked with cypress trees, then cross an equally ancient Roman bridge and keep walking under the deep blue sky, in brilliant sunshine, dreamlike beauty in all directions.

Increasingly, I find myself walking alone. Celine and Sandra, our fellow peregrina from Germany, walk at the same pace, so have fallen quite naturally into walking together. We reconvene at regular stops along the trail. Sandra has prebooked a bed in a private albergue in Villatuerta, about four kilometres shy of Estella, our intended stopping place for the night. Celine, who is still suffering horribly with blisters, would like to stop for the night sooner, rather than later. And though I'd rather walk on further, I am beginning to think there is some merit in not stopping for the day in the places suggested by my guidebook. With so many others, especially North Americans and English-speaking Europeans, using the same guidebook, we end up bunching up in the same places each night. As a result, the albergues are busy. Plus, it would be good to arrive somewhere early enough in the day to get some laundry done.

By mid-afternoon, we make our way to Sandra's albergue in Villatuerta. The lobby is quite beautiful, and so we book and prepay, as is normal, for our night's accommodation and dinner. But then, once we leave the lobby, the beauty of the place begins to unravel. We are shown to the vast attic of the ancient building—a large room with a cracked concrete floor, a sea of single beds, and a couple of dim lights. Some of the windows lack windowpanes and are completely exposed to the outdoors, with only primitive wooden shutters to block out the elements. The single electrical outlet for charging phones is already completely occupied. And to top it off, the bathrooms are on the floor below. This albergue is a bit pricier than the other places we have stayed, and since we haven't seen anywhere else locally open to eat, we are pretty much obliged to dine here and need to reserve so that they know how many meals to prepare.

The last remnants of the afternoon are spent attending to laundry. We spend all of our Euro coins to use the washing machine, then use the change machine to swap bills for more coins for the dryer, which gobbles the coins at an alarming rate. Eventually we run out of cash and hang our limp, still wet laundry on our bedposts in the hopes that it will dry in the damp air of the late afternoon.

Just before dinner, a busload of French tourists appears, and their arrival fills the dorm room to absolute capacity—every single bed in the place is taken.

So much for my theory about avoiding the stopping points suggested in the English-language guidebook in order to find less busy accommodations. And so much for my newfound bravado about staying in cramped quarters amongst so many strangers.

At dinner, there is a very simple green salad. Lettuce and some other lettuce. And if there is a dressing, it is so scant that it is hardly discernible. A dash of oil and vinegar, perhaps? This is followed by a choice of "pollo" (chicken, with no other description listed on the menu) or "bacalao con pimientos y cebolla" (cod with peppers and onions). I would choose the cod but for my pepper allergy. So, chicken it is. What comes are two small drumsticks and about half a boiled potato, no other vegetable, no butter, no sauce, no gravy, not even a sprig of parsley. It looks to me a lot like dinner in the workhouse. I look on enviously at the cod and call the server over to ask, politely, for some bread.

For dessert, there is natillas, the custard served in small earthenware bowls with a plain Marie biscuit (a well-loved European butter biscuit) atop. We had this now familiar dessert back in Saint-Jean-Pied-de-Port, where we started our long walk. The dessert reminds me of something one might expect to eat in a boarding school or in a hospital, and yet it is wonderfully silky and quite delicious. The best part of our meal.

The real saving grace to dinner though, is the company at our table of five: Sandra from Germany; Janine from Ontario; Craig, a pastor from Texas; Celine, and me. Not to mention the two large bottles of wine we share amongst us.

Pastor Craig is a masterful storyteller and keeps us entertained. Somewhat surprisingly, he is more like a stand-up comic than a pastor and has us laughing all the way through dinner. He's not actually walking the Camino but simply sticking around for a while, looking at the local architecture, doing a bit of sightseeing, and generally exploring the area. When I ask him about his work, he says, "I'm taking some personal time, and for privacy reasons, I really can't talk about it." I feel a bit silly for asking. We all agree, a pastor absolutely needs to be able to hold a confidence.

Not long after dinner finishes, with us still sitting at the table and talking amongst ourselves, the hostel staff rush into the dining room yelling at us in Spanish, and then in French, "Montez! Montez!" It seems the upper dorm is flooding, and we all rush upstairs. We fly up the two flights of stairs to find the floor covered in water, our beds soaked, our freshly cleaned laundry sopping wet and tossed onto the floor. The wind is so high that great sheets of rain are coming down horizontally, straight through the open pane-less windows—the water is already a centimetre or two deep on the concrete floors. The window over my bed is neatly lined up with the wind direction. I couldn't have picked a less strategic spot to spend the night if I'd tried. My bed, my sleeping bag, and my backpack, along with all my newly washed laundry have borne the brunt of the flood.

While laughing and talking and lingering on well past dinner time, we entirely missed the fact that it was raining cats and dogs, bucketing down. As it turns out, we were not the only ones to have missed the storm. The whole large group of French tourists are all talking at once, angrily. It seems they have demanded their money back and are about to leave on their bus, in the pitch black and pouring rain. Celine is busy translating the rapid-fire French to anyone listening. "They are really, really mad!" she says. I'm not exactly shocked. I'm pretty annoyed myself. Those of us who don't have a bus are stuck. At least we are just a small group now—in fact, our little table from dinner is all that remains. We start moving our gear to the least wet part of the room.

The joyful laughter and chatter from dinner has evaporated. It is miserably cold and wet in the dorm room, and the staff has brought buckets and mops, along with a load of dirty towels to clean the floor. There is nothing we can do but pitch in to help and make the best of a bad situation. And then, seemingly by providence, another staff member (perhaps the owner?), comes to get us and shows us to a much smaller room on the second floor. It turns out that a group of motorcyclists has failed to show up, so we are going to get their room, and if the bikers show, they will be taken to the dorm.

The hosts put my wet clothes and sleeping bag into the dryer for me. The same painfully slow dryer that eats through euros. It is nearly midnight before I finally get my dry sleeping bag back and climb into bed. Pastor Craig is still regaling us with his hilarious stories and, even better, a massive bar of chocolate that he happily shares. I am a little surprised when he doesn't offer a bedtime prayer or blessing. Truthfully, the chocolate he offers us is the best blessing ever.

Though I haven't known many pastors, Pastor Craig is shattering any illusions I might have about how preachers might behave, even if they are on vacation. Drifting off to sleep, I remember that he did not say grace at dinner, either. It causes me a moment's pause, but then I think to myself, why shouldn't a pastor take a break every now and then? And how very reasonable for a pastor to take a break on the Camino.

Weeks later, after Sandra left the Camino and returned to Germany, I would receive a text message from her. Turns out that she ran into some fellow German pilgrims who stayed at the same place a night or two before us. They, too, met Pastor Craig, only then he'd called himself Dr. Craig. He was, he said, a specialist eye doctor in Texas, but was taking some time off from his work, and while not walking the Camino ("not enough time and he needed a rest") he was exploring the local culture. He didn't want to talk about his work for reasons of confidentiality. Fair enough, they thought, he most definitely needed to respect the boundaries of doctor-patient confidentiality.

"It was one hundred percent definitely the same guy who was our Pastor Craig," Sandra wrote in her texts. "No doubt at all, we compared every aspect him—his height, his build, his hair and eye colour, his accent, his mannerisms, even the things he said."

So, our Pastor Craig was an imposter! I wondered about how many other people he had pretended to be—and if this was how he spent his life or just some sort of vacation act. On the plus side, he had rescued a miserable experience and turned it into a terrific lesson in teamwork and resilience. He'd told the funniest stories. And he shared his chocolate. But I can't help wondering who he really is underneath the facade, and who he might be masquerading as now.

Natillas

Natillas is a quintessential Spanish dessert. It is a cooked, stirred custard, made from milk, eggs, and sugar, and sometimes a little lemon zest and/or cinnamon. Natillas, or natilla depending on the country of origin, shows up throughout much of the Spanish-speaking world, but the dish varies widely from country to country.

Spanish natillas and British custard are variations on the same theme— milk, eggs, and sugar cooked slowly at a consistent low simmer, and stirred constantly to produce a rich, creamy, set pudding. Made properly, this silky-smooth custard will melt in your mouth.

The word custard is thought to have derived from the French term croustade — that is, the pastry crust that held the custard in place. Natillas comes from the Spanish word nata, meaning cream. Natillas is thought to have first appeared in early Spanish convents where chickens were kept for both meat and eggs. Although many ingredients were sparse, eggs were often abundant in religious convents and abbeys. As early as a thousand years ago, the Catholic Church banned the eating of four-legged animals on feast days, resulting in a soaring demand for chicken. And along with the chickens came eggs.

Natillas is often served in small individual pottery bowls or ramekins. The custard is sometimes sprinkled with cinnamon and sugar or topped with a plain sweet cookie such as a Marie biscuit. Served in small bowls, mini canning jars, or even small drinking glasses, natillas is a perfect addition to the dessert selections for a tapas party. It is silky smooth, immensely satisfying, and surprisingly delicious.

This stirred custard recipe can easily be halved or doubled, just adjust your pan size accordingly. Note: be sure to remove the chalazae (the white twisted cord sometimes attached to the yolk) as this will result in a discernable lump in the finished custard.

Serves 4

500 mL (2 cups) milk
1 tsp lemon zest (optional)
½ tsp salt
100 g (½ cup) white sugar
4 egg yolks
15 g (2 tbsp) cornstarch dissolved in 30 mL (2 tbsp) water
1 tsp vanilla extract
1 tsp ground cinnamon mixed together with 2–3 tsp white
    sugar

In a medium saucepan, combine the milk, lemon zest if using (note — do not substitute lemon juice, or you will end up with curdled milk), and salt. Bring the mixture to a low simmer, stirring frequently over medium heat. Once you've reached a low simmer, you should see a few tiny bubbles in the milk and possibly a few wisps of steam. At this point, turn the element off, and with the pan still on the element, continue stirring for another minute or two longer so that the milk on the bottom of the pan does not scorch. Cover the pan, leave it on the warm element, and proceed with the rest of the custard.

In a large glass or heatproof bowl, using an electric mixer, beat the sugar and egg yolks for about 3 to 4 minutes, or until the mixture is thick and pale. Mix in the cornstarch and water slurry and beat gently to mix. Using low speed, slowly beat in about half of the hot milk, leaving the remaining milk in the saucepan.

Now, pour the milk, egg, sugar, cornstarch mixture into the hot milk remaining in the saucepan. Cook over medium heat, whisking continuously for about 15 to 18 minutes or until the mixture is well thickened. The mixture should be the consistency of a crème anglaise or thick enough to coat the back of a spoon. At this point, remove the pan from the heat, and whisk in the vanilla.

Pour the custard into 4 ramekins, mini canning jars, or small serving dishes. Cover immediately with plastic wrap, wax paper, or parchment circles (to prevent a tough skin from forming on top) and refrigerate for at least 3 to 4 hours or until well chilled.

Before serving, sprinkle with a little cinnamon sugar.

CHAPTER EIGHT

Villatuerta to Los Arcos

October 14

> "Let me not be misunderstood. Strength does not come from physical capacity. It comes from an indomitable will." —Mahatma Gandhi, "The Doctrine of The Sword," *Young India*

Before dawn breaks, Celine and I are up and off. Sandra is staying behind for breakfast. It is not just last night's rainy experience in the albergue that has me shooting out the door so eagerly; it is that I find myself waking each day excited to be upright and walking again. I can hardly wait to get outside again, stretch my legs, and see what each day presents. By the time I've walked five kilometres, I'm invariably hitting my stride. In fact, I walk a near constant five kilometres an hour. A pace and a fact I would never have known were it not for the Camino.

To compensate for our shorter walk yesterday, we have further to travel today. And although it does not seem sensible given last night's hostel disaster, we have also decided to try, once again, to stay at Sandra's prebooked hostel, this time in Los Arcos. She has a bed in a two-bunk room, so if we are able to stay with her, there will be, at most, only one other person in the room with us.

Finding places to stay each night, at least for me, is one of the most challenging parts of the Camino. Walking into a strange town every day after a full day on my feet, and not knowing where anything is, much less where best to stay, feels harder than the walk itself. Plus, surviving the flood seems to have bonded all three of us together. Sandra's hostel is neither mentioned nor shown on the map in my English language guidebook yet comes highly recommended by Sandra's German guidebook.

Our first stop is Estella, the medieval town that would have been our destination last night had we not stopped sooner. With a population of nearly fourteen thousand, it is bigger than I expected, and as is usual in towns of any substantial size, we get lost. We end up wasting time and steps, walking backwards and forwards through the streets looking for the Camino and, even more importantly, seeking coffee and breakfast. Eventually we find a yellow Camino marker but realize we are almost out of town and don't want to walk another hour before eating and drinking, so we backtrack yet again.

With no idea where else to go, we head into an unassuming little café that we spotted earlier. At the counter we order our usual coffees, and despite the selection of tempting pastries, we order a large prawn and spinach omelette sandwich to share. What arrives is a perfectly cooked omelette, golden brown on the outside, soft and tender on the inside, and packed full of prawns, creamy melted chèvre, and delicate spinach, served in a large crusty, well-buttered and warmed baguette. Plenty big enough for two and a study in contrast from our dinners last night. "Gracias señor," I call out to the cook/server/owner. We are uncertain exactly what his role is, but he appears to be doing everything in this small café. "El sándwich es perfecto y el café es mejor que perfecto."

"¡De nada!" he calls out, his back turned to us, all the while flipping sandwiches on the grill.

We polish off our breakfast in silence and agree—the best breakfast of our Camino so far, even though we've been lucky enough to enjoy all our café breakfasts.

As we walk back towards the Camino, we happen upon Constance, from Melbourne. She has just decided that she will quit the Camino, finishing off her walk here in Estella. She looks jubilant and announces that she has to scoot off to have her hair washed and styled before she boards the train to Paris. She asks me to email her daughter in London, to let her know that she is safe and travelling to Paris and jots her daughter's email address in my notebook. Then she hands us a small grocery bag containing bread, cheese, and yogurt. "Here, take this," she says, happily. "I won't be needing it now." And with that, she's off. We know that she'll be eating in the dining car, so we take her groceries gladly, despite the added weight, and hug her goodbye. I promise to meet her again in Melbourne someday soon.

We strike off from Estella, buoyed by our breakfast, our chance encounter with Constance, and our unexpected bag full of treats. If we had been just one minute earlier or later, we would never have seen Constance again.

Just beyond Estella, the Camino takes a turn, and we start climbing again, walking uphill toward Ayegui. We are paying full attention this morning, because we don't want to miss the famous fuente del vino—the wine fountain that dispenses free red wine (and water) for pilgrims.

We needn't have worried. Between the signs and the pilgrims gathered at the site, the fountain would be hard to miss. A clearly visible, multilingual sign at the site reads, "Pilgrim, if you wish to arrive at Santiago full of strength and vitality, have a drink of this great wine and make a toast to happiness." And so we do exactly that, all the while smiling for the webcam that monitors the site and posts the footage on the Internet around the clock.[18]

The free wine is a lovely gesture on the part of the Bodegas Irache, which provides one hundred litres a day of wine for the fountain from the wineries founded on vineyards donated to the Benedictine Monastery of Ira014e in 1072, by King Sancho IV of Navarre.

The wine, it turns out, is not that great. No real surprise. Or maybe it's just too early in the day to appreciate it. But still, free wine! Who could refuse? The novelty is too irresistible. I realize later that if I'd thought ahead, the wine would have been perfect for sangría or tinto de verano.

We leave the wine fountain and walk on alongside field after field of grapevines, vineyard after vineyard, interspersed with occasional olive groves and vast wheat fields that have recently been harvested. Once again, we are walking past the raw ingredients that form the bedrock of Spanish cuisine—grapes for wine, olives for olive oil, and wheat for bread. There's something about this that feels so important—so fundamental. The connection between the land and the food on our plate is often so distant, but here, on the Camino in Spain, it is real and apparent and so obvious. We are figuratively and literally eating the landscape.

In these moments, when I recognize these connections, I feel as though I don't ever want to stop walking the Camino. The long walk is changing me. Healing old wounds. Opening me up. I can feel it happening. My brain and feet are fully engaged and synchronized; my entire body feels stronger. I'm grounded, quite literally connected to the earth below my feet. My heart and mind feel open, responsive, every part of me fully engaged. I've fallen in love with Spain and feel as though I belong here in this big Spanish landscape, in a way I've rarely belonged anywhere.

I could never tire of these surroundings. Off in the distance, flanking the vineyards and fields, are the Cantabrian and Basque Mountain ranges—their peaks frame the horizons on either side of the trail. Wide open terrain, incredible vistas. It does something to me—makes me feel alive, connected. There's a link to the actual land here that is no longer the norm in our city lives. And there's a joy that comes with this that I feel deep within myself.

In the small rural village of Azqueta, we stop briefly for a second cup of coffee. In part it's because we need to fuel up before embarking on the walk ahead, and it's also because the ancient stone building and lively patio at the Bar Azketako is impossible to resist. Just as we are leaving, we bump into our German friend Sandra, and the three of us set off together again, heading uphill to Villamayor de Monjardín. We stop briefly in the village to fill our water bottles at the public water fountain, before setting off on the afternoon's walk, said to be one of the most boring, barren, tedious stretches of the Camino—twelve kilometres along a wide flat, gravel trail through a small desert, with nowhere to stop. No villages, no bathrooms, and not even a tree for shelter. And today with no shade in sight, the temperature has once again climbed into the high twenties, and the sun is beating down on us relentlessly.

After a solid hour of walking in the hot sun, we start to look for a place to take a short break. There is nowhere to be found. The path gives way on either side to flat, dry, dusty fields with the spiky remnants of wheat, sometimes hay. We would sit on the trail itself but for the fact that it is covered in small black caterpillars. We must watch our footing continuously to avoid stepping on them, and even so, are routinely crushing caterpillars with our boots. They make a sickening crunch and a slippery mess as we land on them, but there is little alternative; they are everywhere. At one point we see a few rocks at the side of trail and head over to investigate, only to find the rocks also teeming with caterpillars. We push on silently, sweat dripping from our brows, crushing armies of caterpillars as we go. I can't imagine how hot this section of the trail must be in the height of summer, but perhaps it might, at least, be devoid of the caterpillars.

Suddenly the dusty desert-like dirt trail turns into a road, and a battered tin sign on an equally battered old brick wall tells us that we have arrived in Los

Arcos. At first glance the town looks like something from the wild west, where you might expect to see a saloon, with horses tied up out front and cowboys hanging about. We pass a few rustic, ramshackle houses with goats and chickens in the yards. But Los Arcos, population 1,117 (and shrinking yearly), soon gives way to pure delight as we pass through an archway in the stone wall and enter the old city.

Los Arcos (Spanish for "The Arches"), with its winding narrow roads and spectacular central plaza, has Roman origins and has been a main stopping point for pilgrims for more than ten centuries. Though even before the earliest city existed on this site, and before pilgrims walked the Camino de Santiago, the Celtic Druids would likely have walked this route and stopped here because of its strategic situation at the foot of a hill on the banks of the river Odrón.

We walk straight through the centre of town, eager to return and find food as soon as possible. But first we need to locate the albergue for the night and secure our beds. At the front desk, the staff offer us the option of paying for the fourth bed in our two-bunk room so that the three of us, Sandra, Celine, and I, can have a quiet, peaceful night. We jump at the offer and head straight to our room to set up our sleeping bags and park our backpacks. Then we strike off together, heading back to the central Plaza de Santa Maria to find food and explore the village.

In the sunny central plaza, we find a place at one of the many outdoor tables and crank up the umbrella against the late afternoon sun. Minutes later, our waitress arrives, takes our drink order, and leaves us with menus to ponder. Along with a bottle of local rosé, we order a selection of tapas: chocos fritos (fried cuttlefish), a cheese laden pasta dish, and chorizo al vino tinto, small slices of spicy chorizo in a delicious, deep red wine sauce. Then we sit back and take in the stone walls with their arched portals, the cafés and bars and restaurants that line the edges of the central plaza, and the magnificent twelfth-century Romanesque Church of Santa Maria de Los Arcos.

I want to pinch myself. To remind myself that all of this is real. I am in Spain, in this wonderful medieval village, listening to the church bells chiming, drinking a lovely and fruity local rosé, eating tapas, while the sun slowly descends towards the horizon and night begins to settle in. I imagined nights like this on the Camino, but this is more perfect than anything I ever dreamt of.

Before darkness descends fully, we head off to our home for the night.

Back at the hostel Celine heads off promptly to find a computer to make travel plans for her return to Canada. She has to get from Nájera, where we expect to end up two days hence, to Paris, in time to catch her flight back to Toronto. As it turns out, the logistics are far more complicated than she imagined. One of the staff members at the hostel spends a couple of hours helping her. There is a tight timeline to do this because our hostel apparently shuts down both the Internet and the electricity at night. Only the emergency lighting stays on after ten o'clock to light the hallway and the bathrooms in case anyone needs them overnight.

When Celine finally returns, she is shaking her head. "I need a glass of wine," she says. It turns out that making plans from rural Spain for her return to Paris is not straightforward at all. She thinks she can take a bus from Nájera to Logroño and then hopefully find another bus to Madrid, but the details about how and where to find buses, and which buses to take, are complicated. From Madrid, she has booked a flight to Paris. But she cannot find a place to stay overnight in Paris. For some reason, the city appears to be completely booked out, and the only available rooms are several hundred euros.

"I'll have to wing it," she says. For all her calm, intensely competent manner, Celine seems rattled. She might be smart and brave, but she is a lone female with neither clear travel plans nor confirmed reservations for making her way solo across Europe.

I have the greatest faith in Celine and her abilities to navigate almost anything, but even so, I am worried about her return trip home.

Chorizo al Vino Tinto

If tortilla de patatas is the unofficial national dish of Spain, then chorizo al vino tinto should be the unofficial national tapa. Deceptively simple to make, this dish is an absolute star.

Spanish and Portuguese chorizo are not usually hard to find in North America. Most major supermarket chains carry some form of cured chorizo. I like to buy cured, Spanish style sweet chorizo rather than hot chorizo, but almost any cured chorizo will work in this recipe. If you want to add heat, you can always amp it up with a pinch of cayenne pepper. Cured chorizo is ready to eat as is, but don't let that stop you from cooking with it. The finished dish will depend entirely on your chorizo. This dish should not be overly spicy—you want to be able to taste the constituent ingredients.

> Serves 4 alongside another couple of tapas dishes and
> a sliced crusty baguette
> **325 g** (11–12 oz) cured sweet Spanish-style chorizo
> **30 mL** (2 tbsp) olive oil
> **3–4 cloves** garlic, sliced
> **250 mL** (1 cup) dry red wine
> **Pinch** of cayenne or chipotle pepper to taste
> Wooden toothpicks and chopped fresh parsley to serve

Begin by cutting the chorizo into 1 cm (approx. ½ inch) slices. Warm the olive oil in a large fry pan. Add the chorizo and cook until both sides are nicely browned. Add the garlic and cook for another minute or two.

Add the red wine and turn the heat to medium-low. Allow the dish to gently simmer for about 15 to 20 minutes or until the wine has reduced slightly.

Before moving the chorizo to a serving dish, taste the chorizo and add a small pinch of cayenne or other hot pepper if required.

Place the chorizo and wine reduction in a serving dish and garnish with parsley. Tapas can be served with small plates and wooden toothpicks instead of knives and forks.

CHAPTER NINE

Los Arcos to Logroño

October 15

"Solvitur ambulando: It is solved by walking."
—attributed to Diogenes, Greek philosopher
and later to Augustine of Hippo

My alarm goes off early, and Celine and I leave our hostel in the dark, heading back to the central plaza in Los Arcos to find breakfast in a café. We leave Sandra behind to have her breakfast later in the hostel, as is her preference. She is not opposed to the instant-coffee-and-toast breakfasts served in most albergues. Celine and I would rather walk a bit and find a good, strong Spanish coffee and something other than toast.

There are already men in the cafés, drinking beer. I wonder if this is how they start their days or if they've been there all night, but either way, they don't look any worse for it. We order our cafés con leche and croissants a la plancha and shortly after leave Los Arcos, passing the magnificent Iglesia de Santa Maria de Los Arcos and then crossing the old bridge over the Rio Odrón well before sunrise.

Today the path leaves Navarre and crosses into the province of La Rioja, widely regarded as the most internationally acclaimed, biggest, and most famous of all the Spanish wine regions. Like neighbouring Navarre, La Rioja produces Tempranillo grapes, which are said to flourish in Rioja's more arid climate.

Celine and I are both subdued on this morning's trek. We have another thirty-kilometre walk ahead of us, and it is Celine's second last day on the

Camino. She is still contending with her painful, badly blistered feet, and her lack of clear plans to find a way back to Paris for her flight to Canada is weighing us both down.

But the sun is climbing up the sky behind us, warming our backs and making long thin shadows of our bodies on the trail in front of us, leading us onwards. Soon we are trotting along the path at a good pace, once again under another beautiful deep blue Spanish sky.

We are completely in a groove now—leaving before sun-up dressed in all the layers of clothing we have with us, and by mid-morning we are shedding layers steadily. The first twenty-five minutes on the trail are the hardest as our bodies loosen up and ease back into the rhythm. I have learned to put my coat on and take it off without stopping—slinging my pack off one shoulder and slipping out of one sleeve before putting the strap back over my shoulder and sliding out of my other sleeve. After days of walking, I have developed a little system for economizing on stops and starts so that I can focus on maintaining a steady rhythm. The days are beginning to slide into each other, and I find myself losing track of time and of the number of days we've walked. Forgetting from one day to the next about anything much other than walking and maintaining forward momentum.

We pass through the little village of Sansol and shortly afterwards arrive in tiny Torres del Rio, where the Camino heads directly past the front door of the Iglesia de Santo Sepulcro, a tiny but fabulous octagonal stone church built between 1160 and 1170, by the Knights Templar. The church door is open, so we step inside. The priest, sitting alone, immediately gets up and kindly offers to stamp our pilgrim passports for us. "¡Gracias, gracias!" we say as we haul out our passports. He stamps them but sternly demands a euro each from us and holds out his hand until we comply. We dig out coins of course, though somewhat unenthusiastically because it seems a sham to offer what is normally a free service only to cadge money quite so aggressively from us afterwards. "What a racket," I whisper to Celine. "I wonder how much he takes home in a day."

Milling around and admiring the beauty of the tiny church, which is modelled after the Holy Sepulchre in Jerusalem, Celine starts to sing. The acoustics are divine. Her lovely voice floats up to the top of the church, reverberating off the walls, filling the space. Suddenly all my annoyance is gone. If this old priest has done nothing else but help to save this wonderful old building coin by coin by coin, I'm happy to have contributed. Celine is still singing when David and

Camilla stick their cheerful faces in the door to listen, and I wave them in. The priest repeats his offer to stamp their passports and then demands money from them too, of course, and then retreats to a corner, watching us silently. The four of us stand shoulder to shoulder in the tiny ancient church before tumbling out the door to find the sunlight dancing on the path and our hearts lifted. It is only when I get back on the path that I remember that the Catholic Church is said to be amongst the wealthiest institutions and biggest landowners in the world. The next time a priest puts out his hand, I might just shake it enthusiastically and spend my coins tipping the volunteers in albergues, who are most definitely not amongst the wealthiest on earth.

A few hours and about twenty-odd kilometres later, Celine and I walk into the medieval walled city of Viana, population four thousand, founded in 1219. Viana is stately and elegant—full of formal, old buildings, formidable stone walls, Jacobean-style architecture, huge urns of flowers everywhere. Unforgettably lovely in all directions. It is also the last town in the region of Navarre on the Camino Frances and one of the prettiest of the many pretty small towns along the way.

If I were walking a slower Camino, I'd stay here in Viana and explore this beautiful small town with its two municipal palaces and the majestic Church of Santa Maria with its Renaissance portico. As it is, we stop only to find coffee and lunch with a group of pilgrims, and then I press on alone. Celine is finished for the day—she is tired and has decided to take a taxi for the final ten kilometres to Logroño. She will arrive early and find a place to stay. The only problem is that we have yet to plan where to meet or spend the night. All we really know is that Logroño is a big town—population 155,000—the biggest town on the Camino since Pamplona. We organize to meet at the first major municipal hostel. It's a shaky plan, because neither of us has any idea where that might be, nor have we any way of contacting each other once we split up. Neither of us has a European data plan on our phones, so the only way we can reach each other is to hope to find wi-fi somewhere, and message each other, and hope we happen to be connected at the same time.

Celine doesn't even really know where to find a taxi, let alone any idea where to have the driver drop her off. I strike off, leaving Celine to figure out her taxi problems, knowing that she is smart and resourceful. Even when she can't figure out the words in Spanish, she is pretty good at faking it. Over time, we have learned to begin a lot of conversations with, ¿Dónde está...? (Where is…?), at which point we add whatever it is that we need, in whatever language comes to us—English, French, or Spanish. ¿Dónde está … el baño / la farmacia / el albergue / el supermercado / la estación de autobús / la estación de tren / el banco / el cajero automático / el Camino / la comida / el taxi? (Where is the bathroom / pharmacy / hostel / supermarket / bus or train station / bank / bank machine / the Camino / food / taxi?). It's primitive, but it seems to work.

Back on the Camino, I am determined to get to Logroño as quickly as possible. It is just shy of ten kilometres, or about two hours of walking, along what is another notably lonely and isolated part of the trail. Just as I find my way back to the trail, I see a young woman walking alone, and we greet each other and walk along more or less together, mostly in silence. There is absolutely no one else on this stretch of the Camino, and I am grateful to have company nearby. After a while we exchange names. She is Andrea, from Croatia.

Eventually Andrea opens up a little and tells me that she is walking the Camino to try to sort out a few things in her life. Her love life and her career. "Yes, of course!" I reply, "Who isn't?" She is trying to figure how to carve out a path in life and how to find balance. How to know who is right for her—where to put her efforts. "How can I know if this is real love—the kind of love that will last?" she asks me.

I shrug. "If you have to ask, maybe it's not that kind of love," I say, but then I think that sounds far too negative, so I keep going. "Don't take my word for it. I understand this question all too well, and maybe we all do—maybe it's the human condition." Silence ensues. A little while later, she tells me more and asks what I might do in her shoes.

"I'd probably take a really long walk—like, say, a Camino," I tell her. "Maybe it can all be solved by walking?"

Andrea is smiling. "Yes!" she says. "Yes, yes, you are right. Thank you for reminding me. That is exactly why I am here. How is it that I can forget that?" I understand this clearly, too—the ability to forget the very heart of why we're here. It's why I'm here as well. But I don't need to tell her any of that. We are all, pretty much every single last one of us, uncertain or suffering from something and just generally trying to sort out our lives.

Above us the sky is huge and blue, and the sun is beating down. The landscape is wide open, and there is nothing but vineyards for as far as we can see. There is absolutely no shade, and even though it is well into October, it is still fiercely hot. Still, we walk steadily, never slowing, determined, our pace matched. Andrea is a perfect walking partner. We talk a bit, on and off, but also walk in easy, companionable silence. When we reach the outskirts of Logroño, we part ways and bid each other well in life and love, and I head into the local tourism information office to attempt to find wi-fi and track down Celine.

I'm in luck. Using the free wi-fi at the tourism information office, I find Celine. She is at the major municipal albergue, the Albergue de Peregrinos, and by pure fluke has managed to procure two of the last remaining beds in the hostel, perhaps in the entire city. She started by calling in on the smaller hostels and even a couple of small hotels, but there were no beds to be found anywhere, so she doubled back to the main municipal albergue and managed to get there just before the completo (full) sign was posted. She is waiting for me to arrive so we can be shown to our bunk beds.

We have arrived in town in time for the culmination of the grape harvest season, and the city is in full-on fiesta mode. The harvest festival is known officially as the San Mateo Festival, in honour of Saint Matthew (San Mateo), and is celebrated on his feast day, September 21. The festival is informally known as "Gracias." It's a massive thanksgiving party to kick off the grape harvest. Everywhere is full to the brim: the narrow streets of the ancient walled city are packed with young and old, families, couples, groups of Spaniards all eating and drinking and enjoying themselves. Even without the fiesta celebrations, Logroño, capital city of La Rioja, is apparently a bustling university town and dates back to the Roman era, famous not just for its grapes and wine but also for its location along the route to Santiago, and for its production of fine wool, which stems back to the sixteenth century.

The helpful, friendly hospitalero who checks us in at the albergue suggests we try a nearby café that serves a pilgrims' menu for dinner. She also warns us that there was "trouble" in the albergue the night before, and that the police had to be called in. She says that personal belongings including cash and cell phones were stolen.

"Be careful with your things, and keep all your valuables on you," she says, "And do not be late back—the doors will be locked promptly at curfew. If you are not here, too bad for you." Understandably, the staff are apparently in no mood for any further bad behaviour. Later we learn that somebody tried to break into the hostel after it was locked up, and between crashing about and drunken shenanigans and police sirens, nobody got any sleep in the albergue last night. This makes me very uneasy, but since there are no beds to be had elsewhere, what else can we do? I'm not looking forward to a rowdy night, but on the other hand I feel much calmer and more resolved about such circumstances than I did back at the beginning of the Camino.

We set up our bunks in a large room full of bunk beds. Thankfully our assigned beds are along an outer wall so even though we are stacked in like cordwood, it could be worse. I hang my towel at the end of my bunk like a makeshift barrier, since the bunks are not only side by side but also stacked end to end, with no space between. With our sleeping bags set up and our belongings secured as best we can, we head out to explore Logroño and find dinner.

We walk through revellers, families, pilgrims, teens, lovers. All are huddled around outdoor tables eating, drinking, and partying. There are vendors with carts selling food: empanadas, patatas bravas, sandwiches stuffed full of chorizo, and short skewers of grilled meat. We keep walking. Rounding a corner, we are suddenly in a beautiful, quiet bit of the city—a small open square surrounded by boutiques and upmarket restaurants. The angle of the sun is softer here. It's shaded, quieter, with fewer people. We find a table with an umbrella on the terrace of a beautiful bar and order wine. Our lovely waitress recommends a local white for me—a Rioja Blanco. It is as smooth as velvet. This wine, this beautiful terrace, this very Spanish scenario, is what I dreamed of when I imagined Spain.

Eventually we wander off to explore a bit more of the city before heading to the recommended café, where we find a table outside. Since the Spanish do not eat dinner until around nine, the time that most pilgrims are heading to bed and albergues and hostels are locking up for the night, it is often necessary either to cook for yourself if facilities are available or find a place that serves a pilgrim's meal, or better yet a tapas menu or a menu del dia. The pilgrim's dinner is typically an inexpensive, humble three-course dinner: soup or salad followed by something like chicken or pork with French fries and a dessert course that could be yogurt, a small slice of cake, or occasionally ice cream. Pilgrims' dinners almost always include water or wine. The meals are generally quite economical but also usually quite ordinary. We have already grown a little weary of the predictability of these dinners, so we order with relatively low expectations. I might have dreamed of beautiful wine, stunning vistas, and extraordinary food, but, in truth, I've also learned to appreciate the simplicity, availability, and affordability of pilgrims' meals.

Our waiter brings us a full bottle each of house wine. White for me and red for Celine, along with a large basket of bread. We figure that even if this is as good as it gets, we're going to be fine. Next up are the starters—marinated white asparagus for me, most likely canned or bottled, known as a conserva in Spain. Celine's starter is a small bowl of velvety white bean stew with chorizo and small tender pieces of pork. It is memorably delicious. When I ask the waiter what the dish is called, he says, grinning, "Pork and beans." The answer makes us laugh, but I tell him that I'm serious, that I want to know the Spanish name, so I can order it again somewhere. "Pochas," he says, shrugging. "But if you like that—you really need to try fabada." I get out my notebook, start making notes, but he motions at me to stop and takes out his order pad and writes out *Fabada Asturiana*. He hands me the note, then makes the motion of kissing his thumb and index finger. "You will love me forever after you eat this dish!" he says, winking and walking away from the table. He's letting me in on the Spanish reverence for legumes—for lentils and beans. This just endears me to both the Spanish and their cuisine even more.

Instead of mains, we should have ordered a second set of first courses. But it is too late for that, and we didn't realize that ordering two first courses was an option. Ours mains are utterly and predictably ordinary, chicken and fries for Celine and barely recognizable "lamb" stew (definitely mutton) for me. "At the very least..." I say to Celine, pausing to have a drink of wine before finishing my thought, "...our meals are so overcooked that there's little chance of dangerous pathogens."

We're enjoying ourselves regardless—the beautiful setting, our flirtatious waiter, the wine and bread, and the stars in the sky above, and the lively scene going on all around us. So, we clink our glasses and eat up. The main course is followed by a thin wedge of coffee cake dredged in syrup. We linger on the patio, finishing our wine and watching a wandering magician and a juggling flamethrower who is entertaining children at nearby tables as the sky grows inky dark, and more and more revellers join the streets to celebrate the wine harvest fiesta.

Eventually we head back to the albergue, eager not to be shut out for the night. It is only then, on our way home, that we work out our wine must have been watered down, since neither of us felt the slightest effect of alcohol, despite drinking an entire bottle each. We both agree—it's for the best.

Safely back inside the gates of the albergue, we sit out in the courtyard garden under the night sky, admiring the high stone walls all around us, the spires and bell towers above, the fairy lights strung about, and the twinkling stars. The longer we delay the return to our overcrowded room and our bunks the better. We know we'll have to face the dorm at some point, but for now the quiet, walled garden is a perfect refuge.

Fabada Asturiana

Fabada Asturiana, also known simply as fabada, is a wonderfully tasty and iconic Northern Spanish bean-based dish. Like a cross between French cassoulet and baked beans, fabada is akin to a Spanish comfort food. And like baked beans in North America and the UK, fabada is sold in tins in Spanish supermarkets.

But unlike baked beans, fabada is revered as a culinary masterpiece and is hailed as the signature dish of the Spanish region of Asturias—a region known for its outstanding cuisine—and it is part of a revered tradition of canned and bottled foods known as "conservas." The Spanish tend to save the very highest quality ingredients for canning and bottling, and this is the case from lentils and beans to seafood. Unlike many of the beans found in North American and UK supermarkets, beans are held in high regard in Spain, with the best ones often sold in clear glass jars so that consumers can see the quality.

Fabada is normally made with fresh or dried fabes de la granja. Fabes are large white runner beans grown primarily in Asturias, Northern Spain. Fabada also includes several kinds of meat including pork shoulder, pancetta, morcilla (blood sausage), chorizo, and cured pork belly, as well as olive oil, paprika, garlic, and saffron, and other seasonings. Fabada is a wonderful combination of great simplicity and outrageous flavour.

In this very simple version of Fabada Asturiana, I used tinned white cannellini beans, since fabes are not readily available in North America. In place of the long list of meats used in true fabada, I used thick cut smoked bacon and chorizo. The result is delicious and very straightforward to make. Serve with a warm, crusty country-style white bread and cider or a hearty Spanish red wine. The dish is even better reheated the next day or even the day after.

Serves 4

375 g (13 ¼ oz) lean, thick cut, smoked bacon, chopped into bite-sized pieces

350 g (12 ½ oz) cured Spanish sweet chorizo sausage, roughly chopped into chunks

2 medium yellow onions, diced

4 cloves garlic, smashed

Pinch saffron (if available)

2 × 540 mL (18 oz) cans of cannellini beans drained and rinsed (note: reserve 1 cup of the beans to blend)

375 mL (1 ½ cups) vegetable or chicken stock

1 tsp sweet paprika

1–2 tsp cumin

salt and pepper to taste

30 mL (2 tbsp) olive oil for serving

In a large heavy saucepan, fry the bacon lightly until cooked but not crispy. Add the chorizo and brown lightly.

Add the chopped onion (and a tablespoon or so of olive oil if necessary—depending on how much bacon fat is in the pan) and continue to cook on medium-low heat, until the onion is beginning to brown, approximately 5 to 7 minutes.

Add the smashed garlic and cook for another minute or two, again adding a little olive oil if needed. Add the saffron (if using), crushing the threads between your fingers.

In a food processor (or with a hand-held blender) blend the 1 cup of reserved beans with 1 cup of the chicken stock. Add this, along with the paprika and cumin, to the mixture in the pot. Then add all the remaining cannellini beans, ½ tsp salt, and pepper to taste. Depending on the stock, you may need to add a little more salt. Add the extra ½ cup of stock as necessary.

Allow the fabada to continue to cook very gently on a medium-low setting, adding up to another ½ cup of water as needed (the dish should have the consistency of baked beans) for another 20 to 30 minutes, to allow the flavours to meld.

The fabada can then be served or kept warm on low heat either on the stovetop or in a warm oven, in an oven-safe dish. Just before serving, check the consistency, and stir in the 2 tablespoons of olive oil, and add a little more water if necessary.

Serve with cider or red wine and a basket of bread/buns.

CHAPTER TEN

Logroño to Nájera

October 16

> "Whatever happens, your life will find its own path."
> —Rainier Maria Wilke, *Letters to a Young Poet*

Against the odds, my worries about the likelihood of a noisy, disruptive night after all the partying in the streets of Logroño prove unnecessary. Our night in the large municipal albergue is remarkably quiet and tame. We sleep soundly through the night without a single disruption, and both of us awaken feeling refreshed and in high spirits.

By seven o'clock we are up and out the door, as is now our routine. We have another thirty-kilometre day in front of us. Even in the dark, the streets look noticeably worse for wear. It is apparent that the party hadn't fully started when we were locked inside the gates of the albergue last night. Partiers have left their mark on the cobbled roads in the form of broken glass, dirt, and litter. We scurry through as quickly as possible, happy to return to the trail.

Somehow, though, in the darkness and haste, we stumble about and manage to miss both the Camino way-markers and anywhere that might be serving coffee. Entering and leaving cities along the route has become one of my least favourite parts of the Camino, as it is so much easier to manage in the small villages, and even better in the forests, mountains, and fields, and alongside riverbanks. By the time we find our way back to the trail, we've added half an hour and another couple of kilometres onto the day's already long trek. Once on the trail, we keep going forward, trying to put some distance behind us while the day is still young.

This morning, while walking, I am thinking about home. About walking into my own kitchen and putting the coffee on in the morning. About the luxury of not having to get out of my pyjamas to do this. About not having to walk a kilometre or two, or ten, before finding coffee and a bite to eat. I am thinking about all the things I take for granted on a daily basis at home but also about how much I love the trail. Why, I wonder. Why am I so attached to it? Why does walking this trail make me so happy?

It is difficult to explain, even to myself, the pure joy and pleasure I feel walking so many kilometres every day. Perhaps it has something to do with following the footsteps of thousands of others who have walked this same trail for centuries. Perhaps it reminds me of all the hiking I did with my father. Perhaps it is the sheer exertion. Or the endorphins. Or the long days spent entirely outside. Maybe it is the freedom the trail affords from work and routine and constantly being busy. Or maybe it's the time spent away from my desk, offline, disconnected. I feel no need to constantly check my phone, my email. No updates or verifying everything. I love the simplicity of just walking all day long and then finding my mind and body fatigued enough to be able to sleep anywhere. It's like a massive reset, a reboot, a complete recalibration of self. I am driven onward daily—pulled steadily, purposefully, relentlessly towards Santiago—and yet I don't want the journey to end.

A full ten kilometres and two hours later, we finally find a place to have coffee. The Café Cabana is in the middle of the Parque de La Grajera—a sprawling green space built around a reservoir lake. Just as our coffees and pastries arrive, so do David and Camilla. The four of us stay on, ordering another round of coffees, talking and laughing for the better part of an hour. Eventually we take our leave and resume walking. How I love these people.

The path feels long today, and Celine and I walk in silence. Eventually we reach Ventosa and break for lunch in a café, where we join a group of pilgrims, most of whom we have met at some point along the route. We are sitting at a long table all of us together. It seems everyone is feeling the same way—as though they are dragging their feet and bodies along today. Even the air feels heavy.

"Enough!" cries Sandra in her German accent. "We need beer!" Everyone agrees—beer it is. Soon our table is loaded with now familiar foods—bocadillos (elongated crusty buns) stuffed with jamón y queso (dry cured ham and cheese), tortilla de patatas, ensaladas, and patatas bravas (small cubes of fried potato served with a spicy dipping sauce). And of course, beer and coffees. Nobody is anxious to leave. More beers are ordered. And more patatas bravas. I refrain from drinking beer, because I can't imagine walking on a belly full of food and beer, but Celine has decided to stay on a while and take a taxi the rest of the way. She offers to take both Sandra's and my pack with her, lightening our loads and making the rest of our walk so much easier to contemplate. We hang about a while longer, loath to leave the now lively, happy crowd.

Our plan for the night is made. Sandra, Celine, and I will meet at Sandra's hostel close to the bus stop. Celine will organize accommodation. Sandra and I will walk together and meet Celine in Nájera as soon we can. In the meantime, Celine will get her laundry done and her gear sorted in preparation for her return trip home.

Sandra and I set off sprightly into the sunshine, liberated without our packs on our backs. But our sprightliness does not last long. It is just one of those days. And even though it is mid-October, the sun is beating down on us something fierce and the temperature is again pushing up close to thirty degrees Celsius. Over and over, I keep trying to imagine what walking the Camino in mid-summer might be like.

A couple of hours later, we drag our weary bodies into Nájera and find Celine. Only later does it strike me that I have walked every single day since we arrived. I am now averaging at least thirty kilometres a day, and often more, because we inevitably get lost looking for markers. Not to mention heading out in the evening, when we walk at least another couple of kilometres finding supplies and dinner. I wouldn't have thought I could walk so far every day, over and over again, day after day. It thrills me to realize that I can. I want to keep walking forever. To keep moving forward. To keep distilling my thoughts and delving deeper inside myself. I'm thinking on my feet, walking my way to sanity, to happiness, and to Santiago de Compostela.

We pause long enough to clean up before the three of us head back out to locate our dinner. We set out walking back to the riverside. Earlier Sandra and I noticed several pretty, colourful little restaurants along the banks of the Rio Najerilla, nestled picturesquely between a waterfront walkway and a dramatic, massive rocky outcrop. We settle on La Mercería Restaurante, because the menu includes some images of substantial-looking salads, and the sight of them draws us in.

Over dinner, Sandra, Celine, and I drink our final bottle of Spanish wine together to toast Celine's safe travels home. For dessert we order flan, and what comes is a proper Spanish flan—a creamy, silky-smooth, melt-in-your mouth, baked custard in a liquid toffee caramel sauce. It is perfection.

After dinner, we hustle back to the hostel so that Celine can gather up her laundry and pack her bags ahead of her departure first thing in the morning. I am torn about her leaving. I'm worried, both about her return trip to Canada and about how I am going to get along without her. Yet, I also know that I am on the edge of a brand-new adventure—the solo trek I intended in the first place.

She got me to Spain, and for that I will always be grateful.

Flan

Flan is the term used in Spain, Portugal, and Mexico for a dish mostly known elsewhere in the world as crème caramel, though Spanish flans tend to be slightly less sweet. Flan is one of Spain's most beloved desserts.

The only tricky part of making flan is melting the sugar for the caramel portion of the dish. (If you haven't melted sugar before, it is worth watching a couple of videos online before you begin.)

Make this dish the day (or at least several hours) before you plan to serve it. This will allow the flan to set properly and chill and will also allow the flavour to fully develop.

Serves 4

For the custard

2 large or extra-large eggs, chalazae removed

2 large or extra-large egg yolks, chalazae removed

75 g (¾ cup) white sugar

475 mL (2 cups) canned evaporated (not condensed) milk, or 2 cups of 3.25% milk (not skim or 2%) or a mix of both milk and evaporated milk

1 tsp vanilla extract

¼ tsp salt

For the caramel
100 g (1 cup) white sugar
45 mL (3 tbsp) water
1 tsp lemon juice (helps to prevent crystallization of the
    sugar)

Equipment
A fine sieve
A pastry brush and a cup of cold water, for washing down
    the insides of the saucepan
4-6 ramekins (will depend on size) or one 4-to-6 cup flan
    dish.
An ovenproof lasagna dish or similar to use as a bain-
    marie. Check first to make sure your ramekins or flan
    dish fit inside. The bain-marie should have slightly taller
    sides than the ramekins or flan dish.
A paper towel for removing air bubbles from the custard
    mixture.
A wooden skewer or equivalent to test for doneness.

To make the custard: In a large mixing bowl, whisk together the eggs (whole eggs and egg yolks) and the 75 g of sugar. Pour in the milk and whisk gently, and then whisk in the vanilla and salt. Strain the mixture through a fine sieve, and then the let mixture stand while preparing the caramel. This will help allow any bubbles to dissipate.

To make the caramel: Place the sugar, water, and lemon juice in a heavy saucepan. Swirl the ingredients in the pan, and turn the heat to medium or just ever so slightly above medium, and cook without stirring (a gentle swirl now and then should suffice) until the mixture starts to turn light golden (when you might want to swirl the mixture a bit more frequently). You are looking for a golden-brown caramel colour. This will take between 6 and 10 minutes, depending on the distribution and intensity of heat. Don't be tempted to speed up the process by cranking up the heat. You may need to scrape down the sides of the pan with a wet pastry brush while the caramel cooks. Watch carefully, as the sugar can burn very quickly at this stage.

Once the sugar mixture has reached a rich golden caramel colour, remove it from the heat and pour it into the flan dish, or distribute the caramel as evenly as possible between the ramekins. Note that the dishes do not need to be buttered or greased.

If the caramel sets before you finish pouring it, return the pan to the warm element briefly. One completed, set the dishes aside to cool.

Preheat the oven to 150°C (300°F).

Once the caramel is set, gently distribute the custard on top of the caramel in the prepared dish(es). Now set the flan dish(es) into the bain-marie and fill it about halfway up the sides of the ramekins (or flan dish) with hot water. If there are visible air bubbles in the custard, use the corner of a paper towel to gently poke and deflate the bubbles.

Place the bain-marie in the centre of the oven. Cook until the custard is set, about 30 to 40 minutes for ramekins and about 45 to 55 minutes for a flan dish.

Once the top of the custard looks set, test to see if it is ready by inserting a skewer. If the skewer comes out clean, the custard is ready. If not, leave the flan in the oven, checking at 5-minute intervals.

Once set, remove immediately from the hot water bath. Set the flan on the counter to cool slightly, and then place in the refrigerator to cool fully before serving—at least 3 hours and preferably 5 hours or more.

Before serving, run a knife around the edge of the dish and invert the flan(s) onto serving plates. Serve cold or at room temperature.

CHAPTER ELEVEN

Nájera to Santa Domingo de la Calzada

October 17

"It's your road and yours alone. Others may walk it with you
but no one can walk it for you." —Rumi

At breakfast in the hostel dining room, there are so many familiar faces that it feels a bit like a party. After we eat, Celine and I pose together in the hostel lobby for a final photograph before she heads off for the bus terminal, and I embark on the rest of my journey alone. There are no rules for how to handle the shifting dynamic from walking with someone to being alone. For better or worse, it's my journey now.

Just as I am leaving, I see Paul from the Netherlands. I like Paul instinctively. He is tall, dark, and handsome and always looks impossibly well dressed, often with an elegant scarf thrown casually around his neck—as though he is heading off to work at an art gallery and not going for a strenuous full-day hike. His manners are beautiful, and he is softly spoken and seems remarkably thoughtful and intelligent. We've crossed paths a few times, and I find him easy to talk with. It feels safe to strike up a conversation or even a friendship with him, in part because he's quite obviously gay.

I ask him where he is headed for the night. Everyone's journey on the Camino is a bit different—some start and stop early, some start early and keep walking until evening, some only walk a couple of hours each day. Turns out that Paul is heading to Santa Domingo de la Calzada, and then to Belorado the following day. I planned to go further but decide on the spot to finish the day in Santa Domingo and ask him if he'd like to try to meet for dinner sometime. He suggests we meet the following night in the town square of Belorado—assuming there is a town square, neither of us know—at six o'clock, along with anyone else we can gather up.

Since it's my first official day of walking alone, I am a little uncertain how hard to push myself. How I'll feel entirely on my own. By a fluke of timing, Sandra appears just as I am leaving the hostel, so despite my plans for walking solo, for pushing myself to walk fast and far, we strike off together. I realize that what I really need might be some company. It's a learning curve to get things right—the balance between time spent alone and doing what I want versus the safety and companionship of being with someone else.

It is not long before Sandra and I are once again back into the wide-open Spanish countryside, walking through more wheat fields, under more blue skies and endless sun. Beyond the path and the gently undulating fields, far off along the horizon on either side of the trail, we catch glimpses of distant mountain ranges.

Sandra is a slow, steady, methodical walker. Because of all her pre-booked accommodations, she is never in any sort of rush to get into town and find a place to stay. Tonight's accommodation for her is a private room with bathroom at a modern hostel run by Cistercian nuns. On hearing Sandra's plan, I decide on the spot that barring any other brilliant options that might turn up, I will try to find a room at the same place. Having my own room and bathroom sounds so much more appealing than heading into a sprawling dormitory all by myself. I've decided to cut myself some slack. And to do what feels right whether that means staying in private room or in a dormitory.

An hour or so along the track, Sandra wants to stop for coffee. I join her for coffee and admire the village of Azofra. This small village with its old stone buildings dating back to 1199 was once an important and substantial stop along the Camino. Like so many of the entrancing, old, and sometimes crumbling towns, the population has dwindled, and now Azofra is home to a mere two hundred and fifty residents. Its main purpose is to provide pilgrims with sustenance and a place to rest their heads.

It's remarkable to me that those residents who stay are here to service the needs of those merely passing through. The Camino would not be possible without these people, these villages. The relationship between pilgrims and all small Spanish villages is so important. It is also one of the great joys of walking the Camino that these tiny ancient villages continue to exist and serve such a useful and vital function. Azofra has a relatively new municipal albergue with terrific facilities, and all the rooms have only two beds. I make a mental note to record this in my journal and try to stay here next time. It is curious how often the words, "next time I walk the Camino" crop up in my head.

Another eight kilometres or so down the trail, Sandra and I arrive in the outskirts of Cirueña, and set about in search of lunch. Most days I have been travelling with supplies to eat along the trail, but today I'm ill-equipped. I haven't seen any place to stock up on my usual supplies of cheese or chorizo, bread, fruit, and chocolate. Sandra, on the other hand, just wants to find a café.

It is difficult to find a café or bar in Cirueña, which is unlike any place we've seen so far in Spain. After so many picturesque old villages and towns, Cirueña looks like a life-sized movie set for a science fiction film about the end of the world. Great swathes of modern, suburban houses sit completely vacant, out of place with the landscape. We walk past unoccupied apartment buildings, an empty swimming pool, an empty golf course, and an equally empty playground. Everything is "Se Vende" (For Sale), with the signs on almost every single building. Cirueña is the oddest, most unloved place I've seen so far in Spain. It scarcely feels Spanish, or at least not part of the Spain I have been experiencing. Sandra and I plod on. Eventually we find a shabby little bar, in an older but bleak and defeated looking corner of Cirueña. We sit outside eating the least memorable lunch of the Camino, wondering what on earth happened here.

Later we learn that this town was one of several planned communities that never really took off, and when the financial crisis of 2008 hit Spain, many communities like Cirueña were simply abandoned as construction companies declared bankruptcy. The developments remain too unprofitable to sell and too expensive to remove. The result is sad and sobering and seems to be weighing us and everyone else here down.

As I wait for Sandra to finish her meal, I realize that part of why I am sitting here at a shabby café, eating miserable food in an utterly forlorn town instead of striding out through the countryside and eating my picnic lunch sitting on a stone fence under a tree or beside a river, is because I am unsure whether I am ready to strike out fully by myself yet. I think about the tenuous, tentative allegiances we make with others while travelling. I am afraid of what might happen if I am alone, afraid of being anxious, lost, or sick, or hurt or in danger—of outright failure, of being a woman alone in a foreign country, with a poor command of the language. There is both comfort and safety in company.

The reality is that though I imagine pounding down the trail by myself, I am also thinking hard about walking as an antidote for anxiety and restlessness and despair. About the treaty between walking and deep thought, or between walking and repairing oneself. This experience is exposing all my fears and vulnerabilities. I am thinking about this when it hits me that Sandra is only walking for another few days before she returns to Germany. Like so many of the Europeans I've met on the Camino, she is only here for a couple of weeks and will return another year to finish her walk. When she leaves, I will miss her too. I make a decision to simply enjoy, to be mindful and grateful for my time with her. I make a conscious choice to do my utmost to embrace everything that comes my way—whether it is walking alone or having company.

Sandra finishes her meal, and we set off for our afternoon walk. Armed with a plan and a newfound sense of resilience, I am feeling better already and appreciative of Sandra's reliable company. When we arrive in Santo Domingo de la Calzada, it's siesta, and the town is shut tight—even the tourism information office is closed. Nothing will open until around five o'clock. Fortunately, we are able to check into our clean, quiet, and agreeably austere little rooms at the convent and agree to meet at half past five to find dinner together. In the meantime, I take full advantage of my private bathroom to wash some clothes, have a long leisurely shower, and then flop on my incredibly hard, narrow little bed, making cryptic notes in my journal—preserving fragments of another day on the Camino:

October 17. Nájera to Santo Domingo de la Calzada. An easy 22.8 km under clear blue skies and endless sunshine. Made plans to have dinner with Paul on Oct 18th.

Celine is en route to Canada. I am walking with Sandra.

Ciruena—odd, surreal, and an awful lunch. SO unlike Spain.

Convent—basic, clean, austere, oddly modern, and eerily quiet. Very hard twin bed. Checked in by a nun. PRIVATE ROOM!!! My own (very utilitarian!) bathroom.

Sandra and I meet in the lobby and then walk through the old walled city searching for dinner. We find a small, welcoming café serving pilgrims and other early eaters a menu of burgers and sandwiches. We order drinks and hamburguesas—Sandra a cheeseburger and a beer, while I choose a hamburguesa de cordero (a lamb burger) and a glass of local La Rioja white Tempranillo that tastes faintly of honey and citrus. It disappears much too quickly.

Outside night is falling, and the streetlamps are coming on. The days are beginning to grow noticeably shorter as we head into late autumn. We leave the café just as the sidewalks are filling up with Spaniards heading out for the evening. Some of them wave or nod at us and others call out, "¡Buenas noches, peregrinas!" They seem well used to pilgrims and know that our schedules are different from theirs but appear to accept this so willingly.

In a small supermarket, I stock up on my usual picnic fare for the day ahead. Then we head back through the treelined and lamplit city streets to our rooms in the convent.

After so many nights zipped up tightly in my comfortable sleeping bag, a bed with sheets and blankets feels stiff and awkward. The room is quiet and lifeless, and I am listless. I watch the clock. Ten o'clock. Eleven o'clock. I've heard nothing from Celine, and I keep checking my phone, hoping to hear that she's safe and found her way to Paris without incident. Finally, a ping from my phone alerts me to an email from her. She has arrived in Paris, but the trip has been an absolute nightmare. For some unexplained reason, she abandoned the flight she had booked from Madrid to Paris, because of something about timing and connections. Getting to Paris took all day and most of the evening. At times, she was not at all certain that she was going to make it—the bus connections were precarious and unreliable. She met a guy en route who also needed to find overnight accommodations in Paris, so the pair of them set off together in the dark to see what they could find. What they found seems to be the worst room in Paris: a single room with a single bed in a very dodgy neighbourhood, in what sounds for all the world like a flophouse. The room is dirty and barely livable, with a distinct possibility of bedbugs and other things lurking. To make matters worse, it costs "a ridiculous amount of money." Hungry, they dare not leave the place, because the neighbourhood is so rough. He is on the floor—she has the single bed, but it sounds like neither option is very appealing.

I write her back, careful not to tell her about my immaculately clean room in the convent, or my tasty lamb burger and delicious Spanish wine at dinner. Nor my fresh stash of cheese, chocolate, fruit, and fizzy water. Instead I tell her that she is brave and smart, and that tomorrow she will be safely back on an airplane heading home to Canada, and that I am glad she has someone with her. Seeing her note makes me realize how truly grateful I am to be safely installed in the convent, to be continuing on this incredible journey, and how much I adore being on the trail each day. I say a silent prayer for Celine and reach up and touch the crucifix over my bed. I remember witnessing my Catholic mother-in-law perform this small act of devotion many times over the years. Devoted or not, it certainly can't hurt.

It's nearly midnight, and I'm still wide awake, so I sit up in bed and read a tourism information flyer about Santo Domingo de la Calzada. The town was named for Domingo Garcia (1019–1109), an illiterate peasant turned hermit turned priest turned builder and engineer turned saint—and not just a regular saint, but patron saint of civil engineers. Domingo Garcia lived until he was ninety—an astonishing feat all by itself, let alone for someone who was born in 1019. In his lifetime he worked alongside a papal envoy to fight a plague of locusts, was ordained as a priest, and went on to build roads, bridges, and a hospital for the safety of pilgrims on route to Santiago. Then he began work on the church that would later become known as the Cathedral of Santo Domingo de la Calzada. I try to envision Santo Domingo—try to imagine what a man from a thousand years ago was like, what he ate, if he was kind as well as accomplished. And I wonder what record, if any, we will leave of ourselves.

Still wide awake, worrying about Celine's night in Paris, and still feeling that something is not quite right with this sleeping arrangement, I finally work out that I might sleep better in my sleeping bag, and I haul it out and lay it on top of the bedding on the hard narrow twin bed. I turn off my phone and snuggle down for the night, thinking is that if a peasant hermit can end up as patron saint of civil engineers, with a town and a cathedral named after him, Celine can get back to Canada without incident, and I can manage to walk the Camino and sort out my life. Within seconds, I am fast asleep and don't wake again until morning.

Hamburguesas de Cordero

I did not eat a lot of "fast food" in Spain, in large part because I usually ordered pilgrims' meals or the menu del dia—which was generally a much more substantial meal at a very reasonable fixed price. However, many cafés offered various forms of hamburguesas.

Sheep are bred in Spain for meat, wool, and milk. Sheep's milk is used in the production of many Spanish cheeses, including Manchego, Roncal, Cana de Oveja, Queso Zamorano, and La Leyenda. Female lambs are raised to maturity for milking, and male lambs are often used for meat. Because lamb is an expensive meat in Spain (and elsewhere), lamb burgers are an excellent way to make a small amount of meat go a long way. This particular recipe uses a panade, a paste of bread and milk, which helps keep ground meat moist and tender and is especially useful when using very lean meats, such as lamb, goat, or lean beef.

Serves 4

1 slice fresh white bread, torn into small pieces

30–45 mL (2–3 tbsp) milk or milk substitute

½ tsp salt

¼ tsp black pepper

1 tsp cumin

1 clove garlic, finely minced

I green onion, finely chopped

10 mint leaves, finely chopped

1 tbsp Worcestershire Sauce

454 g (1 lb) ground lamb

4 brioche or other favourite buns

Optional extras:

1 tbsp mint sauce

30 mL (2 tbsp) pesto

Place the torn slice of white bread in a small bowl and add the milk. Let this mixture stand for a minute or two to allow the bread to soak up the milk.

Using a fork, mash the bread and milk until the mixture becomes paste-like, then mix in the salt, pepper, cumin, minced garlic, finely chopped green onion, chopped mint leaves, and Worcestershire sauce. If using, add the mint sauce and pesto. Add the ground lamb, and, using the fork, mix the panade and lamb together until evenly distributed.

Divide this mixture into 4 equal-sized portions and then form each portion into a burger, with the centres slightly thinner and the outsides slightly thicker.

Barbeque on a heated grill for 2 to 4 minutes on each side without ever pressing down on the burgers (this will help to keep the juices intact). Alternatively, cook the burgers in a cast iron skillet with a little olive oil, for 2 to 4 minutes per side. The internal temperature should be 63°C (145°F).

Let the burgers rest, covered in foil, for up to 5 minutes before dressing and serving. In the meantime, toast or warm the buns.

Suitable toppings include mint jelly, sliced Manchego cheese, chutney, olive tapenade, mustard, caramelized onion, and aioli.

Serve with patatas bravas, ensaladilla Ucraniana, coleslaw, or a green salad.

CHAPTER TWELVE

Santa Domingo de la Calzada to Belorado

October 18

"The main facts in human life are five: birth, food, sleep, love, and death." —E.M. Forster, *Aspects of the Novel*

Walking out of town, I run into Uda. Celine and I shared a room with her on the very first night of the Camino and then slept across from each other in the dorm in Roncesvalles on the second night. The last time I saw her was fleetingly, in Los Arcos, when we only had a chance to call out a cheery hello to each other. This morning she sees me walking across the plaza in front of the main hostel in town and rushes towards me, calling my name in her German accent. At first I think that she is happy to see me, but as it turns out she is in serious distress. Something happened in the albergue last night, but it is so unspeakable that she is not able to tell me.

"It was terrible," she says, her face all contorted. "I cannot even say the words." I try to calm her down. "Uda," I say, "perhaps you are not quite young enough to be staying in these kinds of places. Maybe you need a room of your own." But she just keeps repeating, "It was so awful, so awful." She is clearly in huge distress, and I cannot even imagine what she has witnessed or been subjected to.

I am not sure what to do. "Should we go to the police?" I ask her and quickly add, "I will come with you." But then she sees her group assembling and says that she must hurry and join them, as they are taking a bus somewhere. She is still frantic and clearly visibly upset.

"I will demand a private room from now on!" she shouts back at me as she crosses the plaza. "I hope we meet again, Lindy." And then she is gone. Poor Uda. I cannot imagine what happened and don't want to let my mind go too far down the path of potential atrocities.

I need to get walking and clear my head. I'm also in need of coffee and breakfast and having not seen a place to stop before leaving town, I want to make haste to get to Grañón for coffee, and it is nearly seven kilometres down the trail. Suddenly I am so thankful for Sandra and her sensible, carefully vetted accommodation choices. If not for her, I realize I might just have ended up in the big municipal albergue where Uda stayed last night.

Sandra and I have already agreed to walk alone today but have planned to meet later, in Belorado, at her prebooked accommodations, if we don't bump into each other sooner. From there, we will head into the village and attempt to find Paul and, hopefully, dinner. I leave town and cross the bridge built by Santo Domingo over the River Oja and begin the uphill climb towards Grañón and breakfast. Long ago, when I was making my plans from Canada, I planned to stay at the albergue at the parish Church of San Juan Bautista in Grañón, rumoured to be one of the friendliest experiences of the Camino, in part because of the shared communal dinner that the visiting pilgrims take part in making. This food aspect, especially the making of food with others, feels particularly important to me.

For as far back as I can remember, I have believed that there is nothing more fundamental than food. This idea began early in my life, when I was little more than a toddler, "helping" my beloved grandfather in his Yorkshire kitchen. He taught me while I was very young how to peel an orange in one long strip, how to shell peas, to bring him provisions from the pantry. As I grew older, he taught me how to make and roll out pie dough, how to roast potatoes and vegetables, and how to cook a leg of lamb or joint of beef. As my skills expanded, so did my love affair with food and cooking.

Equally importantly, I learned about the joy of eating. Decades later, I spent years volunteering as a chef in a community kitchen, and something wonderful happened every time I did this. Cooking is important, life-sustaining work, just as eating together is an intimate, fundamental human experience and, at its best, is one of the great joys of our existence.

When I left the workforce after years of working in universities, I wanted to write. I gravitated towards food writing because I simply couldn't think of anything more important or fundamental than food. What I discovered was that when we write about food, what we are really writing about is the intersection of food and a wide range of topics: from love and death and biological imperatives to the powerful connections between all living things, and from health to the future of humanity. But food is also about history, biology, geography, ecology, politics, and economics. Food writing is about what sustains all life, about the past and present and future of every living thing, and about the future of the planet itself. The production of food is, after all, the world's largest industry and the way we make the biggest impact on the planet.

I had long looked forward to the shared cooking and eating experience at Grañón, but I've decided to let things unfold in their own way. I'm learning to let go of all my preconceived ideas about where I should or shouldn't stay, what I should or shouldn't do. I stop in Grañón long enough to find a small café serving breakfast and am no sooner through the door, when a woman calls out to me, "¿El desayuno, señora?" (Breakfast, ma'am?)

"¡Si, gracias! Con un grande café con leche, por favor," I reply, thinking she will bring me a coffee and a copy of the menu. Instead she returns moments later with my large coffee, an orange juice, and a small plate of French toast sprinkled with icing sugar and cinnamon. I must look surprised because she points at the French toast and says, "¡Las torrijas!" and then waltzes away and leaves me to eat my delicious sweet Spanish French toast. I couldn't have chosen better if I'd had to choose breakfast myself.

I finish my breakfast, pay, and return to the trail, and add the albergue in Grañón to the list of potential places to stay on my next Camino. A list I did not expect to make and yet one that seems to be growing day by day.

Soon after leaving Grañón, the trail crosses the border between La Rioja and into the landlocked, autonomous region of Castilla and León. The landscape shifts, almost imperceptibly at first, but soon I am walking along a level trail flanked on either side by vast corn and wheatfields, both of which have been harvested, and only the remnants remain. I am reminded once again of Josep Pla's comment about Spanish cooking being "the landscape in a saucepan."

Somewhere along the trail, a small and very cute shaggy little dog starts following me. "Shoo," I say, not wanting to lead the pup away from his home. But he will not be deterred. He trots along behind me. Eventually I stop and try to shoo him again, waving my arms in the direction he came from. I don't want to encourage him, but he doesn't seem to need any encouragement at all. He really is the most adorable little dog. He just sits and waits patiently, while I flap my arms about, trying to look menacing and shouting, "Shoo, shoo, go home." Then I try shouting in Spanish, "A tu casa perro, a tu casa. ¡Vamos!" He looks at me sweetly, not moving a muscle. I pull out my water bottle and have a quick drink, trying to think of the best thing to do. I can't help it; I bend over and pat him. Then I pour some of the water from my bottle into my hand and offer it to him. He laps it up. When he is done, I try to shoo him back in the direction we've come from. He keeps trotting along. I decide to ignore him, imagining that he will most certainly get tired and go back home soon. When I sneak a look, he is still following me.

"This is ridiculous," I say to the dog. So, I reverse directions, and he does, too. Okay, this is good, I think. I walk twenty minutes back down the trail, headed in the direction we just came from, and he is still following me. I stop and wait and see if he will keep going. But he stops again and waits for me, his head cocked to one side, looking at me intently, as though he is trying to figure out what we are doing—why we are paused and not walking.

"I cannot keep walking all this way in the wrong direction," I say out loud. "I've got miles to go today." By the time I retrace my steps, I will have taken forty minutes out of the day for a dog, who I am now worried will continue to follow me no matter which direction I travel.

I have to laugh. One of my fears about walking the Camino was of being alone and running into fierce wild dogs. And here I am, walking along with the world's sweetest, cutest, and least frightening dog. And yet I have no clue what to do. I cannot walk back and forth all day, I decide, and surely this tiny pup will get fed up and just go home. So once again, I turn and face back in the direction I am supposed to be heading and keep walking. I am determined not to look at the dog. I walk for about twenty minutes before I check furtively to see if the dog is still following and sure enough, he is. He stays about twenty feet back. I keep going. An hour goes by, and now I am nervous. The dog is getting further and further from home (assuming he has one), and I'm leading him astray. And today of all days I appear to be walking completely alone; there is no one else in sight in either direction.

Eventually hunger forces me to stop and have my picnic lunch. The little dog stops, too. I have a small can of tuna and a bun. I scoop the tuna onto my bun and then put the remains of the tin of tuna down for the dog. He is clearly ravenous and devours the tuna and licks the bottom of the tin even after the tuna and liquid are long gone. I pour some water into the tin, and he laps it all up. We set off.

Sandra's accommodations for the night are a kilometre or so shy of the village of Belorado. This albergue does not look like any of the other places I have stayed so far. It seems more like a small resort than the usual austere pilgrims' accommodations. I check the name twice and confirm that, despite the lovely grounds and the swimming pool, the large deck set up with patio tables and chairs and colourful shade umbrellas, I am at the right place. I head up to the building, find a staff member, and attempt to explain, in very broken Spanish and equally broken English, that I am waiting for a friend who has a booking and that if they will allow us, we would like to share the room. I motion that I will wait for Sandra to arrive and take a seat on the patio. The little dog is still with me. The woman looks at me and then at the dog.

"¡No es mi perro!" I say. "El perro está perdido." (Not my dog! The dog is lost.) Perdido is a word that is well worth knowing when walking the Camino. I perform a small pantomime about finding the dog and the dog following me. The woman looks on, eyes wide. She is grinning, which I find very hopeful. At the end of my pantomime, I recount from my Duolingo Spanish lessons: "Los gatos beben leche. Los perros beben agua." At this point, the woman (possibly the owner) is laughing out loud. A man, sitting nearby eating a large plate of pasta, seems to be enjoying the conversation, too. He has stopped eating and is also chuckling quite loudly. He asks the woman something in Spanish. "Si, si," she says, and with that he puts his plate on the floor for the dog to finish. We are all laughing and talking, when Sandra walks up and makes a beeline for the dog.

With some paperwork, and a jump in the room price, we are allowed to share Sandra's private room with two double beds. We split the cost and get our gear set up. The dog is not allowed in the room, which is fine with me. The woman says they will see if anyone has reported a dog missing in Santo Domingo de la Calzada and, if not, they will see what they can do.

"El perro es lindo," the owner says. (The dog is cute.)

"¡Si, lindo!" I agree, "¡Muy lindo!" (Very cute!)

I leave Sandra lazing in the sunshine by the hotel's pool and set off to walk into the old village of Belorado. The dog is fast asleep on the patio, where he seems to have found himself a new home.

Belorado is small, charming, and very manageable. I find Paul, just as we planned previously, almost immediately on arrival in the village. He is sitting in the sunshine drinking a large glass of white wine in the tiny central Plaza Mayor. For such a small town, the Plaza punches way above its weight. At its heart is a spectacular circular grove of ancient-looking coppiced London Plane trees, surrounded by patios with tables and umbrellas. There are benches amongst the trees, where people are sitting talking or reading newspapers and enjoying the dappled, late afternoon sunshine. A mix of modern and wonderful old medieval buildings forms the perimeter of the plaza. It is absolutely delightful.

I join Paul while we wait for Sandra and whoever else might turn up and join us. I ask Paul to tell me about his life in the Netherlands, and the first thing he tells me is about his wife and family. I don't say a thing to him about the fact that I assumed he was gay, but I do feel a little staggered. In part, it was this assumption that made it easy to ask him if he wanted to have dinner together. Now I wonder silently to myself if he thought I was hitting on him. Perhaps that is why, when I asked him if he'd like to meet, he quickly mentioned, "Yes, along with any others who would like to join us." I'm a little embarrassed about my presumptuousness, but I don't say anything. We move right along, diving into a conversation about walking, working, careers, and the differences between countries and continents. We talk about his European life and my Canadian one. He will be leaving the Camino shortly to return to work and hopes to complete the journey in stages in future years.

Moments later David and Camilla appear and join us. Then Shell from Sweden strolls up, and he joins us, too. When Sandra arrives, we all head indoors and are shown to a large table in an upstairs room, which we have to ourselves. We are having the very reasonably priced prix-fixe pilgrims' meal, and our pretty, and very helpful waitress speaks several languages but claims that being so new to Spain (having recently arrived from Eastern Europe) her ability to speak Spanish is very limited.

With her help, I choose the Ensalada Rusa (Russian salad) for a starter (apparently more popular in Spain than in Russia), and grilled pork tenderloin with fried potatoes for the main. For dessert there is a choice of "flan, flan, or flan." We all order the flan. No sooner than our orders are taken, she returns with bottles of red and white wine and cheerfully refills our glasses.

Dinner is wonderful: not so much because of the meal, but rather the company. We eat, talk, and laugh like old friends until well past sundown and late into the evening. Our roaming conversation covers our collective impressions of Spain and the incredible thousand-plus-year-old history of the Camino, how well the Spanish handle our limited ability to converse, the must-try foods and the wines we've come across, and how best to avoid bedbugs.

We also talk about where we come from and why we're here. For some it's a deeply religious experience. For others it's about the lure of the long walk and the dive into Spanish culture. Mostly we talk about how happy and liberated we feel on the Camino, about what an incredibly positive experience it's been so far.

Eventually, perhaps in a bid to hustle us out, our server asks if we would like an espresso to cap the night off. Clearly we are slightly punch drunk and not ready for this beautiful, joyful evening to end. Without really considering the consequences of late-night caffeine, we all say yes. Espressos gone, cheques paid, we head out the door into the night sky and make our way back to our various beds. It is there, as we discover later, we all toss and turn and curse the late-night espressos. What were we thinking? I lie in bed wide awake, remembering the day of the dog and the blissful evening. Even though I am frustratingly wide awake well past midnight, I am also thoroughly and abundantly happy. Feliz, I think to myself. Yo estoy feliz. (I am happy.) Thoughts, even though very simple, are slowly starting to come to me in Spanish.

Ensaladilla Ucraniana

Ensaladilla Rusa (also known as Ensalada Rusa) is a much beloved Spanish version of an Eastern European potato salad. As a result of the Russian war in Ukraine, the salad has recently been renamed Ensaladilla Ucraniana or Ensaladilla Kiev (Kiev is the traditional Spanish spelling of Kyiv) on many restaurant menus.

This is not the first time the salad has been renamed. In France the salad is known as Salade Olivier, named for French chef Lucien Olivier (1838–1883).

Olivier was trained in French haute cuisine but spent his career working in Moscow, where it is believed he invented the salad.

The salad was and is sometimes still referred to in Spain as Ensalada Nacional. During the dictatorship of Francisco Franco from 1939 until his death in 1975, many restaurants and bars changed the name of Ensaladilla Rusa to Ensaladilla Nacional to avoid the association with pro-Communist sentiments.

In Spain, the salad is served as a first course or as a side salad often presented in a ramekin or similar small dish, and it is also a very popular tapas offering, served in smaller portions. For a tapas party, the salad can be served in small pre-baked tartlets, small serving dishes, or in Asian-style soup spoons.

Serves 4 as a side dish

4-5 medium, red-skinned potatoes, peeled, cubed, and boiled until tender

1-2 large carrots, peeled, cubed, and boiled until tender

160 g (approx. 1 cup) sweet green peas, boiled and drained

180-250 mL (¾-1 cup) homemade or good quality mayonnaise

2 tsp white wine vinegar

1 clove garlic, very finely minced

Salt and pepper to taste

Pinch of white sugar

Optional extras: cooked shrimp, tuna, finely chopped ham, diced cooked beets (add last if using), diced hard-boiled eggs

Garnish: sliced hard boiled eggs, cooked shrimp, sliced olives, sliced pimentos, capers, or a little sprinkle of smoked Spanish paprika

Gently toss the cooked potatoes, carrots, and sweet green peas together.

In another dish, combine the mayonnaise, vinegar, garlic, salt and pepper, and sugar.

Gently add this dressing to the vegetables and stir to coat them. Cover and refrigerate. If adding beets, add these just before serving. Garnish just before serving.

CHAPTER THIRTEEN

Belorado to Agés

October 19

"El vientre gobierna la mente." (The belly rules the mind.)
—Spanish proverb

We leave early, Sandra and I, by the light of a spectacular full moon still high in the sky. We walk for the first hour and a half along the level moonlit trail, ever-present wheatfields on either side of us.

I love these early starts, walking in the dark under the stars—waiting for the slivers of light on the horizon as the sun begins its ascent and the day begins to unfold. It is ten past eight before the sun finally makes its first appearance lighting up the horizon behind us. We are walking in silence. It is Sandra's second-last day. Tomorrow she will walk into Burgos, and from there will return to Germany, and once again I will be on my own. Even my dear little dog was nowhere to be seen as we left this morning. I can only hope that he is sleeping comfortably somewhere, and that his future is safe, secure, and happy.

The map shows a couple of small villages along our route this morning, and so we plan to find coffee and breakfast at the first place we reach. But we do not manage to find a bar or a café open in either of the first two tiny, sleepy villages —Tosantos, population sixty, and Villambistia, population fifty. Perhaps we missed something, but given the size of the places, I'm not sure how that could have been possible. Perhaps we were just too early. Checking the map, nearly ten kilometres down the track from our early morning start, I see that the next village, Espinosa del Camino, is even smaller. Its listed population is a mere forty inhabitants. I can't imagine we'll find much there. But when we do arrive, we are thrilled to find an open café, La Cantina de Espinosa del Camino. The place is packed full of pilgrims, all of them talking in a dozen different languages and eating great plates of ham and eggs, and fried potatoes. The air is laced with the scent of strong Spanish coffee. We fall upon the place gleefully, ordering tortilla de patatas and cafés con leche.

A couple of kilometres down the trail, in Villafranca Montes de Oca, Sandra and I part ways once again. She has opted to take the bus and skip the twelve-kilometre hike to San Juan de Ortega (Spanish for Saint John of the Stinging Nettle)—another long stretch of trail with no facilities of any description. It is not uncommon for modern pilgrims to take buses or taxis, and there are times when it is expedient to do so. I prefer to walk as much as possible, in part because I feel that my father is with me while I am walking, but also because I like the walking so much. My plan is to do the trek by myself and meet Sandra in Agés, later in the day. Tomorrow we will walk into Burgos together, where Sandra will begin her trip back to Germany.

Before I leave Villafranca Montes de Oca, I locate a fountain and replenish my water supply and find a small store where I buy sunflower seeds and chocolate for my afternoon walk. I desperately need to find a bank machine. I've been watching for one for the past couple of days but so far to no avail.

I set off into the woods alone, looking forward to this somewhat remote stretch of trail that passes through the Montes de Oca (Mountains of Geese). A thousand years ago, this section of the Camino was considered to be one of the wildest and most dangerous stretches of the route, known for the wolves and wild dogs, and also for the bandits who inhabited and hid in the isolated, densely forested region. It is also the last mountainous passage before the trail wends its way towards the Meseta—the vast high plains of Spain.

Once the trail leaves the villages and roads behind, the climb is a slow, steady hike through mixed forests of pine, juniper, oak, and ash trees. It reminds me of home—of hiking in Ontario or Quebec or northern New York State—of the thousands of miles of undulating boreal forest.

I am deep in the woods when it strikes me that I have not seen another living soul for quite some time, and I begin to feel vaguely unnerved. Within moments, I come over the crest of a hill, and off in the distance I see a couple sitting at a picnic table. As I get closer, I see that the couple is David and Camilla, who seem to have a knack for turning up whenever I need them most. They are running low on water, so I divvy up my bottle, and we sit a while longer, eating the chocolate and sunflower seeds, before heading off together. We scarcely notice any kind of summit and are soon heading jauntily down the backside of the mountain.

Just before we reach the foot of the trail, a young friend of David and Camilla's strides down the slope and joins us. Tall and leggy, Sebastian from Chile is young, charming, multilingual, and a bundle of joy and energy. He is waving his arms in the air, smiling, and laughing and talking all at once. I like him immediately, instinctively. His arrival reminds me of a chinook—the beautiful warm wind that travels down the Rocky Mountains and raises the temperature in the valleys below.

David, Camilla, and Sebastian are all headed for the albergue in San Juan de Ortega, one of the most famous stops along the Camino. I want badly to stay with them, in part because I enjoy their company so much, but also because this was another albergue high on my list of places to stay along the Camino.

But I promised Sandra that I would meet her in Agés. And that we would find dinner together on this, her last night on the Camino. I add the ancient Albergue San Juan to the growing list of things I will do on my "next Camino."

The Monastery of San Juan de Ortega dates to 1142 and initially served as a hospice for pilgrims. Thought to have been built by the priest and hermit San Juan, a disciple of Santo Domingo, this grand old place has been housing, feeding, and looking after pilgrims for ten centuries. In more recent history, the tradition has involved serving pilgrims a humble dinner of sopa de ago (garlic soup) and traditional bread. Again, it's this communal meal that attracts me so greatly. That and the incredible sense of community and history and continuity, the idea of the thousand-year history of pilgrims who have stayed here, eaten here, and had their bodies and souls tended to.

The elegant old monastery is bathed in sunshine as we arrive. It is even more beautiful than I could have imagined with its lovely sprawling green lawns and gated courtyard. But it is also clearly popular—a long line of walkers is waiting to register for beds for the night. David and Camilla rush off to join the line as I stand on the path outside the gates, alone, watching them and wondering once again if I have done the right thing. This is their second-last night on the Camino. Like Sandra and many other Europeans, they are walking the Camino in two week stretches and will return again to finish the walk next year. Tomorrow night we will all be in Burgos, the biggest city on the path since

Pamplona, and I have no idea where they are staying or, for that matter, where I will be staying, either. Our chances of encountering each other will be slight.

Our goodbye was so swift, and I only realize as I trudge off on my own how lonely it will feel knowing that David and Camilla and Sandra have gone home to their respective countries. Luckily, they have written their address in the back of my journal for me, so that we are able to stay in contact.

I press on. Alone. Everyone else appears to have stopped for the day.

Lost in thought, I suddenly hear from nowhere, "Lindy! *Lindeeee! Wait!*" I recognize the German accent, stop, look around and see the round glasses, the strawberry blonde hair, the massive backpack that always looks as though it might topple her over at any second.

"*Sandra!*" I yell back. We walk towards each other wide-eyed and grinning. Sandra's bus dropped her in San Juan de Ortega, and she was watching for me so that we could walk together for the final few kilometres of the day, into the tiny hamlet of Agés.

So, having once again relinquished all decision-making, I am heading to the same albergue that Sandra is heading to. Agés is so small that the options are incredibly limited anyway. From here on in I'll have to find my own way—not something that I'm entirely looking forward to. I am happy to walk alone all day and don't find that at all daunting. But I can't say the same about finding a decent place to sleep each night.

We book in, stake out our beds in a small room that is way too overcrowded with bunks, and then promptly head off to explore the village and find a drink and dinner. At nearly five o'clock in the afternoon, the very edge of the siesta, absolutely nothing is open. We are sitting at an outdoor table in the centre of the tiny village, drinking the remains from our water bottles and chatting with a small group of pilgrims until a very angry man opens an upper window and yells from above, "*Shut up!*"

"Oh good, he speaks English," says one of pilgrims, and we fall about laughing until we see the shutters reopen, and fearing more wrath from above, we take off like shots, returning to our various albergues and sleeping quarters to wait hungrily and impatiently for things to reopen for dinner later in the evening. Once again, we foreigners ignored the sacred hours of afternoon sleep and silence.

At dinner with Sandra, at the same place where we were yelled at earlier, I order a dish of beans, chorizo, and eggs and a large glass of white wine. The place is completely hopping. Every table is full. When our meals arrive, the food is absolutely terrific.

"It looks so good," says Sandra, nodding at my dinner. "How is it?"

"Unbelievably fantastic, actually," I say, grinning merrily. Whoever is in charge in the kitchen knows exactly what they are doing. My dinner could not be any tastier. Amongst all the wonderful and flavoursome things I have eaten in Spain, this delicious, unpretentious dish chock full of beans and chorizo in a tomato sauce—topped with a perfectly cooked egg, and served with a basket of bread, is easily one of my favourites so far along the Camino. I could eat this once a week and never tire of it.

I know immediately this meal is something that I will want to recreate in my own kitchen. It's simple, so full of flavour, rustic, honest, and wholesome. Dishes like this are my favourite kind of food. I am studying it intently when Sandra says, "You're studying your dinner like you mean business." "Ha! You're right. I'm planning to recreate this one for sure," I tell her. "I can't wait." I'm listing the ingredients in my head: smoked paprika, spicy chorizo, red kidney beans, navy beans. Definitely onion, garlic, cumin, salt, pepper, and a spoonful of honey to smooth and round out all the big flavours. To finish, a little grated cheese, some eggs, fresh parsley. I can hardly wait to get my apron on and start cooking.

After dinner, Sandra and I wait for someone to come and take our dishes away and give us a bill. But it never happens. Eventually I go up to the counter and get out my wallet to pay. "*No, no,*" yells the man (the same man who shouted for us to shut up earlier). I am confused. I just want to pay. I wrack my brain for the words "to pay" but I am so thrown off by all the shouting that I draw a blank. In the meantime, I pull out money. He is still barking at me in Spanish. Flustered and digging through my wallet, I pull out the last of my paper money—a ten-euro note. "Por la cena" (for my dinner), I say.

"¡Oh! ¡Oh! Si. Comprendo. Gracias," he says, seeming to work out that I am not trying to order more food or whatever it was he thought I might have been trying to do. He speaks to me in rapid-fire Spanish—saying a long run of things that I do not understand. What I do understand is that he takes my money and counts out some small change.

"Gracias por la comida muy deliciosa," I manage to get out, haltingly.

"De nada," he says, smiling broadly, and hands me my change. "¡Buenas noches!" He's so handsome when he smiles that I am momentarily unbalanced. "¡Si, si, buenas noches, señor!" We are both grinning at each other. No more yelling.

It's only after I leave that I remember the words I was searching for: "La cuenta, por favor." (The bill, please.) "Yo quiero pagar." (I want to pay.)

Spanish Style Chorizo with Beans and Eggs a la Agés

This quick and easy one-pan dish serves two for dinner with a side salad and a loaf of crusty bread or buns. When fried potatoes are included in the mix, this very popular dish is known as Huevos a la Flamenca. Like so many Spanish bean-based dishes, it is wonderfully delicious.

Serves 2

30 mL (2 tbsp) olive oil

1 medium onion, finely diced

2 cloves garlic, finely chopped

2 (approx. 150–175 g, 5–6 oz) smoked (cured) chorizo
    sausages, cut in half lengthwise, then in chunks

1 tsp honey

1 tsp smoked paprika

1 tsp cumin

½ tsp chili flakes (or to taste)

1 tbsp Worcestershire sauce

398 mL (14 oz) can baked beans in tomato sauce

398 mL (14 oz) can red kidney beans, well drained

4 eggs

Salt and pepper to taste

50 g (1 ¾ oz) grated Manchego (or sharp cheddar)

Fresh or dried parsley to garnish

In a large cast iron or similar fry pan, warm the olive oil on medium-high heat.

Add the onion and sauté for a few minutes or until the onion is starting to colour.

Add the garlic and chopped chorizo and continue to fry for another few minutes or until the chorizo is beginning to brown a little.

Add the honey, smoked paprika, cumin, chili flakes, Worcestershire sauce, baked beans in tomato sauce, and drained, rinsed kidney beans. Stir and allow to cook gently over medium heat for about 10 minutes. If the mixture seems too dry, add a little water to loosen it up.

Using the back of a large spoon, make four indentations in the bean mixture. Crack the first egg into a small bowl, careful not to break the yolk, then gently pour it into one of the indentations. Repeat this with the remaining three eggs.

Season with salt and pepper, and let the eggs cook to desired doneness (at least 6 to 8 minutes for medium yoke). Once the eggs are set, sprinkle the cheese over the surface and garnish with parsley.

Serve immediately.

CHAPTER FOURTEEN

Agés to Burgos
to Hornillos del Camino

October 20

"I exist only in the soles of my feet and in the tired muscles of
my thighs. We have been walking for hours it seems. But where?
I cannot remember." —Virginia Woolf, *The Waves*

All night long, bedsprings are creaking, people are tossing and turning, and our room—packed far too tightly with way too many people—is insufferably hot. I sleep badly, waking and trying to get comfortable, my tossing and turning adding to the general cacophony. First thing in the morning, I am up, packed, and heading straight out the door in the pitch black, hoping to find coffee. Sandra is staying behind for breakfast at the albergue, but I have long since given up on albergue breakfasts. I head right back to the same place where we were the night before.

I find the server and order a café con leche. I don't have enough money to have breakfast and desperately need to find a bank machine. When I go to pay for my coffee, it is, once again, the handsome grumpy man. This time, even though he is still speaking rapid-fire Spanish at me, he is also smiling. I smile back and start counting out my handful of remaining euro coins. He takes my hand, picks the coins out—holding each one up and telling me its value and counting out the total cost: "Veinte, veinte, viente, cincuenta, diez. ¡Aquí esta…un dólar y veinte centavos!" Then he hands all the money back to me. Uncertain, I try to hand it back, thinking that he wants me to repeat and count

133

it all out loud, as he did. But he won't take it. He closes his hands and makes the motion of washing his hands of the money. It's almost as if he intuitively knows how short of funds I am, how desperately I need to find a bank.

"¡Si, comprendo! ¡Bueno! ¡Mil gracias señor!" I say. And then I add, "Adiós, mi amigo."

"¡Adiós, mi amiga! ¡Buen Camino!" he says, beaming at me.

We are like school children making a new friend. I leave feeling inexplicably happy and deeply in love with Spain.

By the time I emerge from the bar, I find Sandra walking towards me, and we set off together. The route this morning takes us uphill past Atapuerca, where a UNESCO world-heritage site is home to some of our earliest human relatives. Investigations are still ongoing, but evidence of hominid life dating back as far as 1.2 million years has been uncovered here. Sandra and I don't even contemplate making the six-kilometre return walk to the famous archaeological site. Next Camino? Maybe?

We carry on, full steam ahead. When we reach the outskirts of town, Sandra says she is going to take the bus into the city to avoid the dreary walk through the outskirts of town alongside busy multi-lane roads with traffic ripping past. The noise and the fumes are a shock after so many days of walking through countryside. Sandra's plan seems sensible, but I am hesitant to start using public transportation at this point on the Camino. And four kilometres is absolutely nothing! I can walk a kilometre in under twelve minutes. Four kilometres will take me forty-five minutes tops, probably more like forty. It would likely take almost that long on the bus, between the waiting and the various stops. "I'll wait with you and see how I feel when your bus comes," I say, still thinking I should just walk into town, when a massive truck hurtles past mere inches away from me, practically brushing up against my backpack. I decide to join her.

Luckily, thanks to my restaurant friend in Agés, I have enough coins to pay for the bus ride. Only later do I learn that this particular stretch of road is notorious for pickpockets, so I did well to miss it. It is my first time *not* walking to my destination, and immediately on boarding the bus and zooming along the city streets it feels like a dangerous slippery slope—it is just way too easy. When I planned my walk, I never once imagined hopping aboard buses. But then neither did I imagine walking into major cities alongside highways and freeways, past industrial parks, dumps, airports, and factories. We are only travelling a very short distance on the bus, but still, when it spits us out in downtown Burgos, mere minutes after boarding, it does feel a little miraculous.

Sandra and I stand on the sidewalk at the bus stop hauling up our packs and organizing ourselves momentarily. Sandra is focused on the task at hand—getting herself back to Germany. She has a schedule to follow and departs with German precision while I am still on the side of the road, trying to get my bearings in this new town. "Auf wiedersehen!" she calls out to me, "¡Buen Camino!" And with true German efficiency and zero sentimentality, she disappears into the crowd, and once again, I am alone. With no idea where I am.

It is so disorienting leaving the Camino. Once you've left the path, it isn't necessarily easy to find it again, especially in a major city. I find myself overwhelmed and feel like crying. I sit down on a bench and get my map out and try to work out where I am. I locate the cathedral and head straight there to walk around the grounds. I note the time of the evening service and plan to return after dinner. Feeling more confident, I embark on a mission to find a bank machine. I find a signpost for the Oficina de Turismo and follow the signs until I get to the office and head straight to the counter to ask about accommodations and a desperately needed bank machine.

The woman behind the counter gives me some instructions—pointing out the window and making gestures in various directions. "A la derecha, a la izquierda, diez minutos..." (To the right, to the left, ten minutes...) is all I can pick out of a long stream of Spanish. On she goes, with more information. I have no clue what she is saying, but it seems too difficult to intervene, so I nod and smile and say gracias, mil gracias, and figure that it will be easy enough once I set off in search of things.

But as it turns out, it is not that easy, and somehow I end up completely lost. I am an excellent walker yet useless with directions, especially complicated longwinded directions in a foreign language. When I try to retrace my steps, I am unable to do so. Nothing is familiar. People stream past in all directions. I keep walking, but it seems clear that I have made a wrong turn, or more likely, several wrong turns.

"Think," I tell myself. Surely there will at least be another sign for the Tourism Office so that I can retrace my steps and start again? Where has the massive cathedral gone? I cannot even see the spires. It seems to have disappeared completely. I walk another block looking at all the signs. Nothing. Nada. No signs for the tourism office. No cathedral. No bank. It's as though

I've walked into another city altogether. Finally, in despair, I approach a well-dressed and rather good-looking older man sitting on a bench.

"Perdón señor, ¿dónde está un cajero automático?" (Where is a bank machine?) I say, cautiously. And then I add, testing the limits of my ability in Spanish, "Yo necesito un banco, por favor." (I need a bank, please.)

He smiles and answers with a long stream of Spanish. The problem, once again, with asking a question in Spanish, is trying to understand the answer in Spanish. I stand there blankly, comprehending words at random. "Si, gracias," I say. But what it is that I am thanking him for telling me, I have no idea.

He gets up and motions for me to join him. This is not what I hoped for, but given that he appears to be at least in his mid-sixties and possibly older, I figure I should be safe enough. As we walk for several blocks deeper and deeper into the city, I am starting to get nervous. The whole time he is talking to me in Spanish and bits of broken English. "I am a millionaire!" he announces, in English, quite suddenly, and apropos of nothing.

I feel myself starting to get increasingly unnerved. Why is he saying this stuff? He reaches out to take my hand, and I pretend I do not understand. Things seem to be escalating in a direction that makes me uneasy. He keeps getting closer and closer and reaching for me—putting his hands on my shoulders or his arm around my waist. I've been in these predicaments before, and things went very seriously awry far too quickly. I think of all the times I simply went along with this kind of behaviour, not wanting to make a scene or seem unworldly. Like many women, I was trained very young for compliance.

It was a beautiful early summer night when I had my first sexual encounter. I had just turned fourteen and finished Grade 8. He was a twenty-one-year-old, third-year college student. I met him at a party I attended with my neighbour Tessa, a girl my parents always said was trouble. At the party, she went off with her much older boyfriend, and I was lost—alone in sea of people I didn't know. When I started to try to leave to walk home, a good-looking, tanned, and shaggy blond-haired man standing on the front porch drinking beer, offered me a ride.

"It's not safe out there for a beautiful young girl like you," he said, introducing himself. I accepted the ride, gratefully, flattered. He drove the family station wagon—an old fake wood-panelled beater of a car.

Partway home, he rerouted. "Wanna take a short walk and see the full moon?" he said. I agreed, probably a little too eagerly. I was always thrilled to see the moon. I had no inkling that this was any kind of metaphor. He parked the car at the side of the road, and we made the short walk to a gravel pit, where he laid me in the gravel, tore my clothes off, and sexually assaulted me.

I never even struggled. I said nothing, even when he told me that I didn't know how to kiss and tried to teach me how it was done. Other than kissing my parents goodnight, I'd never really kissed anyone before. I remember the sharp gravel digging into my bare skin and how badly everything hurt—how I focused so hard not to cry out loud or black out from shock and pain. I remember snippets: being mortified that I didn't know how to kiss, my first actual terrified sighting of a naked man (as opposed to the one in the cartoon-like sex-ed pamphlets), the pain everywhere in my body, and most of all the crazy worry about my parents finding out and my father "thrashing me." I knew technically what sex involved because of sex education classes, but I had no firsthand sexual experience at all and absolutely no language of any kind about sexual consent.

When it was over, we walked back to his car, and he drove me home, silently. I got out of the car and thanked him politely for the ride. Then I walked around to the side of the house and sat for some time in the grassy ditch beside our home, tears pouring down my face, wondering what on earth had just happened to me.

I was terrified my parents would find out. And I was worried sick that I might be pregnant. In the days that followed, I walked alone to the doctor's office and asked to see the doctor. The receptionist chastised me, "You need an appointment," she said, before going on to ask what I needed to see the doctor for. I was standing in the packed waiting room and had no idea what to say. "Cystitis," I finally mumbled—I'd had it before, and I knew it to be in the right anatomical region.

"You'll have to wait until the doctor has seen all the booked patients," she said, and then, "Where is your mother?" I stayed mute, and she waved me towards a chair. As if to prove the point, just after I sat down, one of my classmates arrived with her mother, and I looked on enviously as they sat together, smiling and talking happily between themselves. Finally, after all the patients had been seen, the receptionist called me and took me to an office to wait for the doctor.

I told the doctor, an older English man, as best I could what had happened in the gravel pit. He told me off sternly, voiced his outright disgust with me. "What do you think you are doing hanging around with *these kind of people?*" He said, practically spitting. He took a statement from me, and then wrote out a prescription for birth control pills. "I should tell your parents about what you're up to," he said, as I begged, and cried, and pleaded with him never, ever to tell my parents.

After that, I went a little off the rails for quite some time. I suppressed the truth about what had happened, couldn't name it. When I think back, I realize that this was the point in my life in which I learned to lie to myself and others. All the boundaries had been so badly broken that very little made sense.

For the most part, though, I blocked that catastrophic night out, shoved it down, buried the knowledge and feelings as deeply as I could. There were things I couldn't forgive other people for, and things I could not forgive myself for, either. Looking back, I realize how truly desperate I was to be loved. Little did I know then that the story would never let go of me.

It wasn't the last time I was sexually assaulted. Women who experience sexual violence at a young age are at far higher risk of continued sexual abuse—a phenomenon known as repetition compulsion. The trauma and stigma of sexual assault leaves scars so deep that what are normally rational, instinctive behaviours such as shouting, yelling, fighting back, screaming, calling police, summoning any kind of help, or just simply shouting "NO, STOP!" are lost and completely unavailable and often replaced instead with resignation and compliance. A kind of "let's just try to get out of this alive" mentality. And a normalizing of behaviour that is not normal at all.

Recent numbers in Canada indicate one in three women and one in eight men have experienced unwanted sexual behaviour in public and that more than eleven million Canadians have been physically or sexually assaulted since age fifteen.[19]

But right now, here in Burgos, I am walking along unknown streets, with an unknown man—one whom I approached first. And I am completely unsure of what to do. My inadequate Spanish language skills prevent me from having any sensible discussion with him, so I simply remove his hands and keep walking. On and on we go, deeper and deeper into the narrow old city streets. We appear to have left the city centre and are walking up a steep hill into a residential area. I have lost my bearings entirely, despite trying desperately to spot and remember landmarks. For some reason, there are no banks in sight the whole time. I try to stay calm and focused, reasoning that if I turn around now, I don't know my way and I don't know what will happen. Maybe we are actually heading to a bank?

Then, suddenly, we arrive at a bank. Between words and motions, he indicates that he will wait for me in the lobby while I go and talk to the teller. He says we will go to his house after I am done. At least I think this is what he says, I can only make out the "...a mi casa," which he repeats several times.

I walk through a second set of doors into a large bank and approach the counter.

"¿Habla usted inglés?" (Do you speak English?) I ask the teller. She nods. I make a snap decision to tell her that I am alone, but a man who is a stranger has led me here and is waiting for me in the lobby, and that I am just trying to find a bank machine, and that I am scared. "I just don't trust this man," I say. The words come out in a big jumble.

"There is no bank machine here," she says. The woman is looking at me intently. "Can I help you somehow?"

"Is there another exit?" I ask. "I would like to leave the bank a different way if possible. I just have a bad feeling about this whole situation..." I hear my voice petering out. Uncertain. "Malo," (bad), I add, as if this will explain everything.

She asks me if she should call the police. "No," I say slowly, picturing myself ending up in a Spanish police station trying to explain myself. Trying to explain why a potentially quite kind, respectable looking older man led me to the bank, just as I asked him to do. That he told me that he was rich, and he tried to hold my hand and put his arms around me, and that he invited me to his house. This doesn't really seem like a police-worthy crime. And given my terrible command of Spanish, it all seems too complicated. "I had a bad feeling" likely won't cut it with the Spanish police. I tell the woman that I think I'm okay, but if there is another exit it would be good.

She holds up her index finger and motions for me to wait while she makes a quick phone call in Spanish. With that, she leans towards me and points discreetly to the back of the building away from the lobby: "Go to that corner," she says, in English. "And I will take you out the back door."

I still have no money, but at this point all I want is to get clear of this whole uneasy situation as quickly as possible. I just hope the man in the lobby isn't watching all this transpire.

The teller leads me down a set of back steps and out onto a tiny narrow pathway. "Go straight down the hill all the way to the river. When you get to the river, turn right, and keep going, you will see the Camino," she says, pointing the way.

"Gracias, gracias," I say.

She leans closer—makes the sign of the cross, puts her hand out to touch my shoulder, and says, "Buen Camino." And with that I turn and head as quickly as possible down the steep back alley, towards the river. There is no one behind me. No one in front of me.

When I get to the river, I turn right and keep going, following the riverbank.

It is already past three o'clock, and here I am leaving Burgos behind and embarking for goodness knows where. I planned to stay here and explore town, attend a service at the cathedral, and enjoy a good dinner somewhere. I hoped that I might run into David and Camilla one last time. Or maybe Sebastian. I thought that, at the very least, I would rest up before heading onto the Meseta—the long walk across Spain's high plains, notorious for being the most mentally challenging section of the Camino. But instead, I find myself entirely alone, no other pilgrims in sight, with no food, very little water, absolutely no money, and no real idea where I might spend the night.

Eventually the trail leads me to a bridge across the river. I pause on the bridge momentarily, looking at the river below, where black eelgrass is swirling and dancing in the current. I look behind me. There is nobody. Nobody in front either. In fact, there seems to be nobody at all on the trail. All the pilgrims are sensibly staying put for the night in Burgos.

The experience has left me shaken, and now that I am back out on the path and entirely alone, I wonder at the wisdom of being here. I start to question my thinking. Perhaps I should go back to Burgos and start again tomorrow with a clear head? Although at least if I am robbed out here along the trail, I reason to myself, there is nothing much to take—I have absolutely no money left. And neither is there anyone around to rob me. Chin up, I tell myself. Soldier on.

Twenty minutes further down the trail, I still have not seen another person in any direction. Then, suddenly, I hear footsteps pounding up behind me. My heart quickens. I step to the side, stop, turn, and find Sebastian from Chile. I met him previously when I was walking with David and Camilla—his arrival reminded me of a chinook warming the valley. Curiously, his arrival here feels much the same: reassuring, familiar, and heartwarming. "Lindy! My friend, my Viking!" he says—but his Spanish pronunciation comes out as 'mi biking.' He told me when we first met that I look like a Viking, and the idea has stuck in his head. He's beaming at me. "What are you doing out here at this time of day?!"

"Sebastian!" I am absolutely elated to see him. Of all the people that could materialize, Sebastian's sudden appearance is perfect.

I tell him my Burgos story. I tell him about trying to find a bank. About acting on a feeling that all was not right and hightailing out of town without any real plan. "It was strangely disturbing," I tell him. "I just didn't feel good about it, and I've been in too many of these situations before and sometimes things get out of hand…" I leave it there.

Sebastian tells me that I was smart to act on instinct. He pulls out his wallet. "Okay, first, please take some money," he says, handing me a twenty-euro bill. I refuse. He insists. We repeat. Finally, I accept the money on the proviso that we walk together until I find a bank machine and can repay him.

"No!" he says and insists that he would really like to give me the money, and I truly believe he would. But I am not having any of that. Besides, this way, I will enjoy the pleasure of his company at least until we find a bank machine, which I have to admit, given how few and far apart they are, might be a while.

Sebastian is an excellent walking companion—he is kind and intelligent and fiercely interested in everything and everyone. He is twenty-eight years old and is a veterinarian in Chile but has been travelling the entire world for many months, spending time in all kinds of far-flung places including Russia and other places well off the normal tourist track. He has taught himself several languages, including Russian. His English is excellent, and his accent is delightful. But above all, he's a thoroughly, wonderfully decent human being. His unexpected appearance this afternoon after my experience in Burgos seems wonderfully fortuitous. And my return to the Camino feels deeply calming.

When I ask Sebastian what he is seeking from his travels, he says, "I needed to figure out what I was doing with my life. Being a vet is not exactly what I expected. I started wondering if I was meant to be doing something else, maybe something more meaningful to me. I felt a calling to the priesthood, but I had also imagined a life with a wife and children. It was confusing. So, I left my home and took leave from my job to figure out what I am meant to be doing. The Camino is the last step, and after this and a quick bike ride around Portugal, I will head back home to South America."

We keep walking. Sometimes talking. Sometimes comfortably silent. Either way, it feels so easy with him. But I know that even though I am a fast walker, he is faster again. I'm conscious of holding him back. When I say this to him, he says that the company is the important thing. Sebastian is a gift of a man. The kind of man who restores one's faith not only in men, but in humanity.

Ten kilometres down the track, we walk into the village of Tardajos, where I finally find a bank machine. The absence of bank machines in Spain puzzles me. Why are they so few and far between? And why is there suddenly one here, in this tiny speck of a village? I don't understand the logic. I had, I realize, been acting on the North American presumption that bank machines were pretty much ubiquitous.

I withdraw my funds gleefully, pay Sebastian back, and we head straight to a bar for a celebratory drink. It is late in the afternoon, and I still don't know where I will be stopping for the night, so I order, "una cana," the smallest draft beer, and Sebastian does the same. Before leaving, we fill our water bottles and then head back out onto the trail. Sebastian is planning to walk to Hornillos del Camino, and to stay at the parochial albergue there, adjacent to the church, another full ten kilometres on. If I manage to make it there, I will have walked almost two full days in one and clocked up nearly fifty kilometres since leaving Agés in the morning—even taking into account the four-kilometre bus ride, which I more than added back in during my jaunt backwards and forwards through Burgos trying to find a bank. So now, once again, with no plans in place, I am happy to tag along and simply see what transpires.

With Sebastian for company, it seems like no time at all before we arrive in Hornillos del Camino. Like so many other small Spanish villages with dwindling populations, Hornillos appears bigger than its listed population of sixty. This village, and many like it, provide yet another example of how many small communities have banded together to create the businesses necessary to look after pilgrims. In doing so, they have created a remarkable opportunity for humanity. There are a couple of restaurants, a bar or two, a choice of albergues, a pretty main street with some beautiful stone buildings, and the strikingly austere Gothic stone church of San Roman, with its massive rectangular bell tower.

Walking through town, we run into Hans, a friend of Sebastian's from Austria, and the three of us find the albergue, book in and pay, and grab beds together in one of the bunk rooms. Hans is planning to make his own dinner in the kitchen downstairs, so Sebastian and I head off to find ours. We go straight into the first place we find and head to the bar to order a glass of wine. The bartender asks me where I am from. "Canada," I say.

"I knew it! I spent a few years working in Toronto," he says, pronouncing it "Tor-on-oh," like a local. It makes me smile.

"How did you like the snow?" I ask. He moves to pull out a notebook from a nearby shelf, opens up the book, turns it around so I can see it, and points to an entry in the book.

"This is our weather diary. This day last year, the temperature here was zero, and it was snowing on the Meseta. We had three full days of sleet, hail, and snow. And the wind was terrible—never stopped blowing and raging. Our weather is worse here than it is in Toronto! You're lucky!" he says, grinning away.

He's right, I *am* lucky. The sun has been shining all day today, and for most of the days since I started the Camino. Today I managed to leave an unnerving situation, and I've had the pleasure of Sebastian's excellent company for the rest of the afternoon. And now here I am, safe and happy on the famous Spanish Meseta—the big, golden, high plains of Spain, talking to a Spanish bartender who lived in Toronto, while I drink a glass of silky-smooth Spanish white wine and wait for my dinner. What a wonderful world. And what a contrast to my crazy time earlier in Burgos.

It's only after dinner that I remember there was a vegetarian restaurant in Hornillos del Camino that I'd wanted to try. It apparently served up a fabulous chickpea and spinach dish with Sephardic Jewish roots. But never mind, I'll make it at home to remind me of my beautiful evening in Hornillos del Camino. And there's always the next Camino, I think to myself. My evening was perfect. I wouldn't change a single thing.

The bells are ringing at the old church adjacent to the albergue as we head "home" for the night under the vast starry sky. Inside, Hans is waiting for us with a bottle of wine and a wedge of cheese. I bring along a block of chocolate, and we head downstairs to the communal kitchen, where we stay up late talking, even though there is no common language between all three of us. Sebastian is acting as translator. Hans speaks Austrian and German; Sebastian speaks Spanish, English, French, Portuguese, Russian, and enough German to keep the conversation alive. Somehow the three of us manage to talk about our families at home, about the transformative power of walking, and about all the places we've been in the world. Our evening culminates with us sticking pins into the large world map on the wall—all of the cities and countries and continents we've ever visited. Eventually we run out of pins. Between the three of us, we've been everywhere, except the polar regions. Sebastian has pins from one end of the map to the other.

When we finally head to our bunks, it is very late—the latest night I've had on the Camino. It's been a long day of so many extremes. I look over at Sebastian in the bunk beside me. He's grinning away merrily. Such a good-natured and magnificent being, the kind of person who restores your hope, your happiness, your faith in humanity.

There in the low light—with his long wavy hair, his golden skin, his dark eyes and beatific smile—Sebastian suddenly reminds me of a picture of Christ that was tacked to the wall in the Sunday school that I attended as a young girl. Just then the church bells peal midnight—the last chimes of the day, and everything goes still and dark and quiet.

Espinacas con Garbanzos

Espinacas con Garbanzos is a vegetarian spinach and chickpea stew with a long and significant culinary history, a dish I'd been watching for.

The dish has its roots in medieval Sephardic Jewish cooking and was a staple for Sephardic Jews, although it was also popular with Andalusian Arabs, who are thought to have brought spinach to the Iberian Peninsula from Ancient Persia in the eleventh century.

During the Spanish Inquisition, 1478–1831, Spanish authorities decreed chickpeas (known as garbanzos in Spanish) a Jewish food, and any Jewish Christian converts who were found eating chickpeas were arrested and subject to trial. And yet the dish persisted. Now it is a popular vegetarian dish and often shows up on tapas menus.

Though this is a contemporary recipe, it has elements of the ancient recipes for chickpea and spinach stews, including the small amount of honey used to both sweeten and round out the flavour of the stew. Serve with rice and plenty of crusty bread.

Serves 4

30 mL (2 tbsp) olive oil

1 medium yellow onion finely chopped (approx. ½ cup)

2 cloves garlic finely chopped (approx. 1 tbsp)

2 tsp cumin

1 tsp Spanish smoked paprika (or whatever paprika you have on hand)

¼ tsp cayenne, chipotle pepper, or hot chili pepper powder

½ tsp salt

15–30 mL (1–2 tbsp) honey

480 mL (2 cups) tomato-based vegetarian pasta sauce

398 mL (14 oz) can chickpeas

200 g (7 oz) spinach, washed, and chopped

Garnishes: Toasted slivered almonds, finely chopped fresh parsley

Warm the olive oil in a large fry pan and add the onion. Cook over medium heat for about 6 to 8 minutes or until the onion is just starting to brown.

Add the garlic and continue to cook for a minute or two longer. Turn the heat down slightly and add the cumin, smoked paprika, cayenne, salt, and honey. Stir thoroughly and continue cooking for about one minute.

Add the tomato sauce and stir well, then add the chickpeas. Simmer on low heat, uncovered, for about 10 minutes, stirring occasionally.

Add the spinach, and allow it to fully wilt.

Before serving, taste and add salt and pepper as needed. Top with toasted almonds and a sprinkle of fresh or dried parsley.

CHAPTER FIFTEEN

Hornillos del Camino to Itero de la Vega

October 21

"Life is a balance between holding on and letting go." —Rumi

I awaken with the first church bells at six o'clock, long before first light. I am momentarily displaced, stunned. I don't remember stirring a single time during the night and feel as though I am coming to after a deep coma. And yet, moments later, I'm up, dressed, my gear packed. In the basement kitchen, still drowsy, I find Sebastian, and we partake of the included breakfast—instant coffee, cornflakes, and toast with jam.

The talk around the breakfast table is of last night's noise in one of the rooms. Thankfully we were not privy to a man who was snoring so loudly that nobody got a moment's rest. Some people moved to the kitchen to sleep on the floor, some even left in the night.

"It was the Canadian guy," a man with an English accent announces, shaking his head. "No way anyone could sleep through that," he says. "Snoring like a banshee. He really ought to be staying in a private room. Bloody impossible, that."

I had heard the only other Canadian in the building last night, not due to his snoring, but rather his pontificating loudly to anyone who would listen. It made me feel even more grateful to Sebastian and Hans for being such thoroughly outstanding human beings. Luckily my fellow Canadian does not make an appearance at breakfast, and we don't linger long enough to hear any more. There's a good part of me that feels terribly sorry for him.

Sebastian and I strike off in the dark just before seven o'clock. He is once again planning to walk at least forty kilometres, probably more. I am not. I know that I cannot keep up Sebastian's pace indefinitely, and the last thing I want to do is hold him back.

All around it is dark and still. As the sun begins to rise on the horizon behind us, we keep turning around to watch its progress. First there is the slimmest, merest crack of dawn—a small faint white glow cresting the horizon. A few minutes later, the light grows as the sun begins to climb—to begin with it is just a semicircle, then it is a great glowing ball of red and pink and orange. The early morning sky moves from inky dark through shades of purple, mauve, pink, and soft pale blue. We are surrounded by the soft dun-coloured hues of the Meseta, the stubbled blond wheatfields, the packed dirt trail, the rolling beige hills, the golden sun.

No one else is on the trail. We walk on a wide track, well away from the roads. We sail on past Hontanas—population: seventy; age: ancient; size: tiny —and keep going under a deep blue sky, wispy strands of pure white cirrus clouds high above.

Seemingly out of nowhere the Camino turns a corner, and the trail passes directly under the massive stone arches of the ancient ruins of the San Anton Monastery. It is so gorgeously ruinous that it looks for all the world like a movie setting—though it is too majestic and solid to be anything but real.

I turn to Sebastian. "Can you believe this? It's like a very Spanish dream."

"Yeah," he says, hauling out his camera, taking a video. "You are so right— a very Spanish dream."

"Spain never fails to surprise me," I say. It's true. Like some ancient magic, every day there's something incredible, some scene, some building, some food, a glass of wine, a sliver of cake, the colour of the sky, the vistas, a stallion atop a mountain, pigs frolicking in the woods, or a person that crosses my path. Each of them leaves an incredible and indelible impression on me. It's all so much more than I ever expected. And now this monastery fills my view, my memory, my heart...

We stand there. Reverent and quiet in the face of such beauty and history. Taking it all in. Breathing in Spain. Despite Sebastian busily capturing the scene on his camera, it does not even occur to me to take a photograph. My camera could never do it justice anyway.

The San Anton Monastery, founded in 1146, was built to take care of sick and injured pilgrims on route to Santiago de Compostela. Once upon a time, in the recessed alcoves of the stone arches, bread and other food was left for pilgrims passing through. There is no longer food left here, but pilgrims sometimes leave notes of encouragement for other pilgrims. The ruins now house a simple but much beloved albergue for twelve pilgrims per evening, and in the summer months only. There is no electricity, and therefore no hot water and no lights, no wi-fi, nor telephone. But there is a communal dinner cooked on propane stoves. Pilgrims can take a cold shower and wash their clothes in the nearby river. I add this ancient crumbling monastery to the growing mental list of places to stay next time. Although truthfully, I know I could never withstand walking the Camino in the full heat of a Spanish summer.

A couple of kilometres down the road, we reach the village of Castrojeriz, population five hundred. It is not quite eleven in the morning, and according to my guidebook, this is where the day's walk ends. We have already covered twenty-one kilometres. Sebastian and I pause long enough to find ourselves some tuna and olive empanadas for lunch in a lovely local store. The shopkeepers are eager to talk with us and want to buy some Canadian money off me for their collection of foreign funds. Afterwards, we sit on the front steps of the store, eating our empanadas, and I decide to tell Sebastian that he must strike off by himself. As wonderful as he is, the last thing I want to do is hold him back or monopolize his company. Hard though it is to say goodbye to him, it's time to let him go. We hug and wish each other a Buen Camino and a good life. I watch him stride off, thinking about what an astonishingly beautiful human being he is and wondering if our paths will ever cross again. My life already seems better for the time I've spent in his company.

Just out of town there is a notoriously steep ascent up an exposed track to the top of Alto de Mostolares, straight onto the high plateau of the Meseta. I make the uphill trek behind two Australians, a couple around about my age, perhaps a bit younger. We are all, so far as I can tell, in our fifties. At some point, I say hello and ask them where they are from.

"Australia," they say.

"Yes, that much I knew!" I say. "I lived in Australia for several years and loved it."

Turns out that they live in Melbourne, on the very same street that I once worked on. Even so, the conversation quickly stalls. Fair enough; I let it go. I have no need to talk. I am still full of joy from time spent with Sebastian. But there is no one else in sight, not a soul. And we walk at much the same pace, so we are a bit stuck with each other.

Meanwhile the trail climbs up, up, up. It is a slog of an ascent. Steep, exposed, and brutal. I stop to drink some water, take a photograph—something I rarely do—and purposefully fall behind. I want to respect their need for space, but more importantly, I am choosing to be alone.

Later, when I am once again walking pretty much in lockstep with the Australians, we exchange names. But somehow, any sense of companionship continues to elude us. Perhaps it's the atmospheric conditions—the day is hot, and the air is hanging heavily—or the fact that Sebastian was such perfect company; or maybe I'm just tired from yesterday's fifty-kilometre trek, which has left me with my real first blisters. There is nothing for it except to press on.

Once we leave the villages behind, the scenery gets sterner as we head onto the plateau that is the Meseta. Stark, arid, nearly treeless. I expected it to look like the vast wheat fields and huge blue skies of the Canadian prairies, or perhaps akin to the Australian Outback—red earth and sunshine. The landscape here feels like some ancient, deserted territory, as though nothing much has changed here since the birth of the planet. The sky is boundless, stretching in all directions as far as the eye can see, with nothing in the sightline to interrupt it. I'm learning, once again, to let go of preconceived notions—to try to understand this austere landscape just as it is, without needing to make comparisons.

I turn and slowly rotate through one full revolution. As far as I can see in every direction, there is nothing but sun-parched earth and endless blue skies. Incredibly, the Meseta makes up forty percent of Spain's land mass. Despite this vast high plain that occupies so much territory, Spain is also Europe's second most mountainous country. It is a huge land of staggering contrasts.

I am reminded of how most of the books I read about the pilgrimage noted that the Camino Frances is divided into three separate phases, each with their own unique topography. The first phase, from Saint-Jean-Pied-de-Port to Burgos, is known as the physical phase. Here you get used to walking all day long, often through rugged and mountainous terrain. It's exciting and exhilarating and exhausting.

The second phase begins as you walk onto the Meseta. This section is known as the mental or emotional phase. Here the crowds have thinned and dispersed, and the scenery changes from mountains to the high flat plains and vast sky. There are few distractions, and the walking is less challenging, making it easier to clock up more distance. This is a time of reckoning, for sorting out why one is actually here, walking from sunup to sundown each day. The Meseta is the part of the Camino notorious for soul searching, for figuring things out, for building internal fortitude, for tying up all the loose ends of our lives and making sense of them. It's a wide-open landscape that lends itself well to introspection, to intensity.

The final phase is known as the spiritual phase, and it coincides with entering Galicia, with its deeply lush, earthy, forested, mountainous landscape and its fifty shades of green, probably more. In this phase of the Camino, there is said to be great joy at entering the final days of the long walk. Many pilgrims report that by this stage, they feel a new connection to the earth, along with profound feelings of empathy, love, and compassion for others, plus a greater understanding of their own lives.

So far at least, all of this seems spot on.

It's late afternoon by the time I arrive in Itero de la Vega. I've walked on and off for most of the afternoon either just behind or just ahead of the Australian couple. Because we walk at roughly the same pace, and there's nowhere to stop, we keep overlapping. Throughout all this, we haven't really said much of anything to each other, a respectful spacing, pacing. I'm enjoying the silence, the landscape, the walking.

At this point though, when we descend upon this strange, very foreign, rather austere-looking village, we are all in search of an albergue. The first place we enter is nothing but a massive open room with a cracked concrete floor. The entire place is packed full of what look like army cots. It's miserable. There is no one around, so we turn around, and without even saying anything, we all walk straight back out.

The next potential hostel is smaller and has some rooms with just two or three beds. We take a room with three beds and book in for dinner. Only afterwards do I realize it might have been easier if we'd stayed at the place with concrete floors and army cots—I could have disappeared more easily into the crowd. I don't want to impose myself on any of my fellow walkers, and I get the sense that something is going on with my fellow Australians—but what it is, I am not sure. I wish I'd been more able to speak up and simply book myself into a bunk room, let them take a room to themselves. "But it's just one night," I tell myself. "We can definitely make this work…"

The Camino is full of chance and temporary allegiances. Some are tentative, fleeting, and purely matters of convenience. Others are surprisingly profound and meaningful and enlightening. Some make you feel alive and connected and joyful; others make you feel far lonelier than you'd have felt if you really were alone. All of this, I'm finding, is strangely helpful.

The Camino really is like a microcosm of an entire life—all of it condensed into bite-sized pieces along eight hundred kilometres. Unlike in our everyday lives though, we pilgrims converge here from all over the world and come together on this journey, all travelling towards Santiago de Compostela—all following the same yellow trail markers. We are all searching for more or less the same thing: food, shelter, and belonging. And, quite often, for a bathroom. We are all just finding our way as best we can. Sometimes it works, sometimes it leaves you perplexed. Sometimes you belong, and sometimes you don't. Sometimes you're winning and inexplicably joyful, and sometimes you're failing, losing, floundering, lonely, and lost.

I have to keep reminding myself that I'm going somewhere. I'm on a mission. And that mission is simply to walk and keep walking, relentlessly, solidly, unequivocally west, towards Santiago. And yet, as simple as that seems, I keep getting derailed by mere human interactions. There are bigger things at stake here. I'm often deeply lonely and longing for connection, yet I also want to be able to go on alone—to have time to sort out some deeply buried matters that I need to think through. I'm not even sure what all the deeply buried matters are. They just *are*. Some I know and can't bear to confront. Others are waiting to surface. A lifetime of baggage just lurking about. I thought by walking I'd manage to figure a few things out, but so far I seem mostly to lunge from one day to the next, merely trying to get through and figure out where to eat, where to stay. And trying not to end my days entirely alone. Perhaps, though, this struggle to find one's place amongst others, no matter what journey you're on, is just simply the human condition.

My plan, I decide once again, is just to let things continue to unfold. Tomorrow will be a new day, and I'll keep walking. One foot and then the other. Hour by hour. Day by day. Week by week.

At dinner in the albergue, there are eight of us at the table. Three quiet, well-behaved, thoroughly decent Canadian men from Sarnia who are all missing ice hockey; lovely Alistair and Kate, who have a home in Edinburgh, but seem to have lived and worked all over the world, including some long stints in Africa; the Australians; and me. We are a motley crew but have a lively enough conversation along with plenty of wine and another standard pilgrims' dinner—bread, salad, chicken, and for dessert some kind of processed cheese with quince paste. Using my imagination, I can see how given the right cheese (a wedge of blue, a sliver of old cheddar, or a piece of sharp, salty Manchego), this dessert could be absolutely sublime. After walking over eighty kilometres in two days, though, I am just happy and grateful to be sitting at the table, drinking a nice Spanish red wine and eating every single thing that is put in front of me. With gusto.

With dinner over, I don't know quite what to do. I don't want to head straight to the room, and neither do I want to take myself for a walk after so much walking. But there's really nowhere to go and nothing at all to do in this tiny hamlet. So, I head outside and find a seat in the garden and watch the darkness fall all around me before turning in for the night, alone but not alone.

Membrillo y Manchego Tapas

Quince trees, members of the rose family, are native to Iran, Turkey, and possibly also to Greece and the Crimean Peninsula. The quince fruit, which looks like a cross between and apple and a pear, cannot be eaten raw but is delicious when cooked. It is very popular in Spain, France, Turkey, and parts of Asia. Quince cheese or quince jelly, known as membrillo in Spain, is a well-loved sweet and is often served with Manchego cheese.

Though quince is not indigenous to North America, many varieties can be grown, even in zones that have a real winter. If you can grow a peach tree in your area, then it is likely that you can also grow a quince tree. And thankfully, quince are self-fertile, so a single tree is all that is required.

Quince trees are relatively rare in North America, though this was not always the case. They are wonderful small, umbrella shaped trees that produce both beautiful, fragrant blossoms and a delicious and useful fruit. Quince fruit are astringent and high in tannins, but when cooked, they transform in colour, character, and consistency. Their flesh turns from a pale peach colour into ever-deeper ruby red, and the longer the cooking, the deeper the colour. They make excellent jams, jellies, and chutneys, as they are rich in pectin, and yield themselves well to desserts. If you've got a garden and room to grow a small fruit tree, it is worth planting a quince tree, or two.

But even without a tree, quince paste can be found in the international section of many major North American grocery stores and some European style delicatessens. Quince paste, or quince cheese as it is sometimes called, can be served as either a light dessert or as part of a tapas menu. These easy-to-assemble skewers make an excellent addition to a tapas party and are both vegetarian and gluten-free.

Makes approximately 32 individual tapas (allow 2–3 per person)
225 g (8 oz) pasta de membrillo or quince paste
225 g (8 oz) Manchego cheese (or substitute blue cheese, or
    a sharp cheddar)
75 g (½ cup) roasted almonds or walnuts, finely chopped (a
    food processor works well here)
Small wooden skewers or toothpicks

Cut the cheese and the quince paste into 2 cm (¾ inch) cubes. Roll the quince paste cubes in the crushed nuts. Spear the cheese and quince paste so that the cheese forms the base.

CHAPTER SIXTEEN

Itero de la Vega to Carrión de los Condes

October 22

Solivagant: [L. *solus* alone + *vagans* wandering.] Wandering alone.
—*Webster's Dictionary*, 1913

After a long, stuffy, somewhat sleepless night in the small room, I'm anxious to get up and get going. I pause long enough to drink some instant coffee with my Australian roommates and then pack quickly and hit the trail. I set off alone, solivagant, on purpose. I am determined to get better at walking alone and being alone. I make it my mission.

The landscape leaving Itero de la Vega is like a post-impressionist painting—gently rolling fields of wheat stubble, with the remnant indentations of tractor trails. All around me are shades of gold and beige and muted green, dotted here and there with vibrant autumn wildflowers. Above, a deep cornflower blue sky dotted with small fluffy white clouds look as though a painter has taken too much brilliant white paint and just daubed it about thickly, casually, childishly. It's a happy landscape, perfect weather, and an easy walk. I plan to end my day in Carrión de los Condes, a very manageable thirty-four-kilometre walk.

Just before the first village of the day, Boadilla del Camino, I run into Alistair and Kate again and join them for a quick coffee break. They are such good company, but I am determined to continue on alone. I soon find myself back on the Camino, striding out along the lovely, level, tree-lined banks of the Canal de Castilla—an agricultural irrigation canal built in the eighteenth century.

Perhaps it's simply that the scenery today is more than usually magnificent and that I am seeing everything in double because of the perfect reflections in the still water of the canal. My walking alone means I can focus on the details of the landscape, rather than on any companions or even my own internal dialogue, and everything seems so breathtakingly beautiful, so exquisite.

The canal is my companion until I arrive in Fromista. I am standing at the top of a dramatic set of steep locks looking down at the five sets of locks below me, admiring this feat of engineering (the locks allow boats to be either raised or lowered as they travel either up or downstream), when a man strides up and introduces himself as Guy, from France. I'm only half paying attention when he mentions that he is from somewhere near Le Puy, or perhaps Paris. Frankly I'm more interested in the locks. He is chatty. Older. Graying, balding. A little paunchy. Enthusiastic. Nice enough, but oblivious to signals.

My French isn't great, and though his English is better, our conversation is limited. I don't want company today. I'm determined about this. But my subtle, and later less than subtle, rebuffs don't seem to put him off at all. We walk on together, mostly silent. Still, he persists.

"Où vas-tu?" (Where are you going?) Guy asks. "A Carrión de los Condes," I answer, honestly but reluctantly. It's another twenty kilometres down the trail on top of the fourteen-and-a-half kilometres I've already walked. And I really don't want company for the next four hours. "Me too!" he says, beaming. "Let's walk together!" I repeat that I'd really like to walk alone today. But Guy just waves his hands and keeps talking, he can't seem to hear me even when I am very direct. I stop talking. I really don't want to tell him anything more.

I have a bad habit of simply going along with people at times. Of not trusting my own judgment or going with my intuition. This has happened too many times in the past and at times with lousy and even terrible consequences. When I set out today, I was determined to walk alone. And now, only a couple of hours into the day, I find myself ineffectually trying to fob off a Frenchman. He's probably a perfectly reasonable man, but his persistence bothers me. I tell him several times that I planned to walk alone, but it's as if he only hears selectively. And he keeps asking me quite personal questions. He wants to know how old I am. What I do for a living. If I have children. If I am married. And why I am walking the Camino.

"Trop compliqué…" I say, trying to shut the discussion down. It is, in fact, complicated. I don't want to explain my life, the messy, gritty truth of my relationships in broken French and English to someone I do not know. And I don't really want to hear about his circumstances, either. My head is swimming.

The truth is that I married very young, while I was still an impoverished under-graduate at university—in part because being married meant I would qualify for a grant to keep attending university; and also because the handsome young man who was my housemate seemed as lost in the world as I was. He kissed me once at a party, and I fell for him based on that one kiss. We were young and naïve and foolish. In some wild way, we were also soulmates. We just seemed to work together, so we eloped at City Hall and embarked on a crazy life together.

Before long we had our first daughter. We moved to Melbourne, Australia, where we both embarked on new careers. Chris was studying for his PhD in engineering, and I worked in the university's public affairs department while doing night school classes towards a master's degree in communications.

Along the way, our second daughter was born. Immediately after she was born, before I'd held her or even seen her, I had a post-partum hemorrhage in the delivery room and went into cardiac arrest. I was a "code blue," and sent to a cardiac intensive care unit with a sea of medical personnel and the defib-rillators on my chest. I was later told that I had technically died on the way to the unit. I was passing in and out of consciousness, coming to and finding myself hooked up to intravenous drips, heart monitors, and machines beeping and whirring all round me.

A doctor, mere inches from my face, kept repeating the same words over and over. "I'm Dr. Short, head of cardiac intensive care. You've been in cardiac arrest. Speak to me when you can." When I finally spoke, it was to ask what happened. I remember the collective sigh when I finally spoke, but what I didn't remember yet was that I'd had a baby. That realization came later, when they brought me back to the maternity ward and put my baby in my arms.

I was a miracle—the hospital chaplain later told me—one of the lucky ones to survive after losing so much blood. He went on to tell me that I'd restored his floundering faith. That I'd given him a reason to go on. "You are such a gift, and your baby is absolutely perfect," he said, as we both wiped tears from our eyes.

Even though I lived to tell the tale and made a full recovery, our daughter spent much of her childhood in and out of hospitals and at specialist appoint-ments. Eventually she was diagnosed with life-threatening seizures, thought to be caused by birth trauma. But undeterred, she went on, like her sister, to become a medical professional and emerged triumphant and beautiful in every possible way.

Now well into our fifties, with so much of life behind us, things have fallen apart between my husband and me. We moved three times to Australia and three times back to Canada, dozens of times across both countries, from coast to coast, south to north. We uprooted ourselves and our two daughters, selling up house after house, always questing after some new job, some step up the ladder, some new adventure. Some elusive thing that we could not define. We truly were each as lost as the other.

For years I lurched through life, slumbering between crises, through babies, jobs, and transcontinental moves. Through renovations and nightmares, seizures, and illness. All of life's various and sundry explosions, the minuscule and the monumental tragedies of everyday life. Somehow along the way I became hypervigilant, hypersensitive, and probably hyperbolic.

Our marriage was the casualty of all the stress. Or maybe it would have happened anyway. Who knows? And yet, if there was one thing I knew, it was that I still loved him. I just couldn't see how we could make it work after years of drifting further and further apart. I wasn't interested in other men. Outside of my beloved paternal grandfather, there had been only two other men in my life whom I'd really loved—my handsome intelligent loyal teenaged boyfriend who'd gone on to a dazzling career; and then at university, another handsome intelligent loyal man—the one who became my husband. When our marriage broke down, I wasn't interested in another man. But I didn't want to spend the rest of my life alone, either. I wondered about a companionable existence with a woman. But that didn't work out how I expected either. I felt like a failure at love. The single thing I believe matters most.

It was this last bit—trying to make sense of what I wanted and the failure of my marriage—that I wanted to think about on the Camino. Of how to let go of the past, live in the present, and somehow embrace the future. Of how to simply go on...

But try as I might, I seem to keep getting distracted and perhaps distracting myself from my own agenda, and instead of using the Camino as a mechanism for sorting out my life, I end up walking with other people and somehow abandoning my mission. It's not that I am particularly conforming, and I do want companionship, of course, but striking the balance—both here on the Camino, and in my regular life—seems to be such a challenge. The truth is, I've long been afraid to embark on my own path. I've let a great many fears and insecurities stand in my way for so long. Really for most of my life.

So here I am, determined to walk on alone and sort through my life, and yet Guy, this socially oblivious Frenchman, seems to have other plans entirely. He is still talking to me, but I am no longer listening, let alone attempting to decipher his French. It's as though I am sleepwalking, putting one foot in front of the other. Everything else is irrelevant. Partway through the afternoon he falls silent, and then shortly after this, we approach a village, and he asks me if I would like to stop for a drink. I consider this. Would I? Yes, as it turns out, I am quite thirsty. I am not actually feeling great and think a drink might help.

We head into a bar, where I insist on ordering and paying for my own drink, despite Guy's offers to buy me wine. What I would like is a Gatorade or a ginger ale, but I have no idea if either of these might be available or if so, how to order any such thing. So, I ask instead for a fizzy water—una agua con gas—and when it comes, I use it to take two acetaminophen tablets. I just want to quench my thirst, get back on the trail, and find a place to crash for the night.

The day seems interminably long, and for the first time on the Camino I am thoroughly exhausted. When we do finally make it to our destination, I am too tired to talk. I let Guy take charge of finding accommodations. He is heading to the Real Monasterio Santa Clara—where the beds, he tells me, cost seven euros. All I want to do is get horizontal and sleep. I'm worried that I am coming down with something.

We walk across a massive courtyard, and a robed priest comes forward to greet us, and takes us into the building. I don't even try to follow the conversation and am surprised when the priest takes us to a small private room with two twin beds. The bathroom is just down the hall and only shared by another couple of twin rooms. It's luxurious compared to most albergues.

I did not anticipate being in a private room with Guy, who quickly explains that this room is for couples but costs the same per person as the bunk rooms. I weigh my options and realize that it might be better than being in a dorm, as I am really not feeling at all well. All I want to do is climb into my bed and get some sleep. I put my pack on the floor and climb on top of my bed fully clothed and am out like a light. When I wake up, a couple of hours later, it is early evening and Guy is sitting on his bed reading. "Do you want to get something to eat?" he asks. "Yes, I think so, but nothing much," I reply. "Maybe a sandwich or a bowl of soup?"

We head out into the night and walk straight to the nearest bar, where I order more mineral water and a bowl of lentil soup. When it arrives, it is thick, like a stew—simple, delicious, and soothing. The dish seems to revive me enough that I suggest that we attend a church service at the monastery. I find the services and the beautiful ancient churches remarkably peaceful. I'm also not in a rush to be alone with Guy in our small twin room, and I figure a dose of a Catholic church cannot do either of us any harm.

After the service we head back to the room, and I go straight to bed. I am feverish again and exhausted. I take more medication with the hope that I will be well enough to walk in the morning. Moments later, Guy starts snoring loudly. I put my wax earplugs in and say yet another silent message of gratitude to Camilla, who kindly gave me the earplugs way back in Puente la Reina.

Lentejas

Lentejas is a beloved and iconic Spanish dish that is a cross between a soup and a stew. It is found throughout Spain, with slight regional variations. It was the Spanish and Portuguese explorers who first introduced lentils to the Americas in the early sixteenth century. Canada is now the world's largest producer of lentils.

Lentils have been sustaining humans for thousands of years. They are the oldest known pulse crop and one of the first domesticated crops ever grown. Amongst their many qualities, lentils are remarkably high in protein and fibre—inexpensive, delicious, very nutritious, flavourful, filling, and low in calories.

Serves 4 as a main or 6 as a starter
30 mL (2 tbsp) olive oil
1 small onion, chopped
2–3 cloves garlic, minced

1 large carrot, peeled and diced

2 small potatoes, peeled and diced into small cubes

300 g (1½ cups) dried green or brown lentils, well rinsed, or
  540 mL (19 oz) can lentils*

796 mL (approx. 3⅓ cups) can crushed tomatoes

Approx. 1.5 L (5–6 cups) vegetable or chicken stock

1 tsp cumin

1 tsp sweet paprika

1 fresh lemon (juice and zest)

Salt and pepper to taste (amount will depend on your stock)

Chopped fresh parsley to garnish

In a large pot, heat the olive oil over medium heat.

Add the onion and cook for 2 to 3 minutes, until it is starting to sweat. Then add the garlic and cook for another couple of minutes, being careful not to burn it.

Add the diced carrots and potatoes and cook for 10 minutes or until they start to soften.

Add the lentils, crushed tomatoes, 5 cups of stock, cumin, and paprika. Bring the ingredients to a simmer and cook for about 30 to 40 minutes, or until the lentils are soft. If you are using canned lentils, you can shorten the cooking time to about 25 minutes (check that the potatoes are tender). If you are using dried lentils, and your lentils are old, they may take slightly longer to cook, up to 45 minutes.

If the mixture starts to look a bit too thick, add the remaining cup of stock.

Once the lentils are thoroughly cooked, you can either use a potato masher to partially mash the mixture gently enough to thicken the soup OR use a hand-held blender and give the soup a couple of very quick whizzes to thicken it. Be careful not to turn the soup into a giant purée. Or you can skip this step altogether and just serve the soup/stew as it is.

If the soup is too thick, add a little water. If it is a little thin, continue cooking it down and mash it lightly again. Before serving, season with salt and pepper and add the lemon zest and a tablespoon or two of lemon juice. Ladle into bowls and garnish with parsley. Serve with a loaf of warm bread or a basket of bread rolls and butter or olive oil for dipping the bread in.

CHAPTER SEVENTEEN

Carrión de los Condes to Terradillos de los Templarios

October 23

"If you don't know where you are going any road can take you there."
—Charles Lutwidge Dodgson, aka Lewis Carroll, *Alice in Wonderland*

Sometime in the middle of the night I wake up coughing non-stop. A deep, nasty, hacking cough. Guy snores on, oblivious to the world. I'm thankful that he is such a sound sleeper and would feel so much worse if my cough kept him awake. I cough for what feels like half the night. In the morning I drag myself from bed, pack up my sleeping bag, and tell Guy that I am too sick to go on. He says that he will stay and look after me, but that is the last thing I want. "Please," I say, "I'm so sorry. I don't want you to catch this bug, and I really just need to be alone."

"Write me your email address," he says, handing me a piece of paper and a pen. I am cornered. There's nothing wrong with Guy, but he seems to want something that I'm not looking for, and he is clearly unable to take a hint. I'm not interested in a fling, or any kind of relationship, and his words and actions indicate that he is. I contemplate giving him a fake address, but my hand works on its own, and I hand him back the slip of paper with my name and email address. I am feeling queasy, probably from all the gut-wrenching coughing. I just want him to leave.

The thing is, though, it is a general rule that you cannot stay two nights in an albergue. In most albergues, especially the parochial ones like this one, you have to be out by eight o'clock in the morning, so that the cleaners can come through before the next batch of pilgrims arrive. So despite my condition, I pack my gear and wander around the grounds trying to find someone who can tell me how to book back in for a second night. There is nobody around who is able help me. When the cleaning staff arrive, I approach one of them to see if staying on is a possibility. She talks to me loudly in rapid fire Spanish while I look on dazed, my head swimming. I have no clue what she is saying. Finally in exasperation she shouts, "¡VAMOS!"

I remember the word "vamos" from years of watching Speedy Gonzales cartoons as a child. This particular ¡VAMOS! certainly seems like a stern invitation to get a move on and quit wasting her time. It's not even nine o'clock yet and everyone else has long since left the premises. I take my leave as well, with no clue what I'm going to do.

Before I leave the monastery grounds, I run into an English couple about to take a bus somewhere or other. As I listen to their complicated plan, I don't recognize the place names, nor can I figure out what they are talking about. My head is too muddled from coughing, lack of sleep, and whatever plague I'm fighting to be able to follow their story. I ask them if they know how I could book in for a second night, and as it turns out, they were told that this albergue does not reopen until afternoon. There's no way I can spend half the day waiting outside in the cold and the wind, hoping to be let back in again. Not knowing what else to do, nor where I'm heading, I decide walking might just be easier.

I find the familiar signposts to the Camino and start once again, walking west. I have absolutely no idea where the day will take me and have not even checked the map to find out what lies ahead. I haven't had coffee or breakfast, but I plan, as has become my usual, to stop at the first nice place I encounter.

The trail on this part of the Camino is a wide, flat gravel path with stubble on either side. The sky is grey and threatening rain, and I find myself walking directly into a stiff head wind. I walk for an hour and see nothing of note. No villages, no trees, nothing whatsoever alongside the path. Everyone else left the albergue long before me, so I am walking entirely alone. Eventually I stop to pull out my guidebook and discover that the nearest village, Calzadilla de la Cueza, is just over seventeen kilometres from my overnight stop in Carrion de los Condes, and there is nothing, not even a toilet block between the two villages, let alone a place to find coffee or a bite to eat. This is the bleakest, most miserable day yet on the Camino. I am not sure if I need this punishment for some reason, but on I go, slightly dazed, one foot then the other. Plodding, slogging, trudging on.

I arrive in Calzadilla de la Cueza shortly after noon and head into one of the albergues to see about staying. Although it seems too early in the day to stop, the place is almost full already, and the only bed I can find is an upper bunk in the middle of the vast dormitory. If my cough is anything like last night, I will keep the entire huge room awake. And neither can I imagine staying here for an entire long afternoon and evening with nothing to do, and not even a book to read. This will never work. What I need to find is a pharmacy—una farmacia—and preferably a room of my own, but neither is available here. So once again, despite utter fatigue and wanting neither to stay nor go, I pick up my pack and head back to the path, without even bothering to try to find food or coffee.

It's only about another ten kilometres to Terradillos de los Templarios. I decide to walk there as quickly as possible and find myself food and a bed for the night. By the time I get there, between the combination of whatever I'm ailing from and the walk, I should be so utterly fatigued that I'll be able to sleep through anything, even the horrible cough I seem to have developed.

As I approach Terradillos de los Templarios, I'm so glad I walked on. The tiny village is golden in the late afternoon sun, which has finally made its appearance after a long grey day. Silke, a German woman whom I met along the path an hour or two earlier, said that she was heading to the Albergue Jacques De Molay, and that it came highly recommended by her German guidebook. The mention of this made me smile. I've experienced more than I ever expected of German recommendations along the Camino. I tell her I'll find the albergue and look for her at dinner.

Terradillos de los Templarios is Knights Templar territory. Jacques de Molay, for whom the albergue is named, was the head of the Knights Templar when King Philip IV of France outlawed the Knights Templar in France and confiscated their vast assets. Jacques de Molay was the last Grand Master of the Knights Templar, and in 1314, he was burned at the stake in front of Notre Dame Cathedral in Paris, by order of the King. At the time of his death, De Molay, aged seventy, was considered exceptionally old. Average life expectancy of the era was about thirty-one years. Many of the Knights Templar outlived the average life expectancy of the time, often by decades—leading many to think that they had been granted a special divine gift. Contemporary scholars believe that the Templars' longevity might have been due to the strict dietary and sanitary rules they were forced to follow; handwashing, for example, was mandatory. The Templars followed a semi-vegetarian regimen, with meat only allowed three days a week, they drank modest rations of diluted wine, and on Fridays eggs, milk, and other animal products were banned. Eating fish, however, was allowed and encouraged.

It doesn't take me long on arrival in the tiny village to find the albergue. It has a picturesque walled garden with a neatly trimmed lawn and a clothesline. I book in and am shown to an empty room with four single beds. I pick a bed in the corner along a wall, underneath the window and away from the other three beds, which are lined up against the back wall, side by side. I set up my sleeping bag and use the communal bathroom down the hall to have a quick shower. It's better than being in a room with twelve or twenty or fifty others, but it makes me think of how luxurious it will be to return home after all this and have a bedroom and bathroom entirely to myself.

By the time I emerge, the room has filled up. By luck, Silke has one of the beds, along with two men—Benedict, also from Germany, and Bruno, an interesting looking, exceptionally hairy older man with a thick black beard and long black hair. He seems to speak no English, German, Italian, French, or Spanish. We never do find out where he's from or what language he speaks. The four of us exchange rudimentary greetings, and with that out of the way, I set off to wash and hang my clothes to dry. It is an endless job trying to get clothes clean and dried on the Camino, especially in late October, when the days are short. Many days I have my still damp spare socks and undies safety pinned to my backpack, drying in the sun as I walk, exposed for all the world to see. (Best to remember that when you pack your underwear to walk the Camino.)

With my laundry done and my bed made up, I find my way to the restaurant on the main floor of the albergue and order a long-awaited coffee and a slice of tortilla de patatas (known outside of Spain as tortilla Española), which has rapidly become my favourite Spanish comfort food. It's widely available and, even though it varies slightly from place to place, is predictably tasty, inexpensive, nutritious, and filling with its copious amount of olive oil, eggs, and potatoes. It works for breakfast, lunch, dinner, or tapas. In this case, since

I haven't eaten all day and it is now closing in on dinner time, the tortilla de patatas is taking the place of all three meals and it could not be more perfect.

The dining room here is one of the most convivial I've seen on the Camino. There's Spanish music playing, drinks flowing, and an excellent tapas menu. And not only that, but there is cheerful table service. I find myself starting to perk up and feel a bit brighter.

Before long Silke comes and joins me. I contemplate taking a walk around the tiny village before nightfall, but I am so happy and comfortable right here that I decide to stay put and order a glass of wine and a second serving of tortilla, along with a salad. The food is rustic, flavourful and nicely presented, and the company is lively. Between the two of us, Silke and I know many of the people staying in the albergue, and we enjoy a very happy, sociable couple of hours. However, my previous long night of coughing and equally long day of walking are catching up with me, so I take my leave to head outdoors to gather up my damp laundry and then head off to our sleeping quarters.

I am asleep before the others come to bed. But several hours later, in the dead of the night, I awaken, coughing so badly that I can scarcely catch my breath. I don't want to wake the others, but it is too late. My hacking cough is relentless. Everyone is wide awake. I feel awful, but I have no idea where I can go so that they can sleep. I try to sleep sitting propped up in bed, but I still cannot stop coughing. Eventually Benedict gets up and rummages through his bag. He brings me a pill and tells me it will help my cough. As touched as I am, I have no idea what kind of pill it is and am reluctant to take medication that I do not know. What if I have a reaction? What if it is something illicit? I've never heard of a pill that stops coughing, so I hesitate, and Benedict, understanding, reassures me as best he can, that the pill is fine.

"I do not know the name in English, but I have taken these many times. It will help, and you will get some sleep," he says, kindly but firmly, then adds, "And that way, maybe all of us will get some sleep." Benedict looks and seems calm, reasonable, and intelligent. He is very clean cut and somehow seems safe. But it is the last bit of his comment that gets me. I really do not want to keep everyone else awake. So, I quell my misgivings and swallow the pill down with some water from my water bottle and pray that this all ends well for everyone.

Tortilla de Patatas/Tortilla Española

It would be difficult to visit Spain without encountering the ubiquitous culinary staple tortilla de patatas (or tortilla Española as it is often called outside of Spain)—one of the key national dishes of Spain.

This humble potato and egg dish is not in any way related to the corn or flour flatbreads which bear the same name across the ocean in Latin America. Tortilla de patatas (often just referred to as tortilla) is tasty, simple, inexpensive, nutritious, filling, and as a side bonus, it is also vegetarian. As Penelope Casas says in her classic book *The Foods and Wines of Spain,* "The tortilla is a way of life in Spain."

Tortilla de patatas is one of the most popular dishes along the Camino, where it can be found almost everywhere—in cafés and albergues, in bars and restaurants, on pilgrim and regular menus, for breakfast, lunch, dinner, and also when cut into small pieces and skewered, on tapas menus. Spanish tortilla is made with potatoes, liberal quantities of olive oil, eggs, salt, and sometimes (though not often) onions. Spanish chefs cannot agree on whether onions belong in the tortilla de patatas. Tortilla may vary slightly from place to place but is nearly always unadorned by any extras.

Mastering the flip is the only challenging part of making this dish. One important thing to note is that in some Spanish regions, a less-cooked, runnier version of tortilla de patatas is preferred to a fully cooked version. Recent food poisoning scares in Spain have resulted in a reinforcement of Spanish government's guidelines for cooking eggs that include either using pasteurised eggs, or if using fresh eggs, cooking to an internal temperature of 75°C (167°F).

It's much easier to start with a smaller tortilla, like this one. The dish is not complicated, but it is best to get used to flipping a smaller version before graduating to a larger pan and flipping a larger tortilla. For a completely traditional tortilla, much more olive oil is used—in which case, after cooking the potatoes, the oil is drained and reserved. The important aspects are the eggs, potatoes, and plenty of olive oil. It is the generous quantity of olive oil that will give the dish its beautiful creamy consistency and flavour. In my kitchen, I use less oil, and so I don't drain or reserve the oil. You can experiment with this recipe a little to find out what works for you. Be sure to use the best olive oil possible—it's what makes this dish so incredibly satisfying.

A note on slicing: Spanish cooks tend to cut the potatoes into thin discs. However, I've found it easier to cook and flip the tortilla if the potato is cut in half lengthwise and then cut into slices about 1 cm or ½ inch thick. I also like my potatoes a little more browned (and less anemic looking).

Serves 2

60 mL (¼ cup) extra virgin olive oil

3–4 small potatoes, preferably Yukon Jack or Russet, peeled and sliced

4 eggs, beaten

30 mL (2 tbsp) of water

Salt and pepper

Warm the olive oil gently on medium-low heat in a medium-sized non-stick pan. Add the potato slices. Season with a little salt and pepper.

Cook, moving the potatoes about with a spatula, until tender and just beginning to turn slightly golden. This will take approximately 12 to 15 minutes or longer, depending on how crowded your pan is.

Beat the eggs until slightly frothy, and whisk in the salt, pepper, and water. Pour this mixture over the hot potatoes in the pan.

Cook over medium-low heat until the eggs are set around the edge and starting to set in the centre (about 3 to 5 minutes, depending on your stove).

When the bottom is browned and the top is mostly set (centre should not be fully set—this will help keep your tortilla tender), it is time to flip the tortilla. To do this, either place a slightly larger pan over the medium-sized pan and carefully flip the two pans together, then remove the medium pan. Alternatively, if you don't have two appropriately sized pans, place a large flat plate over the pan and invert, and then slide the tortilla back into the pan. Either way, you want to cook the tortilla on both sides before serving. The second side should take about 3 minutes to cook, though this will depend on the temperature of the element.

Serve the tortilla with a spoonful of aioli or spicy mayonnaise, along with sliced olives and/or a side salad. Do not overdo the accompaniments. Let the beautiful simplicity of this omelette speak for itself.

CHAPTER EIGHTEEN

Terradillos de los Templarios to Sahagún to León

October 24

"Above all, do not lose your desire to walk: every day I walk myself into a state of well-being and walk away from every illness; I have walked myself into my best thoughts and I know of no thought so burdensome that one cannot walk away from it." —Soren Kierkegaard, from a letter to Henrietta Lund, 1847

I awaken to find the curtains drawn and the room awash in sunlight. Ribbons of sunlight dance across my sleeping bag. Everyone is up, dressed, and packing their gear. This is the first time I've slept so late while on the trail, but when I check my watch, it is only shortly after eight o'clock. Benedict walks into the room and asks me how I'm feeling.

"Better, much better—thanks to you," I say, and I do feel better, but then I felt quite a lot better during the day yesterday, too. The hacking cough seems to be a mostly nighttime affliction.

"That's a very bad cough," he says, authoritatively. "I think you should see a doctor when you get to a bigger town. But in the meantime, take these extra couple of pills with you." And before I can ask what the pills are, he puts a little blister pack of pills on the top of my rucksack and is out the door. "Get well. Buen Camino," he calls out as he heads down the hall. I reach out, grab the blister pack, and turn it over—it says nothing. I still have no clue what the mystery pills are. Codeine, I wonder?

Our fourth roommate, Bruno, looks at me, bows his head, and makes the sign of the cross. I viewed him somewhat suspiciously when I first saw him, but he's been a perfect gentleman. As he picks up his bag, I wish him a "Buen Camino," and he smiles broadly and bows deeply. Then he stands up and puts his hand to mouth and demonstrates a little fake cough, and we both burst into laughter.

Silke asks me if I'm heading to the dining room for breakfast. I am. Having walked the entire day yesterday without eating, I am taking no chances going forward, and despite my vow to quit paying for lousy albergue breakfasts, I had prepaid for breakfast when I booked last night. It still seems that no sooner do I make my mind up about something then I change it again. "I'll wait! I'm in no rush," she says as she spreads her gear all over her bed. I head to the bathrooms to splash water on my face and brush my hair. When I come back, she is sitting on her bed waiting for me.

Breakfast is simple—a proper brewed (not instant!) coffee and a croissant. But it feels like such a luxury after yesterday's experience of walking for hours and hours with no food whatsoever. Over breakfast, I agree to walk for a while with Silke, and true to her words, she really is in absolutely no rush. She pokes about packing and repacking her gear and then decides that perhaps she needs another coffee. I tell her I'll see her down the trail and set off alone.

The plan for today is a twenty-three-and-a-half-kilometre walk, which at this point on the Camino feels relatively short. But by the time I've walked to the town of Sahagún, about twelve kilometres down the trail, I'm beat. The bug I'm fighting has finally worn me down. My feet are sore. I'm achy and exhausted, and obviously more unwell than I thought. Pressing on relentlessly is in my nature but seems foolhardy given the circumstances. Unsure of what to do, I make a snap decision and head to the nearest tourist information office to ask about trains to León.

There's one other visitor in the Sahagún tourist information office. A woman, speaking English. Unbelievably, she is asking the attendant about trains to León. I walk up and join her, "¡Hola! ¡Yo tambien!" (Me too!) And to the woman behind the counter, I add "¡Buenos dias!"

"You are friends?" she asks.

"Sure," I say. "We are now!"

"I'm Donna," says my new friend.

"Lindy." We shake hands and grin at each other.

The attendant shows us the train schedule. We can get on the next train to León in just over two hours. She explains carefully and patiently, as if she has done this many times before, where to find the train and how to purchase our tickets.

When I left to walk the Camino, I never once dreamed of using public transport to get about. I imagined that I would walk every single step of the way or die trying. But just as I didn't imagine walking alongside major highways, garbage dumps, or tracts of land labelled "Zona Industrial," I also didn't imagine getting ill. As disappointed as I am, I know that if I keep going, I'll likely develop pneumonia, if I haven't already. I've had two or three bouts of it in the past, one serious enough to land me in hospital. I'm hoping that I can find it in myself to be sensible, to rest up a little so that I recover enough to keep walking. I haven't planned any further ahead than getting on the train, and I intend to figure out the rest once I get to León.

Donna and I leave the tourist office and set off to explore a bit of town before the train departs in the early afternoon. Sahagún is the halfway point along the Camino Frances. It's a medieval city, famous for its beautiful early Mudéjar architecture and ornate art. The Mudéjar were the Muslims (known as the Moors by European Christians) who stayed in Iberia after the Christians reclaimed the land during the Christian Reconquista following the nearly eight-hundred-year Muslim occupation of Spain.

Donna has been in Sahagún for a couple of nights. She's walking a slow Camino, taking time along the route to explore the sights. She purchased a one-way ticket to Spain in the United States and is planning to buy her return ticket when she's finished. Unlike me, she has no deadline, and she's in no particular rush.

The one thing Donna hasn't yet had a chance to visit in Sahagún, is the Santuario de la Peregrina, a former Franciscan convent turned museum. The massive, sprawling brick edifice is perched high atop a hill at the far end of this historic city. Construction began circa 1245 and the convent was offically founded in 1257. The walk gives me a chance to see almost all of this beautiful city. With a population of 2,800, it is the biggest place along the Camino since we left Burgos. Because of our pending train departure, we don't have time to tour the museum, but we do stop long enough to admire the building and get our pilgrim passports stamped.

On our way to the train station, Donna leads me along a small street full of restaurants and small stores. We head into one of the stores and are greeted by a woman, who seems delighted to serve us. In a glass case are a vast selection of glorious-looking savoury pies and empanadas.

When it's my turn, I ask for "Una empanada sin pimientos, por favor," and then I add, "Soy alérgica a los pimientos." (An empanada without peppers, please. I am allergic to peppers.) It is the same thing I ordered back down the trail in Castrojeriz, when I was with Sebastian, and where afterward the two of us sat and ate our picnic lunch of empanadas on the wide front porch of the delightful little tienda.

This kind Spanish women in Sahagún begins diligently cutting open all the empanadas, checking for evidence of peppers. I feel terrible that she is doing this. I want to tell her to stop and just give me something else—a simple sandwich—whatever is easy. She is ruining a whole selection of pastries just to make sure she does not give me one with peppers. It is such an extraordinary kindness, but I wish she would stop. Every new empanada she slices open is no doubt costing her or someone else money. I don't have enough money on me to pay for all the ruined empanadas. Eventually she finds one and exclaims, "¡Por supuesto! (Of course!) ¡La empanada de la reina!

"¡Aha, la reina!" I say. "The empanada of the queen!"

"Si! ¡La reina! The queen!" she says, smiling happily.

I am thrilled to understand what she is saying, but less thrilled that she's had to cut open so many empanadas to find one that meets my needs. I add some clementines, a bar of chocolate, and a bottle of fizzy water to my order, and she packs all of this carefully into a bag for me, smiling sweetly the whole time.

"¡Mil gracias!" I say and repeat a couple of times, attempting to convey the full weight of my gratitude and enthusiasm and unable to conjure up any other words to try to thank this lovely woman adequately enough for hacking into so many empanadas on my behalf. It is yet another situation where my inability to communicate properly in Spanish leaves me woefully lacking.

In the train station, while Donna and I wait for the train to arrive, I read through my guidebook and decide to try to stay at the Convent of the Benedictine Sisters in León.

Donna has plans to find a hotel room and asks if I want to stay with her. When I tell her that I thought I'd go to the albergue at the convent, she surprises me and says she'll join me. To be fair, I have no real idea why I have chosen this albergue, but for whatever reason, I'm determined to head there.

Maybe after a night at the convent, I'll find a room for the night in a nearby hotel, find a doctor, rest up a little. The plan is to take it day by day and see how I am as things progress. I'm hoping that by not walking all day today, I might feel a little better tomorrow. One thing I know is that I am too sick to keep walking at the pace I've been going.

We're all alone in our train compartment, so we tuck straight into our picnic lunches. The empanada is divine—a filling of beef, carrot, onion, peas, and olives—all lightly spiced and wrapped in the softest, most tender pastry. And sure enough, no bell peppers. Donna, who is vegan, is eating bread and olives. We finish off with the sweetest, most perfect clementines we've ever eaten. It's peak citrus season in Spain from October to May, so we are eating citrus both in season, and more or less in situ, even though most of the citrus crops come from further south in Andalusia, Catalonia, Murcia, and Valencia.

For the rest of the short trip, Donna and I are doubled over laughing at one thing after another. The train ride seems to have reduced us both to hysterics, and we can't seem to stop. Perhaps I am too giddy and overtired from all the coughing at night to be sensible. Taking the train instead of walking makes me feel like a school kid cutting class and having a grand illicit adventure. The idea of this makes us laugh so hard that neither of us can straighten out. We just start to pull ourselves together when we start up again. I haven't laughed this hard for years. I'm having fun. Actual fun, like the kind of fun I had as a youth but seem to have largely forgotten how to have as an adult. And it's not the first time I've had fun on the Camino either. The long walk is proving as much about finding a way back to myself as it is about finding my way across Spain.

And then just like that, Donna and I arrive in León. Right off the bat, León is strikingly beautiful, sophisticated, and immaculate. The architecture is a fantastic mix of spectacularly ornate grand historic buildings and sleek modern bars and restaurants with floor-to-ceiling windows. This city seems easier to navigate than some of the other biggish cities we've been in. It also helps that there are two of us. And that Donna is such excellent company. We make our way along the city streets, admiring the cathedrals and convents and museums, the bakery windows, the plazas where people are gathering to talk, or sitting reading the newspaper while children are playing. There is something to see in every direction, the formal gardens, the ornate lampstands, the stone walkways, the patios, and narrow, old back streets lined with shops. Bathed in the afternoon sunlight, all of León seems glorious.

Eventually we make our way to the Albergue del Monasterio de las Benedictinas. Men and women are separated in this albergue, and it is made very clear that we are not to enter the male dorms. I am quite happy with this arrangement—after all it is not usually the women making a snoring ruckus all night long, even though it has been me, lately, keeping everyone awake with my coughing.

The place is a little on the austere side, bordering on grim, but nonetheless, we register and pay, and are shown to bunks in the middle of a room full of bunk beds. I implore the hospitalero, likely a volunteer, who takes us to our beds, to give us a bunk bed up against a wall, in a room with fewer people. I try to explain, in English, that I have a bad cough. I have no idea what the words are in Spanish, so I demonstrate by coughing. He jumps back and looks vaguely alarmed.

Donna, meanwhile, is using her phone to translate everything into Spanish and is able to tell him what it is that I have been trying to tell him in English along with my bits of Spanish and my coughing demonstrations. Finally, very begrudgingly, he takes pity on us, and takes us to a smaller room, partitioned off from the main room, and assigns us some beds up against a wall. We set up our gear and climb into our beds for an afternoon nap. In the larger room beside us, separated by a mere pretense of a wall that is scarcely more than a curtain, someone is coughing like a fiend. I recognize the cough—it sounds exactly like mine: fierce, hacking, and unrelenting. Unable to nap, I take Benedict's precious pills from my bag and enter the room to find the person coughing. I give her one of Benedict's pills and keep the last one for myself.

"What is it?" she asks. I shrug, "A cough pill. Take it, you will feel better," I say, hoping that I am right and that it does her no harm. I have no idea what the damn thing is, and frankly I'm worried that I'll need it as badly or worse than she does, but I hand it over and she takes it. Half an hour later, the dorm is quiet. All thanks to Benedict and his little German miracle pills.

Our naps interrupted, Donna and I head out to find a bite to eat and see a little more of the city. León is the third biggest city along the Camino (behind Pamplona and Burgos), with a history dating to the first century BCE. It was founded by Romans serving under Caesar Augustus during the final stages of the Roman conquest of Hispania. León is known for its architecture, including the magnificent thirteenth century Gothic-style Catedral de Santa María de Regla de León, and for Catalan architect Anton Gaudí's Modernist Casa

Botines, which was built in the late 1800s and now houses a museum dedicated to Gaudi. But León is also widely renowned for its food scene, and has more bars and taverns per capita than any other Spanish city. Many of these establishments serve free tapas to those ordering drinks.

Donna and I have only walked a couple of blocks before we stumble across a sleek bar looking out onto a large open plaza. Unable to resist, we enter the bar and sit up at the counter on high stools and order wine, settling on a local white wine known as Rueda Blanco, made from locally grown Verdejo grapes, many of which are grown in centuries-old vineyards. The grapes are harvested at night because the lower nighttime temperatures help protect the grapes from browning. Night harvesting is said to improve both the colour and clarity of the finished wine. The wine is soft, smooth, light bodied, dry, and very delicious.

No sooner do we have our glasses in hand that the bartender turns around and shaves a few slivers from a leg of ham hanging over the bar. He lays the meat on a plate along with some slices of baguette and brings the plate to us. "Aquí esta jamón ibérico. ¡Tapas!" he says, proudly. It is after all, some of the finest ham in the world.

When it comes to jamón, jamón ibérico is the pride of Spain. This cured ham belongs in a category of its own. All at once tender, firm, salty and sweet, the meat is so full of flavour that it needs the bread as a counterpoint to offset the intensity. The only ham more prized than jamón ibérico is jamón ibérico de bellota— referring to meat from the black-footed free-roaming pigs who feast on acorns. I can't help thinking of the pigs I've seen in Spain, romping freely in the forests and meadows, rummaging about for acorns and herbs and grasses.

The more I think of it, between the pigs in the forests, and the fields of wheat and corn and barley, and the orchards of olive and fig trees, and the vineyards, the more I feel that walking across Spain is like walking through a supermarket in the wild. Donna, who is vegan, pushes the plate of meat towards me and orders a bowl of olives and a basket of bread. Here in this elegant bar, we are eating Spain on a plate.

We sit in the last of the late autumn afternoon sun, enjoying the bar, our wine, and our delicious tapas, when quite suddenly I start to cough and am completely overcome with it. I stand up and put myself into a corner. I am coughing relentlessly, can scarcely take a breath. The cough is coming in great heaving spasms. I am worried I will throw up from coughing so hard, but I cannot move because I am so overtaken with coughing. Finally, the cough abates, subsides, and I can move again. I sit back down, exhausted, involuntary tears rolling down my face. Down the bar, I see the hospitalero from the albergue having an espresso. He looks over at me with real concern. At least now I am sure that he believes that I do have a cough, and that I wasn't just angling for a more private space to sleep.

Donna wants to go and find some proper dinner, but I just want to go back to the convent and not risk another terrifying and humiliating public coughing jag or spreading my germs any further afield. We agree to go our separate ways for the evening and head to the cash register to pay, only to have the bartender tell us our tab was already paid. He nods towards the hospitalero, who looks up and smiles at us, then makes the sign of the cross. Another humbling act of grace. The generosity of which floors me and brings more tears to my eyes.

"¡Gracias, mil gracias, señor!" I say. Once again I am feeling frustrated and woefully inadequate over my limited ability to fully express my gratitude for this act of caring and generosity. I promise myself that I will learn to speak Spanish far more fluently before I ever return to Spain, if only so that I can thank the Spanish properly for their kindness and remarkable hospitality.

Back at the convent alone, I plan to have a very quiet night and if I am well enough, I want to attend the nightly chapel service given by the Benedictine Sisters. In order to avoid another spate of coughing during the service, I take the last of Benedict's mystery pills. Then I sort my gear on my bunk bed and get ready to find the chapel when I hear a voice in the hallway, a voice I'd know anywhere. I head out to the common area to try to find him and call out, "*Sebastian?!*"

Before he even sees me, he yells back, "*Linndddyyy!!!*"

Sebastian is also going to the service in the chapel, so we head in together. Afterwards, we sit in the courtyard, a group of us, talking and laughing and eating a collection of potato chips, candy, and chocolate which we have scrounged from our backpacks and brought to the table. Someone arrives with a bottle of red wine, and someone else goes to find glasses. The stars are shining above. The moon is out. It's a perfect beautiful evening, and I know now, with absolute clarity, why I was so drawn to staying at the Benedictine Convent—I must have known on some deep unconscious level that I'd find Sebastian here. I never imagined seeing him again. For the second or third time today, I cannot believe how deeply happy and thankful I feel. What does one call this kind of pure, inexplicable happiness that feels beyond measure?

Empanadas de la Reina

Empanadas, which are immensely popular throughout Spain, Portugal, and much of Latin America, have their roots in Galicia. The first documented historical record of empanadas comes from a cookbook published in Spain, in 1520[20], although references to related dishes (breaded dishes containing either fat, meat, or fish), appeared as many as two centuries earlier in a book on Jewish law. Contemporary empanadas are thought to be a variation on the Arabic meat pies that first appeared in the Iberian Peninsula during the Moorish invasions (711–831 AD).

Empanadas can be made as full-size pies, or as smaller hand pies. The fillings vary widely from place to place and may include tuna, cod, sardines, eel, chicken, beef, pork, chorizo, onion, garlic, tomato, potato, carrots, peas, and other vegetables, and a variety of spices, all contained within either a bread or pastry casing. They may be either fried or baked. Smaller empanadas, served as tapas, are often called "empanadillas." In Spain, the suffix illa generally denotes something little.

Empanadas are perfect highly portable picnic fare, but also great for lunch or tapas, and even for dinner, served with a substantial salad. This recipe is my very basic recreation of the empanada from the beautiful store I stopped at in Sahagún.

Makes 10–12 empanadas (allow 2–3 per person)

30 mL (2 tbsp) olive oil

1 small onion, finely chopped

2–3 cloves garlic, finely chopped

225 g (8 oz) ground beef

1 medium carrot, peeled and grated

55 g (¼ cup) of frozen peas

1 tsp cumin

½ tsp paprika

¼–½ tsp hot chili powder, depending on how spicy you like things

½ tsp salt

½ tsp pepper

60 g (⅓ cup) stuffed green olives, roughly chopped

30–45 mL (2–3 tbsp) olive brine
450 g (1 lb) frozen puff pastry sheets, thawed
1 small egg
1 tbsp water

Add the olive oil to a large fry pan and allow to warm gently on medium heat. Add the onion and cook until softened and just starting to brown. Add the garlic and cook another minute or two, stirring often so as not to let it burn or scorch.

Add the ground beef, and break the mixture up, stirring the beef into the onions and garlic. Keep the heat on medium and continue to stir until the beef is cooked.

Turn the heat to medium-low, and add the grated carrot and frozen peas. Cook for about 3 minutes or until the carrot has softened.

Add the cumin, paprika, chili powder, and salt and pepper. Stir in the olives and olive brine and remove from the heat. Set aside while you prep the pastry.

Preheat your oven to 190°C (375°F).

Using a 13 cm (5 inch) bowl as a template, cut the pastry into as many circles as possible—rerolling the leftover pieces to make extra circles when needed. You should be able to cut about 10 to 12 circles.

Divide the filling between the circles, careful to keep the filling away from the edge, otherwise it will be difficult to close the empanadas.

Using a pastry brush, brush the edges of the pastry with water, and then fold the pastry to make a semi-circle. With a fork, press down to crimp, and seal the edge.

When all the pasties are sealed, beat together the egg and 1 tablespoon of water and brush the tops of the empanadas liberally with the egg mixture.

Place on a lightly greased baking sheet and pop into the hot oven for 25 minutes, or until the pastry is puffed and browned and the internal temperature has reached 73°C (165°F).

CHAPTER NINETEEN
León to Hospital de Órbigo
October 25

"Walking is man's best medicine."
—Hippocrates, *Journal of the Royal Society of Medicine*

I am up at half past six in the morning. Still coughing, but perhaps not quite as badly as I was. Mostly, I am sure my cough is better because of Benedict's German mystery pills. I really wish I knew what on earth they were so that I could find some more.

Guidebook in hand, I make the decision to continue on today. I could stay and try to find a doctor. I could see more of León, attend a service in the cathedral, and rest up somewhere, but the pull to keep walking overrules everything else, including any possible reason to stay. Donna, meanwhile, is staying in León for another couple of days and plans to visit the cathedral, soak up the sights, and enjoy a hotel room by herself.

For me, the lure of the trail is so strong that I am seemingly helpless to stop myself, even when it seems to make little sense, considering the state of my health and my terrible cough. "Onwards, onwards I go," I say to myself, and even as I make the plan, I feel myself climbing down from the ledge of anxiety and back to the reassuring certainty of walking. Walking will be my cure.

The walk out of León is a steep climb along busy roads, past rubbish dumps, and through the inauspiciously labelled, "Zona Industrial," on my map. I decide to avoid all this and take a city bus to the outskirts of León. It's the path I'm longing for—the forest, the trees, the dirt beneath my feet again. Not walking beside busy highways through the zona industrial while garbage trucks and buses fly past me on the busy, narrow roads. The city bus will take me a few kilometres, to the outskirts of León, where the last suburb merges with countryside. From there, I will be able to rejoin the Camino again and walk on to the village of Hospital de Órbigo.

Before I head off, Donna and I find a café and have coffees and a fare-well breakfast together. A chocolate croissant for me and pan con tomate for Donna—essentially a thick slice of rustic bread, grilled or toasted, liberally brushed with olive oil, topped with garlic and rubbed with a fresh ripe tomato. Pan con tomate is a beloved Spanish staple, found widely throughout the country. It is served for breakfast, lunch, and tapas, and is one of those simple dishes that is so much more than the sum of its parts.

After our breakfast, Donna helps me find the bus stop, so that she, too, knows where to head when she leaves León in a couple of days' time. The bus driver knows the drill. He spies my backpack and says, "Camino?" He's obviously used to pilgrims wanting to skip the uphill walk through the zona industrial.

"¡Si, Señor! La Virgen del Camino por favor." And with that, I'm back on my journey. When I climb off the bus, the bus driver points me in the direction of the trail, and within minutes I'm back on the path once again, thrilled to feel the earth under my feet.

The trail runs alongside the road for most of the day, but somehow, somewhere along the line, early on in my walk it seems, I have managed to veer off the trail and am completely and eerily alone and nowhere near a road. I check my watch and guess that I've been walking for an hour or two, though I'm not exactly certain what time the bus dropped me off. I was more focused on making sure I got off the bus in the right place than the time when I hit the trail. Even with a map, I am stupidly prone to being both physically and metaphorically lost. Sometimes both. I often "come to" after marching along for hours and realize that I have lost track of time and space and have no real clue where I am. It's as though I'm existing beneath conscious thought, somehow merging into the landscape. When I check the guidebook, I see that there are two trails—the main trail which follows the road and an alternative, much more remote and slightly longer trail, which I seem to have found my way onto. I cannot even recall seeing a single waymark. I start searching for one, anxiously. Slightly desperately.

I haven't really felt seriously afraid on the Camino until right now. I realize that not only can I not remember seeing a yellow waymark or one of the traditional scallop shells marking the trail, but I also have not seen another pilgrim, nor another person of any description, since I left the bus.

I fight the urge to backtrack, since I have no idea how long I've been on the wrong trail. I have a moment of panic about wild dogs before pulling myself together. I check the map again and see that at some point, I should have passed a café and possibly a fountain. Somehow, I have bypassed all this. I have been walking through forests and fields, and the only consistent thing has been the complete absence of any indication that I am actually on the Camino.

"Keep moving forwards," I order myself. And even more sternly, "Don't panic." I say this out loud and keep repeating versions of the same words. "There is no need to panic," and "Stay calm." I know that all of this is probably "lost person behaviour." I've read enough about this to know that lost people often start off with shock and disbelief before moving onto irrational and fearful thoughts as well as embarrassment and a sense of urgency or panic. Often when people fear they are lost, they start making questionable, illogical decisions and just make matters worse. In the worst case there is a tendency to turn back, or, worse yet, head off the trail entirely and simply bushwhack.

I stop and look at my map again, shaking my head at my own stupidity. I hold the map in the direction I'm supposed to be heading and search the sky for the sun to get my bearings—nothing, it is completely overcast—making it impossible to make any kind of informed decision. The safest decision seems to be to keep going.

I don't recall any sort of sign indicating that I was heading onto an alternative trail. My best guess is that I've been on the alternative trail since Virgen del Camino—the last suburb of León, where the bus dropped me off. I blame myself, for taking the bus. It's always a bit challenging re-finding the Camino once you leave it. Had I walked out of town, I would been able to follow the way-markers the entire time. Self-recrimination is useless, I tell myself. I'm in the middle of nowhere now, and to make matters worse, I am travelling with no supplies since I planned to stop at one of the many small villages along the main route to buy food. The only thing I have with me is a small bottle of water, half full. There are no villages along the alternate route.

"Onwards," I say, out loud. It has become my mantra. After all, what other options are there? Saying it aloud helps. It makes me feel strangely calm, resilient.

Then, abruptly, I arrive at a roadway—and pass a closed, or at second glance, possibly abandoned, café and study the map. Now at least, I think I know where I am. The building appears to be marked on my map. I am almost certainly on the alternate trail, and once again there is nothing for me to do but to keep going.

Another half a dozen kilometres or so later, I pass through the pretty little village of Villar de Mazarife. Now I know exactly where I am.

I could stop. I could get a late lunch or at the very least some supplies. But I can't seem to bring myself to do anything except keep walking. All I can think about is getting back onto the main trail, which I will rejoin in Hospital de Órbigo, another three hours down the path. It's where I'm planning to spend the night. So, once again, I press on, relentlessly, somewhat recklessly, but somehow also quite certain that I'm going to be okay. So much so that I don't even stop to try to find a place to refill my water bottle.

It's closing in on dinnertime before I finally set foot on the Puente de Órbigo, the bridge where the two trails finally merge. The relief is sweet. The Puente is a thirteenth-century two-hundred-metre-long bridge with twenty stone arches, built over an earlier Roman bridge. It has been here, helping pilgrims cross the Órbigo River, since medieval times.

I head straight into the first decent looking albergue I come across. The owner is a displaced Venezuelan who speaks excellent English. He shows me to a bunk, and so far, at least, I am the only one staying. The albergue looks new, clean, and empty. After so many days immersed amongst crowds of people, it feels disconcerting to have been alone all day and now to find myself still alone in the albergue. I am slightly uneasy. Where is everyone? I find myself actually hoping that someone else comes to join me.

After setting up my sleeping bag, I head out to find food. Of course, it's siesta time in this sleepy little village, and nothing appears to be open. I'm famished, as all I've had to eat or drink all day was my chocolate croissant and a cup of coffee first thing in the morning. I pass by a closed restaurant and notice a side alley, where a door is open to the kitchen. I hear water running, pots clanking, and people talking. I'm not sure what possesses me, but I walk up the side alley and call out into the kitchen, "¡Hola! ¡Buenas tardes!" A fine Spanish face peeks out from behind the corner. "¡Hola! ¡Buenas tardes!" A whole slew of Spanish follows. I stand there uselessly trying to pick out words. When he finishes, I say, "¿La comida? ¿Hay comida, por favor?" I don't even know where the words are coming from. I think I've said something along the lines of, "Food? Is there food? Please."

"Si..." he replies, and more incomprehensible words in Spanish ensue. I am not sure what he is saying, though he is still smiling broadly, so I can only presume that he is not telling me to get lost, or come back later, or go to hell. I am pretty sure the place is closed before the dinner service starts, but I am so hungry I cannot think straight, so I say the first thing that pops into my head: "Señor, me gustaría un gran bocadillo de chorizo y queso, tostado, por favor." (Sir, I would like a big, toasted chorizo and cheese sandwich). I'd like a drink, too—a ginger ale or even a glass of wine. But wine won't come in a portable container, and I have no idea if ginger ale even exists in Spain. So, I go ahead and continue with my wish list: "¿Y una cerveza? Por favor."

The restaurant is clearly not open, and yet this man, grinning wildly, says, "¡Si, si, si!" and then motions for me to sit down at one of the tables in the dark, empty restaurant and wait five minutes. He holds his hand up, all his fingers splayed, palm facing me—the universal sign language for "gimme five minutes!"

Sure enough, five or so minutes later he comes out with a giant sandwich on a half baguette, wrapped in tinfoil, and a tin of beer. Six euros and several rounds of "¡Gracias Señor, mil gracias!" All met with, "De nada," and "¡Buen Camino, peregrina!" and I'm out the door with my sandwich and my beer and heading back to my home for the night, ravenous and thrilled out of my mind. It's not just the food itself, it's also the act of generosity that feels so important, so nourishing. He watches as I leave. Still grinning and waving. "Only the Spanish," I think to myself. Only the Spanish could be so extraordinarily kind.

Back in the dorm, I have a new roommate. Jo is a twenty-three-year-old female nurse from Germany. We are the only two staying in the albergue. Jo has already eaten, so I sit down alone with my rustic sandwich packed with layers of warm, lightly spiced chorizo and melted cheese. Despite my hunger, I eat it slowly, savouring every delicious bite. The beer is a perfect accompaniment. I don't know if it's the Spanish beer or all the walking, but I've seldom appreciated beer the way I do here in Spain. I really couldn't be any happier or any more satisfied in a Michelin starred restaurant. Now all I want is my bed, a long quiet night, hopefully without any coughing.

Bocadillo de Chorizo y Queso, Tostado

Un bocadillo de chorizo is one of Spain's most popular sandwiches. Typically, it consists of sliced chorizo and other toppings, such as cheese, served on a Spanish baguette known as barra de pan, and may be served as is, warmed, or lightly grilled. It is also great cut into thin slices and skewered with a cocktail stick and served along with Cava (Spain's answer to Italy's Prosecco) at a tapas party.

If you're ordering a bocadillo (pronounced boke-ah-DEE-yo) in Spain, typically you will just get the barra de pan and the chorizo (and cheese if you've requested it) and nothing else. It is delicious as is, but if you're making this at home, feel free to add extras.

Serves 2

1 large baguette, sliced into two equal lengths, or two demi baguettes

30–45 mL (2–3 tbsp) olive oil

225 g (8 oz) dry cured Spanish-style chorizo, finely sliced

Additional toppings: sliced Manchego (or other favourite cheese), aioli, sliced tomatoes, caramelized onions, chopped olives, etc.

Cut the baguette or demi baguettes in half horizontally.

Using a pastry brush, coat the outsides and insides of the bread lightly with olive oil. Layer the inside with chorizo (this can be warmed gently in a frying pan before adding to the sandwich if preferred) and other fillings as desired.

Press the top half of the baguette down firmly, place the sandwich in a large fry pan (preferably cast iron), and warm over medium-low heat for about 3 to 4 minutes on each side, watching that the bread does not burn.

Wrap the sandwiches in foil and keep warm in a low oven if you are not serving immediately.

CHAPTER TWENTY

Hospital de Órbigo to Rabanal del Camino

October 26

"Pursue some path, however narrow or crooked,
in which you can walk in love and reverence."
—Henry David Thoreau, "Life Without Principle"

The night in Hospital de Órbigo was blissfully quiet. My cough woke me a couple of times, but thankfully my roommate, Jo, managed to sleep soundly through everything. Breakfast was included at the albergue, so after coffee and toast with Jo, we strike off separately.

I've made the decision: I will take a bus *one last time.*

I've already skipped too many of the places I wanted to see and stay at. This particular bus will take me from Hospital de Órbigo to Astorga, about fifteen kilometres, and will cut three hours of walking from my day. From Astorga I will walk to Rabanal del Camino, where there is an albergue where I want to stay, for two reasons: one is to be present for the Gregorian chants sung at a church there in the evening. The second reason is the communal afternoon tea for which this particular albergue is known. This albergue feels important, and I am determined not to miss it. I know that if I walk from Hospital de Órbigo all the way to Rabanal, I'll only end up more unwell. I need to heal, and if taking a bus partway so that I don't overextend myself helps, then so be it. This still leaves me with at least twenty kilometres to walk today, most of them uphill.

I wait at the bus stop with a group of high school students dressed in uniforms. They seem remarkably polite and well-behaved, and actually step aside to motion me get on the bus first. As the bus hurtles along the highway en route to Astorga, I feel as though I'm finally managing to do my own version of the Camino. It's liberating. I'm solo in Spain. I'm doing it!

Twenty-five minutes and one-and-a-half euros later, the bus pulls into the terminal in Astorga. I clamber off with my pack and set about finding my bearings. Astorga, population twelve thousand, has two thousand years of history. It is compact and straightforward enough to navigate easily. And it's stunning, so picturesque. As in so many towns I pass through, I find myself thinking, "*This is the prettiest town so far.*" I've lost track of how many times I've thought this, only for another even lovelier town to follow.

Of course, it helps that the sun is shining, and the sky is a deep cerulean blue, but it's the architecture in every direction that takes my breath away—the beautiful crumbling remnants of ancient Roman walls and portals; the Roman Catholic Catedral de Santa María de Astorga, built over three centuries starting in 1471; and the remarkably ornate Bishop's Palace (Palacio Episcopal), built in the late 1800s and designed by the internationally famous, and by all accounts extremely eccentric, Spanish Catalan architect Antoni Gaudí.

Everywhere I turn, I am tempted by small stores selling cheese, or wine, or flowers; by tiny old fashioned grocery stores and cafés and chocolate shops, and by the wares in bakery windows—glorious looking iced buns, pastries, tarts, croissants, and some small plain cupcakes known as Magdalenas, said to be named for a young woman called Magdalena who baked and served the small, lemon cakes to pilgrims en route to Santiago de Compostela.

Astorga is a thriving small town bustling with people all busily shopping—their market bags overflowing with flowers and baguettes and neatly bundled packages. This is the traditional market town of the Maragatos, a distinct ethnic group, thought to be the last Moorish people in Spain. The Maragatos are the descendants of the Berbers of North Africa, who crossed into the Iberian Peninsula in the early eighth century. They are an ethnically distinct culture and community who have hung onto their distinctive food, dress, and beautiful medieval architecture—especially the ancient stone homes with dry-stone walls and large doors.

I imagine for half a second, that I, too, could live here. I could learn to speak Spanish properly, cook local dishes, walk daily amongst the spectacular buildings and gardens and the gloriously ruinous city walls, carrying my own overflowing bag full of wares from the markets, bakeries, and famous chocolateries of Astorga. I've had this feeling before: while hiking in the wild, rugged mountains of Tasmania; in the moors in Yorkshire, where I lived as a small child; and then again in a small village on the coast of Queensland, where I imagined that I might grow old wading in the ocean and riding my bicycle into the sunset. Somehow, though, I know that I'd never truly belong in Spain. I'd be forever grasping at the language, trying endlessly to make myself known and attempting to understand others. Still, I think to myself, perhaps a sabbatical here?

Leaving Astorga, there is a short steep descent before the trail turns and heads upwards again. Just at the bottom of the hill, in a bus shelter, I stop to readjust my pack and find that someone has written out a pilgrim's prayer, in English. The prayer feels so companionable that although it is not like me to do this, something causes me to pause and copy out the text into my journal—all the while wondering to myself. Why? Why have I stopped to write this of all things into my journal? What has possessed me? There must be some reason, but I cannot put my finger on it.

Jesus, my Lord, my friend,
You, the Icon of God,
You fountain of communion, of freedom, of love,
You who are my servant, walk always with me.

Beyond the bus shelter, the trail begins to climb, and there are trees again, a sure sign we've left behind the golden-brown sun-drenched fields of the Meseta. There's a woman way out in front of me wearing a pair of unmissable, vibrantly lime green running shoes. Happy shoes. The colour makes me smile. Eventually I catch up and say hello and introduce myself. Kathy, from Florida, is as lively and cheerful as her shoes. We stop to have lunch together at El Caminante, a restaurant in Santa Catalina, population fifty. There are enough pilgrims stopped to eat and drink here to nearly double the village's tiny population.

This is the second small Maragato village I've passed through today, and the stone building, with its double-wide solid wood doors and beautiful flagstone interior courtyard, is a perfect example of Maragato architecture. Not surprisingly, the pilgrim lunch menu does not include the famous local dish, Cocido

Maragato—a notoriously laborious, long-cooked stew made of potatoes, carrots, cabbage, dried chickpeas, stock, garlic, pimento, and at least seven types of meat including shin of beef, ham hock, chicken, bacon or salt pork, sometimes pancetta, pork trotters, pork ears, pork ribs, and chorizo. The dish is found on the dinner menu though. Next Camino, I think to myself, making yet another mental note.

The Maragato diaspora in Spain includes approximately four thousand Maragatos, spread throughout about forty villages in Northern Spain. The Maragatos are believed to be the last Moorish people in Spain. They converted to Christianity at the time of the Reconquista—the Spanish, Portuguese, and Galician military campaigns between 718 and 1492 to take back the Iberian Penininsula, which had been lost during Muslim conquests. In 1502, the Spanish Crown ordered all remaining Moors to be forcibly converted to Christianity. All those who continued to adhere to Islam were expelled from the country. It was during this time that eating pork was seen as evidence of conversion. The widespread availability of pork during the fifteen and sixteenth centuries made the meat a popular ingredient, hence its inclusion to this day in dishes such as Cocido Maragato.

Kathy and I order from the lunch menu, which offers the standard list of sandwiches and hamburgers along with drinks and coffee. We sit on the lovely outdoor patio, thoroughly enjoying our lunch in the glorious sunshine. Afterwards we go our separate ways. Kathy is another pilgrim who has chosen to walk a slow Camino, doing things at her own pace, and is in no rush whatsoever. Whereas I am always anticipating the next town, the next thing, the final destination, constantly walking away from somewhere and simultaneously walking towards something new.

On the Camino, leaving is a given. I don't want to linger. I want to keep moving forward, keep my momentum. I don't know exactly where this behaviour comes from, but I am pretty sure it is related to a lifetime of moving, of constantly anticipating the next thing, the next target, the next city, county, country, continent. *Move* is a word I know intrinsically.

I was born on a business trip, to British parents working temporarily in the United States. At ten weeks old I was already crossing oceans, moving countries and continents. By the time I was three, I'd lived in three countries on two continents. The concept of moving, so engrained in infancy, seems to have become a pattern that has ruled my life. As an adult, I have moved back and forth between Australia and Canada three times, with multiple moves within both nations. I am currently living in the thirty-first—or perhaps it's the thirty-fourth or forty-third—house in my life. There have been so many addresses that I've lost track.

I'm still wondering where I'll end up. Still wondering about life in another city, another province, another country and continent. It's obvious to everyone including myself that I'm searching for something. But what it is that I'm searching for, what hole needs filling, what emptiness I cannot seem to assuage—escapes me.

Sometimes I awaken, tears running down my face, my pillow damp, having dreamt of a bit of my past—left in another place. I am filled with longing to see something or someone I left years ago and countries away. I leave pieces of myself like a trail of crumbs, scattered across continents. My heart seems always to be left in the last place or lurching forward towards the next.

The fragments I awaken dreaming of have always surprised me. They are often of places or things I have not thought of for years. Mostly they are of remarkably insignificant hidden things, like memories within memories—the ravine I walked through to get to school as a child in Ontario; the gravel path in the terraced rose garden down to the river behind my grandfather's Yorkshire home; a narrow, winding road up the dales.

Sometimes I awaken lost and in a panic. Where is Weber Street in Waterloo? Have I lost my way on the drive north to the cottage on Georgian Bay? What is the name of the ancient pub in Hebden Bridge, Yorkshire? The Pack Horse Inn, of course. But where is Far Flat Head Farm? And what has become of my oasis—Crescent Beach in Vancouver? Or Marysville, the little mountain hamlet that became my private Australian sanctuary. And always and above all, I miss my beloved Yorkshire grandfather, his old stone home on the river, his beautiful face, and his remarkable kindness and generosity.

I stride off, mad keen to reach Rabanal del Camino in time to secure myself a bed as well as a spot at afternoon tea in the gardens at the Refugio Gaucelmo, where I will start planning the next day's journey.

For the rest of afternoon, I walk uphill through exquisitely beautiful countryside drenched in soft late autumn sunshine, through picturesque stone villages, past gardens full of late season brassicas: kale, giant cabbages, and towering stalks of Brussels sprouts. Yards alive with pigs, chickens, cats, and dogs. High up above, massive, comical-looking stork nests perch precariously atop chimneys and rooftops, sticks and twigs pointing in all directions, and swallows darting about everywhere. Alongside the trail on either side lie ditches filled with wildflowers and wild raspberry and blackberry patches, and beyond that spread steeply rolling pastures of grazing cows. Further off in the distance stand stunning views of the rocky, rugged, craggy blue grey peaks of the Cantabrian Mountains. A dream landscape.

As I approach the village of Rabanal del Camino, there are more and more trees, more greenery, once again reminding me of the changing landscape. The mountains and lush greenery are such a stark contrast from the Meseta. And even though the Meseta has its own arid and monochromatic beauty, this new landscape appeals to me deeply. I watch the countryside transitioning all around me. I am submerged in all this when I round a corner and see a large German Shepherd heading straight towards me. I freeze on the spot. Terrified.

As a young girl, shortly after moving to Canada, I was chased and then bitten by a German Shepherd on my way home from school, and I have been afraid of dogs ever since. And even though I live with a dog, she is a very domesticated, sweet, loving animal and is as afraid of other dogs as I am. So, when the German Shepherd starts coming straight towards me, I have no idea what to do and find myself resorting instinctively to the prayer I'd copied out earlier in the day. Especially the last line, "You, who are my servant, walk always with me." I repeat this line out loud, the only line I can actually remember, as I head deliberately towards a bench up against a large stone wall at the side of the road. When I get to the bench, I climb atop it and stand there, awkwardly. The dog lumbers over slowly and sits below the bench, like a prison guard.

"Good dog," I say, several times, before remembering the dog does not likely understand English. I try again with an encouraging, "¡Buen perro!" And then once again, remembering my Spanish lessons, I slowly remove my backpack and take out my water bottle and pour a small puddle of water onto the ground below me. The dog laps it up. I pour more water. The dog laps that up too. Finally, I empty the entire water bottle onto the ground and the dog drinks all the water. "¡Buen perro!" I keep repeating. "¡Buen perro! ¡Los perros beben agua!"

I lower myself slowly, so that I am sitting on the bench beside my pack, still talking to the dog. He puts his head on my lap and lets me pat him. Slowly,

slowly, I stand up and put my pack on and start walking again. The big, handsome dog walks by my side until I approach the albergue where I'm spending the night. Then he moves into the shade and lies down. He has been my protector, and we are, it seems, friends.

The Refugio Gaucelmo, a donativo (pay what you can), is operated by the Confraternity of St. James in London, England. It has thirty-six beds in total, and so even now, in late October, I am aware that all the beds may be taken. I'm in luck, however, and manage to get there in time to pick a lower bunk along the wall in the corner of the room. I roll out my sleeping bag and spend some time before the five o'clock afternoon teatime showering, washing my clothes, and exploring the tiny village—finding some new sunscreen to replace the small tube I brought with me and have used up, and locating internet in the bar, where I order a glass of wine and send a couple of quick messages back home.

Afterwards, I head out to the lovely sweeping green lawn behind the old stone building that is home to the refugio. Tables and chairs are set up in the small apple orchard at the back of the lawns. About a dozen of us from all over the world have shown up for a late afternoon tea and are treated to homemade apple cake, made from the apples of the trees we are sitting under, and pots of hot tea. This tradition appeals to me so deeply. Partly, perhaps, because of my English background, but also because I am always enamoured of all the food traditions that bring people together to eat. The coming together and sharing of food is such an important and fundamentally human experience.

Around the table, we are in the midst of what I have begun to call "The Camino Questionnaire." Whenever two or more pilgrims meet up, there is a set of what feel like obligatory standard questions: Where are you from? Where did you start? Where will you finish? How far do you walk each day? Have you been sick/got blisters/encountered bedbugs?

In the middle of all this, my Chilean friend Sebastian strides up, grinning widely and just generally lighting the whole place up. He has a way of cutting through everything and connecting with everyone. And also, of getting immediately to matters of substance. The Camino Questionnaire session ends abruptly with his arrival, and we move on to loftier and more interesting topics. Immediately we're talking about food, wine, and twelfth-century knights. About the merits of hermit life. About cattle farming in Chile and whether social media is a source of evil or good. About declining common sense and the parallel demise of religion. And about rational thought and whether intuition is real. About the pros and cons of socialized medicine. And how to quickly learn a new language.

Like me, Sebastian plans to attend the evening service at the Romanesque church across from the Benedictine Monastery next door to the refugio. I've looked forward for a very long time to attending this evening service sung in Gregorian chant by a group of Benedictine monks. But, as it turns out, the very modern monks are away, at a conference, out of town. There will be no chants tonight. As disappointed as I am, I go to the chapel anyway, and a delightful young priest conducts a welcoming service in both Spanish and English. It's not the same as the chants, but I'm happy I came, even if just to experience the small barrel vault church, La Iglesia de Santa Maria. The term barrel vault refers to the rounded arch ceiling that looks like the roof of a tunnel, in this case, one built from stone in the twelfth century, by the Knights Templar.

The arched barrel roof reaches down the interior walls of the church and wraps around us, holding us in what feels like a different space and time. We're ensconced in the small, atmospheric chamber with its spectacular acoustics, flickering candlelight, and crumbling ancient stone walls. There's a presence here that seems distinctly otherworldly, and it feels as though there is something extraordinary, or at the very least ancient, at work.

I have come into the habit of using the churches. I use them for prayers that I do not fully understand. For silent, solitary conversations to an unknown god. I light candles for family and friends back home. For my mother. For my ex-father-in-law, who is elderly and very unwell. For my family, my daughters, and my ex-husband or estranged husband—I am no longer sure how to think of him, what to call him. I bow my head, remember them, see their beautiful, intelligent faces, say their names silently to myself, in the glow of the candlelight.

At the end of the service, I suddenly remember with great clarity that it was here, on this fiercely gorgeous stretch of path from Astorga to Rabanal del Camino, that American pilgrim Denise Thiem, age forty-one, went missing on Easter Sunday, 2015. She was later found murdered, having been lured off the path by false way-markers—a horrific, senseless crime. I read about Denise before I set out on the Camino, and it occurs to me that this may be why I've been on some sort of high alert all day. It's odd that it comes to me now, but not remembering earlier seems to have kept me insulated from walking all day in fear. I wonder if it is the reason why I copied out the prayer into my notebook, earlier in the day, or perhaps even the reason why the prayer was posted there.

I light one last candle for Denise and return to my pew to remember her and her family.

When I look up, Sebastian is watching and waiting for me. "Join us," he says, as he introduces me to a beautiful young female doctor from Brazil. What a pair they would make, I think to myself, though it is clear they are just friends.

"We're going to have something to eat and a nice glass of wine in a restaurant nearby," Sebastian says. So, I join them, grateful for the pleasure and safety of their company, and I order a single glass of Godello, the beautiful Spanish white wine made from Galician grapes, before heading back to the refugio and calling it a night.

Pastel de Manzana

This is such a lovely, simple, flavourful cake—and it comes together so easily and quickly. You can use fresh apples, or if, like me, you have an apple tree or two in your yard and a freezer full of chopped apples, it can also be made with thawed, frozen apples. It makes a simple, rustic, flavourful, one-layer European style cake and is particularly delicious served with whipped cream or ice cream.

4–6 servings
125 mL (½ cup) olive oil
100 g (½ cup) white sugar
2 large eggs
30 mL (2 tbsp) brandy (or 1 tbsp vanilla extract)
120 g (1 cup) all-purpose flour
1 tsp baking powder
1 tsp cinnamon
¼ tsp salt
2–3 good-sized cooking apples, peeled and chopped
    (approx. 2 cups)
1–2 tbsp icing sugar to dust the cooked cake

Butter and parchment-line a 20 cm (8 inch) shallow round pan, preferably springform.

Preheat the oven to 175°C (350°F).

In a medium-sized bowl, using a hand mixer or wooden spoon, beat together the olive oil, sugar, eggs, and brandy (or vanilla).

Next add the flour, baking powder, cinnamon, and salt. Fold gently to combine. Add the apples and stir gently to distribute them through the batter.

Using a spatula, scrape the batter into the prepared pan. Place in the centre of the oven, and bake for 30 to 35 minutes, or until the top springs back, and a skewer comes out clean. Allow the cake to cool before dusting the top with icing sugar. Serve with whipped cream.

CHAPTER TWENTY-ONE

Rabanal del Camino to Ponferrada

October 27

"I felt my lungs inflate with the onrush of scenery—air, mountains, trees, people. I thought, 'This is what it is to be happy.'" —Sylvia Plath, *The Bell Jar*

We seem to awaken collectively in the albergues. Once one of us is awake, it is only moments until everyone is awake. Yet again though, it was a surprisingly quiet night, and my upper bunk mate seemed not have moved all night long.

Given that today's walk is long and steeply up and down, thirty-three kilometres if I make it to Ponferrada, I need to get going. I scramble out of bed, pack my gear, and head to the bright communal kitchen for the breakfast laid out for us—coffee, tea, toast, and apples from the trees in the garden. Miraculously, here in the middle of rural Spain, there's an incredibly large jar of Vegemite alongside the usual jam. I'm thrilled to bits to find the Vegemite, apparently a gift from one of the volunteers at the refugio.

After breakfast, I say a fond farewell to the Refugio Gaucelmo and put my money into the collection box. Then, once again, I hit the trail alone. At 7:45 it is still pitch-black outside, as dark as the middle of night, and though the moon is still up, I walk with the flashlight on my cellphone turned on to see my footing.

An hour later, as the sun is climbing up behind me, I reach Foncebadón, population thirteen, the highest village (though not the highest point) on the Camino. It is one of many former ghost towns along the Camino enjoying a resurgence of interest thanks to increasing pilgrim foot traffic.

Before the great revival of the Camino, which began in the late 1970s, the road was mostly unmarked, and guidebooks were few and far between. The "father" of the modern Camino (which follows the ancient route) was Father Don Elias Valiña Sampedro of O Cebreiro parish, who in 1967 completed his doctoral thesis, *The Road of St James: A Historical and Legal Study*. Father Don spent the next three decades working on restoring and promoting the Camino as well as adding the yellow direction arrows. At least in part because of his work, the Camino de Santiago was declared a UNESCO World Heritage Site in 1993.

Before the number of pilgrims began to increase dramatically in the mid to late 1990s, Foncebadón nearly met its end. If not for a woman named Maria, there would be little if anything left of the remote village. In the early 1990s, Maria and her son were the last two remaining residents. When four civil guards and two priests arrived in the village to remove the church bells, Maria climbed atop the church roof, where, armed with a stick and the roof tiles that she hurled at the interlopers, she defended the bells, telling the priests that the bells were required to toll her own death knell. Maria's story made the front page of Spanish newspapers, and as a result, the bells remained.[21] Since then, the village's permanent population has grown to at least thirteen and now includes a small store, and according to my English Camino guidebook, as many as half a dozen albergues (some of these are no doubt rooms in private homes), plus a pizzeria, a tavern, and a restaurant.

Maria was not the last person to make Foncebadón famous though. Shirley MacLaine wrote about the village and its wild dogs in *The Camino*, published in 2000. The story left its mark on many, myself included. For years the thought of encounters with wild dogs just helped to cement any other fears I had about walking the Camino. More recently, it's been said that the wild dogs were purely fictional, but nonetheless the legends about wild dogs on the Camino persist.

Despite my fears, I pass through Foncebadón without incident and keep climbing. Soon enough, I come across the Cruz de Ferro—the iron cross that sits atop a five-metre wooden pole that is often falsely said to mark the highest point along the Camino, at 1504 metres. In fact, the highest point of the Camino, at 1520 metres, is just a couple of kilometres past the iron cross, and along a short detour from the trail.

There is a pilgrim tradition of depositing a stone at the base of the Cruz de Ferro in memory of someone, or as a symbol of letting go of something such as a loss or painful emotion or leaving a burden behind. Here, now, it is my turn to do so. I place the small, round, smooth stone taken from my parents' Georgian Bay property on the pile of rocks and think about my parents for a moment, trying to imagine what emotion or burden I am releasing. Somehow though, the gesture feels mostly empty.

It's only later that I learn so many "sorrow stones" are deposited at the Cruz de Ferro, the stones themselves have become a burden, requiring regular removal at no small effort and cost.

I liked the stone and later will wish I'd kept it. Having it felt like having some small part of my past with me, only better, because it seemed even smoother than it had when I first found it. I liked the metaphor. Liked thinking of myself with my own rough, sharp edges gone. And I liked the idea of having my parents along with me. But more to the point—it was my talisman, an anchor, a piece of my life—free of imperfections, comforting, and grounding, in the way that rocks are. Sometimes along the trail I caught myself reaching in my pocket and rubbing the smooth surface like a worry stone, narrating a story in my head. Hours could go by like this. Perhaps it's normal, I'd think to myself. What else is there to do on these long days of walking alone except go over the stories of one's life and make sense of them? It felt unavoidable, inescapable, and necessary. A sorting mechanism—a large part of the reason I wanted to walk the Camino. And once the stone is gone, I miss it.

For the first half of the day, the trail climbs into spectacularly mountainous territory, until I walk out onto a high plateau flanked all around by distant mountain ranges. It feels as though I am walking across the very top of Spain. Alongside the path are carpets of heather and purple loosestrife, fall crocuses, asters, brambles, and late season daisies. The sky is the most vivid blue imaginable. The air is sweet and fresh and cool. This is some of the most exquisite scenery along the Camino so far, though I've lost count of how many times I've had the same thought in other places.

I feel as though I'm falling for Spain—for the landscape, the food and wine, the people, the history, the language, the climate, the villages, mountains, and forests. The trail. All of it. But what is it that I love so much? Perhaps I'm just euphoric because of all the exercise and sunshine? Or from the long days spent outside. Our lives rarely ever afford us the luxury of simply spending days and weeks out of doors, walking, wandering, thinking. Life on the Camino is magnificent in its simplicity. You travel, by foot, in one direction, following the trail markers, doing whatever it is that comes next. At night there are places to eat and sleep and shower. Wine to drink. Ancient churches to visit. Sceneries and vistas to rival the previous ones. And people to talk to, if you care for any such thing.

Eventually the trail heads sharply downhill, and I calculate that I have about fourteen or so kilometres before I arrive in Molinaseca, where I aim to find some food first and then make a decision about where to stay for the night. At this point on my trek, walking through towns makes me less euphoric than walking through the countryside or staying in rural villages. First there's the navigation and then all the various people to deal with, coupled with my inadequate grasp of the Spanish language and all my incredibly inarticulate attempts to converse or make my wants known. Out in the country, away from people, my lack of ability to communicate adequately in Spanish ceases to be a problem. I find that I am enjoying long silent conversations with myself.

By the time I get to Molinaseca in the early afternoon, I'm ravenous. As I cross the medieval stone bridge into town, I can see people sitting at patio tables in the sunshine. There appears to be a line of cafés along the riverbank. Between the ancient stone terraces, the shallow rushing river, and the cobblestone streets, this village is just too picturesque to pass up. I wander up to a café with lots of open tables and wait for someone to seat me. There are well-dressed families here and plenty of couples, but no pilgrims. Nobody seems particularly keen to deal with me—a solo female walker. Dressed in my hiking gear and hiking boots, with my backpack, I stand out and feel scruffy and embarrassed and completely out of place. I'm not really surprised to feel so incongruous, and yet this is the first time since I arrived in Spain that I have felt quite this unwelcome. Eventually, I seat myself, only to be quickly moved somewhere else and given a lengthy explanation in Spanish—which, of course, I do not understand. It's as though I have foolishly missed a "Pilgrims Not Welcome" sign.

Ever since I left Foncebadón earlier this morning, I've been fantasizing about food and making an astonishing and evolving list in my head of things I'd like to eat. I realize that my dinner last night consisted only of the cake and tea served in the late afternoon and a glass of wine and a few olives later in the evening. And that my breakfast this morning—a cup of coffee and a slice of toast with vegemite—was twenty-five kilometres and five hours ago. For a good half of the walk, I've been adding new foods to the list, trying where I can to think of the Spanish words. I call this game, "Me gustaría…" (I would like…) A homemade egg salad sandwich on buttered brown bread; tarta de manzana; a Montreal bagel, well toasted and buttered, with cream cheese and lox; tortilla de patatas; a raisin and walnut butter tart. Homemade sausage rolls. My list goes on, and my mouth is watering at the thought of it all.

I'm so hungry that I don't even know where to begin. So when the waiter asks me impatiently what I want, and does not present me with a menu, I ask for the only thing that I know how to order off the top of my head. "Me gustaría un bocadillo de jamón y queso y una cerveza, por favor," I say—imagining a sandwich stuffed with ham and cheese. The waiter says nothing, and as he walks away, I realize that damn it, once again, I don't want a beer. I have no idea why I tacked this on, why I keep ordering beer when I don't really want it. It's probably because I ordered the same thing successfully back in Hospital de Órbigo, and the Spanish words come easily. But what I really want, *and need*, is a good strong, large coffee. I haven't had anything since the single cup of instant coffee in the refugio several hours earlier. "Perdón señor," I call out to him, but it's too late to retract. He's easily still in earshot but keeps going and never looks back.

Ten minutes later the grumpy waiter returns with my sandwich, which seems to be cold bacon with cheese. And a beer. He plunks it all down unceremoniously and leaves without a word or a smile. A few moments later, he's back with the bill. It's far more expensive than anywhere else I've eaten so far. All this seems so distinctly un-Spanish to me. It feels like the antidote to my love affair with Spain—the sobering wakeup call that nothing is perfect—the reminder to never get in over your head. Mere hours ago, I was swooning over the wonders of life in Spain. But isn't that just exactly how love works, great crescendos of happiness followed by constant reality checks?

The sandwich is big and filling, but one of the least remarkable sandwiches I've eaten so far this trip. Nonetheless, I eat the entire thing and drink the beer and then leave the money with the tab on the table even though, to the best of my knowledge, this is quite unusual in Spain. And then I head back to the trail. I thought that perhaps I'd call it quits for the day in Molinaseca, but my experience at lunch feels like a clear message to just keep walking.

It's three o'clock as I head out of town. I'm slightly nervous, because I know with a population of around sixty-nine thousand, Ponferrada is one of the bigger towns along the Camino, the last major town before we reach Santiago de Compostela. So far I've found all the bigger towns so much more challenging to navigate and deal with than the smaller rural ones. But moments later I'm in luck when I run into three others heading off in the same direction. "Are you heading to Ponferrada?" one of them calls out.

"Yes! Bit late in the day, but too early to stop!" I reply.

We fall into walking together. Cynthia is from the United States. Kim and David are from Holland. They are headed for a private albergue in Ponferrada that has rooms for four, and they ask if I would like to join them. Once again, I don't have any kind of plan, and I'm happy not to have to make another decision and find a place by myself, so I agree, gratefully.

When we arrive in Ponferrada, we find the albergue almost immediately, mostly thanks to David, who has been leading our little expedition from Molineseca. A room with two bunks is available. It has a private bathroom just outside the room. The place is quiet and immaculate, with fresh sheets on the beds. I haven't slept in sheets for weeks. What luxury!

Our beds sorted, we deposit our backpacks and walk into town to have a look around. The walk takes us along the Río Sil, which bisects town and flows under the iron bridge that gives Ponferrada its name—from the Latin pons (bridge) and ferrata (iron). Several times we catch a fleeting glimpse of the magnificent twelfth-century knights templar castle looming in the distance. But it's food that my roommates are after, so in a small square, near the river, we stop at a patio bar for something to eat and drink. The local specialty is botillo—a pig intestine filled with seasoned pork offal, usually served with boiled potatoes and bitter greens. I'm still not hungry because of the oversized sandwich at lunch, so I can't even face the thought of botillo. I order only a glass of local Bierzo white wine and a tapas plate of patatas bravas to share. Later in the evening, on the way back to our albergue, I stop to replenish my picnic supplies for the next day: fruit, cheese, and my daily ration of Spanish chocolate.

Back in our room, we head straight to bed. For ages I lie still, trying not to move about in the bunk below Cynthia. Once again, I cannot sleep. Perhaps I'm missing my sleeping bag, or maybe it's because I'm sleeping in such a small, airless room after so many nights in big open dormitories. Whatever the reason, I lie wide awake, once again watching the hours roll past. It is well past midnight, and my roommates are all sleeping soundly. For a while I contemplate getting up and finding my sleeping bag, but I don't want to risk waking everyone up. So I refrain and instead lie quietly, waiting, concentrating on slowing down my breathing and following my breath in and out, in and out again, slowly. Slow deep breath in, hold, hold, hold, hold; long slow, slow, slow release. Repeat. Repeat. Repeat. Forget about everything. Forget your sleeping bag. Forget frustration. Forget the roommates. Forget the airlessness. Forget Spain. Focus on breathing slowly in and out. Follow the breath...

Patatas Bravas

Potatoes have been called the crop that changed the world. They were cultivated first by the Inca of Peru between 8000 and 5000 BCE, and the Spanish Conquistadors who travelled to Peru in 1536 CE are thought to have brought the first potatoes back to Europe. The potato is now the third-most consumed crop in the world, with rice and wheat being the first and second.

Spain's relationship with the potato is evident in the many beloved potato dishes in Spanish cuisine, such as patatas bravas and tortilla de patatas. Patatas bravas—made from bite-sized cubes of potatoes shallow or deep fried (or sometimes roasted), and served with a spicy tomato sauce, aioli, or spicy mayonnaise—originated in Madrid and is now one of the most popular tapas dishes in Spain.

Serves 3–4 as a side dish
3–4 medium potatoes (russets and Yukon gold both work well)
45–60 mL (3–4 tbsp) olive oil and more as needed
Salt and pepper to taste

Peel and cut the potatoes into small cubes (approximately 2 cm or ¾ diameter). Rinse and drain the potatoes thoroughly and pat them dry with a paper towel.

In a large fry pan, warm the olive oil over medium heat.

Add as many potatoes as can fit comfortably without overcrowding the pan. (Keep any extra potatoes in a covered bowl until you are ready to cook them.)

Brown the potatoes on all sides, then season with salt and pepper and reduce the heat slightly, to let the potatoes cook until quite tender, about 20 minutes. Continue to flip the potatoes intermittently to avoid burning. When quite tender and browned on all sides, remove the potatoes from the pan to a serving plate and keep warm on low heat in the oven.

Repeat with any remaining potatoes.

Serve the potatoes with aioli, spicy mayonnaise, or homemade bravas sauce.

Bravas Sauce

Bravas sauce is similar to gravy in consistency, and though it varies widely from place to place, generally it is slightly sweet and quite spicy. Some prefer aioli or spicy mayonnaise.

30 mL (2 tbsp) olive oil
1 tsp smoked paprika
1 tsp sweet paprika
1 tsp garlic, minced or dried
⅛ tsp cayenne or chipotle powder
1 tbsp flour
125 mL (½ cup) vegetable broth, and a little water if needed
30 mL (2 tbsp) tomato ketchup
Salt and pepper to taste
A dash or two of hot sauce (optional)

Heat the olive oil in a small saucepan over medium heat. Add the smoked and sweet paprika, garlic, and cayenne or chipotle powder. Stir until combined. Cook for a minute so that the flavours start to meld.

Add the flour and stir for another minute or so.

Slowly add the broth, and continue stirring until the mixture thickens to the consistency of gravy. Once thickened, turn the heat down, and stir in the ketchup. Add salt and pepper to taste. If the sauce is too thick, whisk in a little water.

If the sauce lacks flavour (will depend on the intensity of the spices used) add hot sauce, a dash or two at a time.

The bravas sauce can be drizzled over the plate of cooked potatoes just before serving.

CHAPTER TWENTY-TWO

Ponferrada to Villafranca del Bierzo

October 28

"I am extremely happy walking on the downs....I like to have space to spread my mind out in." —Virginia Woolf, September 5, 1926, *The Diary of Virginia Woolf, Volume Three: 1925–1930*

For the first time on the Camino, I awaken trying to remember where I am. What city I'm in. Where I'm headed next. Or how many days I've been on the trail and how many days I have left. It takes a minute or so to remember that I'm in Ponferrada and headed today to Villafranca del Bierzo. I'm the first up again today, but my roommates soon follow. Within twenty minutes we're all packed, ready, and heading out the door. The plan is to find breakfast together and then head off for the day—walking separately.

In a very upmarket little bakery café near the famous castle, we are tucking into some seriously sophisticated, beautifully presented brioche (mine is coffee and almond, swirled through with marzipan and drizzled with coffee icing and toasted almonds) alongside our grande cafés con leche. It's all so good that I contemplate having the same all over again: second breakfast, right after first. But the draw of the walk is even stronger. Sunlight is streaming in through the café windows, and Ponferrada beckons. It's time to get a move on, explore this town, then hit the trail.

Ponferrada is a place that has been conquered, destroyed, and rebuilt time after time after time. In the nearby hills, the open pit gold mines of Las

Médulas—now a UNESCO World Heritage Site—were once the largest mining centre in the vast Roman Empire. The ancient Romans' hunger for gold left a two-thousand-year-old gaping wound in the landscape, a permanent reminder of human impact on the planet.

I'm quite taken with this compact city and its incredible history. Ever since the twelfth century, Ponferrada has been dominated by the Castillo de los Templarios, an enormous, fantastical, sprawling stone castle that sits high atop a hill, looming grandly over town. With its towers and turrets, moat, and drawbridge, the castle looks like something straight off the pages of a children's storybook. But this former fortress turned castle is very much the real thing. It came under the jurisdiction of the Knights Templar in 1178, when King Fernando II placed both the town and fortress under the Templars' jurisdiction, with the goal of providing safety to all pilgrims. The Templars immediately set to work extending and improving the fortress. Their reign, though, was not to last. By 1312 the Catholic Church had disbanded the Knights Templar, at least in part because of their growing wealth, power, and fame. By 1314, King Philip IV of France had ordered most of the remaining Templars to be burned at the stake, while those who lived were imprisoned for life.

I walk through town admiring the remarkable buildings bathed in morning sunlight. Everywhere I look there are pilgrims and tourists, locals out shopping and having coffee, and hordes of lively Spanish school children visiting the castle, running up and down the gangplanks whooping and yelling, and spilling out across the sweeping castle lawns. I could stay here, I think to myself. Another time, I could stay longer, explore the castle. Learn more about the Knights Templar and about pilgrimages of yore. I could take photographs, like everyone else. I could eat in all the local restaurants, sample all the local foods, like the botillo with its intestine casing. But when I reach the end of Ponferrada, I don't stop, I don't look back, don't take a single photograph—not even of the storybook castle. All I want is to hit the trail, to keep walking. To keep heading towards the distant mountains that frame the horizon in all directions. "Get thee to the mountains," I say aloud to myself, grinning. I cannot wait to stand amongst them.

I'm finding things in myself.

After years of stress and worry; of moves around the globe, across countries, of back-and-forth passages between Canada and Australia, while searching desperately for some place to call home, some place to belong; of leaving and starting jobs; of profound and useless worry about my seriously ill youngest daughter; of struggling, and of merely trying to survive amidst all the baggage of life—here, in the Spanish countryside, deeply immersed in the outdoors, pushing myself physically every single day—I have found something new.

It is not a sense of contentment or self-satisfaction, nor is it revelling in my own strength, though I do feel all of these things, too. It's more about all I'm letting go of—self-doubt, hurts, old wounds, worry, sorrow, loss. Letting go because there is no need to carry them, not here. Incredibly, much of what I'm finding is a new ability to feel deeply, even intensely happy.

I tell myself it's the endorphins, but it feels like more than that. Away from everything I know, displaced, and largely alone for long stretches of time, I am able to see more clearly and think more deeply. It feels like I've reset my brain, my body chemistry, and at the same time, I've archived a lot of tired, old matter. It feels powerful, healing, transformative. It feels like what I came for, for the incredibly curative power of walking, of the brain-foot connection. I feel free, wide open, full of joy and possibility.

Tomorrow the trail leaves the autonomous region of Castille and León and crosses into Galicia, the fifth and final region of Spain along the Camino Frances.

I'm nearly there, closing in on the final leg of my walk, but I won't let myself say or think anything further. I don't want to get ahead of myself. *Just keep going,* I say, musing aloud. Just keep going, step by step, one foot after the other, village by village, day by day, night by night, week by week. One month sliding into the next. Slow and steady wins the race.

After the first ten kilometres of the day, I am walking through endless beautiful rolling vineyards—all of them turning various shades of red and burgundy in the late autumn sun. Somewhere along the way I stop to look at my guidebook. It seems I've passed by villages without ever noticing. I've found this occurring more and more lately, the further I go down this trail. I don't feel as though I am missing out by not taking note of these places. I know that I am absorbing Spain on an entirely different level. By this point on the Camino, I am deeply involved on focusing inwards, on sorting out my life. From the very beginning, I viewed the Camino as a sorting mechanism. The further I've walked, the more this process has evolved naturally and on its own accord, thanks in large part to the brain-heart-foot connection.

I am giving birth daily to a new, stronger state of mind and body. I feel lighter, stronger, more content and, equally importantly, less anxious, less burdened by worry. My feet and brain seem to be synchronizing. Sometimes I start off thinking about walking as an antidote for anxiety, restlessness, and despair—about walking as a way to repair and heal. Sometimes I think about walking as meditation—about walking being such a fundamentally human activity. Before I know it, hours have passed, and I'm not clear as to where I have been geographically, physically, or mentally. It is almost like being in a different state entirely, devoid of conscious thought. As though I am transitioning from mere observer into becoming part of the landscape itself. Or perhaps I'm simply merging into the long history of walkers who have trekked this path for over a thousand years.

Shortly before I arrive in Villafranca, I pass the most elegant, striking white house, perched high atop a hill in the midst of a sprawling vineyard. I wonder about its occupants and their Spanish life amongst the grapevines. It's one of those places that imprints on the memory and feels a bit like a dream. All of it so stunningly beautiful. The house is a Camino icon, although I only find that out later, when I hear others talking about it and the glorious Mencía vineyards.

Mencía is a red grape variety, indigenous to Northwest Spain (and Portugal, where the variety is known as Jaen). The old vines are perfectly suited to the Bierzo region's high-altitude terroir, and the grapes produce highly sought-after red wines that are attracting global recognition. There's a rumour that the vines originally came from France, giving Villafranca del Bierzo its name, but DNA testing has recently disproved this theory. The grapes predate humans. They have always been here in this remote mountainous region. They were here before us and will very likely outlive us too.

I have a loose plan with Cynthia, made before we left Ponferrada in the morning, to meet up at the end of the day in Villafranca del Bierzo, at the Albergue de la Piedra, a private hostel owned and operated by two former pilgrims who left behind their big city life in Madrid for a very different existence along the Camino. Whoever gets there first will book a room or beds in the dormitory, whatever is available. I wonder how this will work, but Cynthia assures me she will arrive after me and ask the proprietors if I've checked in. She's right. I get there first and book us a room for two, explaining to the owners that I think there will be two of us, but that it might end up only being for me. They are remarkably accommodating. If Cynthia does not show up—no problem—I will have a room to myself. If she shows, I will have company. Either outcome will be perfect. The room has a double bunk bed and a window overlooking the pretty street and river. There's a clothesline in the window for hanging our wet clothes and a very decent bathroom down the hall, plus a well-equipped communal kitchen. What more could we possibly want?

Villafranca del Bierzo was founded in the eleventh century by French monks establishing a monastery to care for pilgrims walking the Camino de Santiago. It's a picturesque, prosperous-looking mountain village, complete with a winding river and a meandering main street full of lovely old stone buildings. At the ancient Romanesque Iglesia de Santiago, pilgrims too sick and injured to continue could, and still can, pass through the church's Puerta del Perdón (door of pardon) and receive absolution along with their certificate of Compostela, the certificate normally only obtained by those who walk on, to Santiago de Compostela.

Even our albergue seems rather special. On the first days of the Camino, booking into places for the night, I didn't see what I see now. I saw a mass of people and beds. I saw primitive facilities and a lack of space and privacy. I wasn't used to sharing bathrooms with so many strangers. It hits me that after so many days and nights on the Way, my perceptions of what I require to be comfortable have shifted. Now it seems I have everything I need, and I want for nothing.

Cynthia arrives, finds me, and declares that she would rather cook than eat out tonight. We set off together to buy supplies for dinner. In a tiny shop on the main street, we wander the aisles, formulating a plan. Cynthia proposes chicken tortillas on account of the fact that the store stocks tortilla wrappers. We buy wine, chicken, tortillas, an onion, a can of corn, a tomato, and a small head of lettuce. Back in the albergue kitchen we find oil and spices and cook up a small feast. When others drift in, they eat the leftovers and offer wine and chocolate and conversation in exchange. There's Will from London, who "likes a drop of red." And Leo from Finland, who is cycling the Camino on a tiny folding bicycle, wearing a watermelon helmet—impossible to miss. Others too stay on and join the conversation. It's a beautiful, celebratory evening. All of us are eager to be entering fabled Galicia tomorrow—the culmination of our journeys are now very nearly within reach. I can feel my own excitement building.

Tex-Mex Chicken Tortillas in Spain

A tortilla in Spain is a potato-filled omelette, while in Latin America it refers to corn or flour-based round flatbreads. And just as tortilla de patatas is a way of life in Spain, flatbread tortillas packed with tasty ingredients are a cornerstone of Mexican and Mesoamerican cuisine.

I wouldn't have thought of making Mexican-style tortillas in Spain, but the tiny grocery store on the main street of Villafranca del Bierzo had flour tortillas. And with a little improvising on ingredients, we had the fixings for a dinner for two, with plenty of leftovers for other pilgrims who wandered in to find out what was cooking in the albergue kitchen. It was a fun, easy dinner to share with others, and the evening ended up being a very sociable kitchen party. Change up the ingredients for the fillings as you see fit.

Serves 3–4 (or more)
8-12 (1 packet) flour-based tortillas
30-45 mL (2-3 tbsp) olive oil
1 large onion, diced
2 large boneless, skinless chicken breasts, cut into thin
    strips
salt and pepper to taste
½ tsp paprika
½ tsp cumin (or more)
small pinch of cayenne

340 mL (approx. 1 cup) can corn, drained

1 large tomato, diced

1 small head of lettuce, washed, drained, and finely sliced

Other ingredients as available: grated cheese, hot sauce, olives, avocado, etc.

Preheat the oven to 165°C (325°F). Wrap the tortillas in a clean, damp tea-towel or foil, and when the oven comes to temperature, set the wrapped tortillas on the middle shelf. Set the timer for 15 minutes. In the meantime, prep everything else.

Warm the olive oil in a fry pan at medium heat. Add the onion and chicken strips. Season with salt, pepper, paprika, cayenne, cumin, or whatever appropriate/preferred spices are on hand. Cook for at least 8 to 10 minutes or until the chicken is completely cooked (no pink remaining; juices should run clean, internal temperature 71°C (160°F). Keep warm on the stove, stirring occasionally.

Drain the corn and place in a bowl. Wash and chop the lettuce and tomatoes and place in bowls. Grate cheese if using. Assemble extras such as olives, hot sauce, avocado, etc.

When the tortillas are hot, remove from the oven and keep wrapped.

Assemble your own tortillas!

CHAPTER TWENTY-THREE

Villafranca del Bierzo to O Cebreiro

October 29

"From there we came outside and saw the stars."
—Dante Alighieri, *Inferno: The Divine Comedy*

Today the Camino leaves the province of Castilla y León and enters mythical, rugged, ancient Galicia, the final region of Spain along the route. Even though there are a couple of possible routes to O Cebreiro, there is no particularly easy option. All the routes to O Cebreiro are notoriously long and challenging. I pick the shortest, steepest route, which, adjusted for altitude, is about thirty-three kilometres, with at least part of the day spent walking alongside a busy highway. After the trail leaves the roadways behind, the remaining walk is a notoriously long, very strenuous, and steep climb to the ancient mountain village of O Cebreiro.

Many pilgrims choose to split up this gruelling day or organize to send their backpacks along by one of the various courier services that operate along the route. But sending my own pack on ahead would have meant needing to know where I was staying overnight *and* having a second smaller pack in which to carry my raincoat, water, and valuables with me. Splitting the day up did not feel like an option. And since I neither booked my accommodations in advance nor have a spare backpack to carry my valuables, I have by default chosen to walk the whole way in one day, carrying my pack.

Well before first light, I am up and on the Camino, leaving Villafranca del Bierzo behind, as are many of my other fellow peregrinos. An hour later I pause for coffee and breakfast in the pretty little village of Pereje. While I am there, Leo, part of the kitchen party from the night before, cycles up on his small folding bike. He joins me at my outdoor table, sporting his distinctive watermelon helmet. Within minutes, a crowd of pilgrims has gathered around, all curious about Leo and his bicycle, his helmet, his life in Finland. Leo is a one-man travelling road show and soon everyone is talking and laughing at once. I am loath to leave the lively conversation and welcoming café, but I am conscious of the long walk ahead and must keep moving.

For the next couple of hours, the trail hugs a major highway before wending its way gently upwards, past increasingly small villages full of ancient stone buildings with gardens full of kale and exuberantly coloured late-season geraniums. The narrow roads are little more than stone or dirt paths, and there are few cars but plenty of livestock, especially cows, and cow pies aplenty. I walk past the villages, past the animals, through vividly green fields into dense forests of oak, chestnut, and Spanish firs. Everywhere I look it is lush, beautiful, and as green as Ireland. I am obsessed with this landscape.

After the village of Herrerias, the trail begins to ascend steeply for the final eight kilometres, towards O Cebreiro, which sits atop the 1,293-metre pass. Occasionally there are wide open vistas across pastures and meadows, with views to the mountains beyond. Then the forests close in again, and the path continues climbing, winding upwards. I find myself walking through rugged mountainous farmland, past sharply sloping fields of cows kept in place by ancient stone walls known to Galicians as chantos. The air is deeply scented, earthy, grassy, mossy, with notes of pine and often pungent with manure.

For a time I walk with a young Korean girl who introduces herself as Kim. She is twenty-eight, the same age as my eldest daughter and one of a series of twenty-eight-year-olds I have walked with along the Camino. Kim is not an especially strong walker. She reminds me of a pair of English girls I met in the first few days on the Camino. The English girls were beautiful, blonde, and very fit looking, but within days of starting, they quit. One had developed tendonitis and could not go on. They left together. I ran into them just as they made their decision to quit. They were sitting in a bar, drinking beer—a crowd of men gathered around them. Shortly after that, another young pilgrim I met in the first days of the Camino dropped out. I began to realize there was something about the sturdiness of maturity and the ability to pace oneself and endure that helps immeasurably on the Camino.

When I stride up behind Kim, she is trudging along, painfully slowly. When I say hello, she joins me, matching my pace temporarily. She tells me immediately that she hates this day, this walk. "I came for the partying," she says, "I did not know the walking would be so hard." She had read a popular Korean book about the Camino before coming, and it had made the walk sound so fun, so wonderful. Before we have walked ten minutes together, she starts to cry, tears running down her face.

"It is *sooo* hard," she says, sobbing. It's true, we are walking steeply uphill, and there is no relief in sight. But the walk is also spectacular, and, unlike Kim, I am strong from years of walking. "Just look down and place your feet, one after the other," I tell her. "Do not look up at the trail—that makes it so much harder. Soon we will be at the top, and you will be happy."

But Kim is not buying any of this. She keeps up a steady stream of complaints. I tell her to drink some water and have a short rest. "Stay with me," she says. So, I stop and wait for her, even though today, of all days, I want nothing more than to keep walking alone at my own steady pace. This is a day I have looked forward to since before I even left home. Stopping and starting just makes it harder, and I really want to be alone to focus my energy and attention on the walk and the spectacular scenery. I can scarcely get enough of the views—this is what I dreamed of when I imagined the Camino. But I cannot just up and leave Kim behind. Even though if it were the other way around, I'm sure she'd leave me behind in a heartbeat.

When we resume walking, I encourage her along for the better part of an hour, but it does very little good. She is obviously struggling. She tells me I am walking too fast, though I am walking along at a snail's pace. "Kim," I say, firmly, "you must do this at your own pace, and I will do it at my pace. If you stick to the trail, you will be fine. Going slow is absolutely fine—it is not a race. Just follow the trail, one foot after the other. Keep going. We are almost there." I try to be encouraging, hoping that I am right but knowing that we have some way to go yet.

I tell her to take another rest and then continue when she feels more ready. I pull out the chocolate bar that I am carrying as my emergency rations and offer it to her. "I want a beer," she says, and sulkily rejects the chocolate. Just as I am wondering whether it is morally wrong of me to leave her on her own,

I see a young couple coming up the path behind us, about a hundred feet or more back. The timing is perfect. I have not seen anyone other than Kim all afternoon. "Look, Kim," I say, "There are some other people coming along. You will have new company to walk with." She brightens and waves at the young couple heading up the hill. Even though I feel a bit guilty for leaving, I stride off, and before long I find myself entirely alone again. Once again, it feels like I am walking across the top of Spain. Every time I break out of the forest and into a clearing there are magnificent mountain vistas in all directions, deep green valleys below, wisps of white clouds in the blue, blue sky. I am so happy to be alone—to be out here immersed in and consoled by the mountains and trees and sunshine, absorbing all the impossibly beautiful landscape.

After all these days of walking and of being outdoors, I have walked myself back into my body. Walked myself into an altered state. I am physically stronger. And that strength seems to be helping me let go of some of the losses of my life—of youth and old dreams, of lost friendships and family members, of miscarriages and misfortunes. I've also let go of old hurts, resentments, and a lack of faith in myself. I've remembered to walk for myself, of myself, with myself. This is part of the gift of the Camino, that while I have been busy walking and gaining physical strength and fully occupied with moving forwards, I have also begun to leave other things behind, or file them away. I can feel the weight of my life starting to slide away.

Before long I run into a sign telling me I've crossed into Galicia. This rugged, verdant corner of northwestern Spain is home to some of the most spectacular scenery in Europe, and also to one of the world's most dramatic coastlines—the famous "Coast of Death" along the Atlantic Ocean. It's an ancient land of pagan myths that, like much of Spain, has been occupied by the Visigoths, the Romans, the Moors, the Berbers, and the Celts. Galicia is legendary for its history, its ancient buildings, its mountain ranges and dense forests, wild beaches, and steep rugged pastures.

But it's equally well known for its beautiful wines and distinctive cuisine—especially its seafood. And for its empanadas and caldo Gallego—a rustic, regional soup made with local vegetables, meats, beans, and stock; and one of the best-known desserts in Europe—the tarta de Santiago—the stunningly delicious almond torte, typically decorated with the Cross of St. James.

Abruptly, after a full day of walking, I follow the path around a corner into O Cebreiro, population thirty, and pass the first of the ancient round stone buildings with their thatched roofs. These famous hobbit-like houses of O Cebreiro are known as pallozas. And then, there right in front of me, is the Santuario de Santa Maria Real, thought to be the oldest church on the Camino Frances. Established circa 840, nearly twelve hundred years ago, this small stone church is said to have been the home of the Holy Grail during the Middle Ages.

I am here! I am actually here in this incredibly beautiful old mountaintop village, which I have been dreaming about for so long. A place where there is evidence of a pilgrims' refuge dating back to the mid-800s, mere decades after the tomb of St. James was discovered in 813 CE, a thousand long years and more before Canada officially became a country.

I walk straight past everything and join the long line-up to book into the Albergue de Peregrinos O Cebreiro, operated by the Government of Galicia. When the staff person arrives to sign us in, she seems positively hostile. When it is my turn to proceed forward towards her, she says one word to me: "Pasaporte." I hand it over and wait silently. She writes down the details and then gives me a slip of paper with my bed number on it and the fee in euros, which I hand over in change. Then she quite literally shoos me away, incredibly efficiently, with a flick of the back of her hand. Who needs language, anyway?

The albergue, which houses one hundred and four pilgrims, is disappointingly big and modern. The free wi-fi is non-functional. The bunk beds are cheek by jowl. When I visit the bathrooms, I see that the shower stalls are entirely devoid of curtains. But it's too late to change my mind—I've paid my money, and it's already five o'clock. I plan to spend as little time as possible in this place, so I shower as quickly as I can, dress, and set up my bed.

Just as I am getting ready to head out for the evening, the couple staying in the bunks beside me arrive and introduce themselves. They are Spanish and are around about my age. He is tall and handsome and speaks perfect English, and she is very pretty and speaks Spanish but tells me, grinning, "¡Yo hablo Spanglish!" (I speak Spanglish!)

"¡Yo tambien!" (Me too!) I say, grinning right back.

He warns me that he has a terrible cough and demonstrates this for me—a great, deep bark—which makes everyone around us look over at us, alarmed.

This makes me laugh, since earlier on the route, I, too, tried to demonstrate my cough with mixed results. I tell him not to worry, that I've already had that nasty cough and can sympathize completely. It's just such a shame I don't have any of Benedict's mystery cough pills left.

The wife asks me if I would rather have her upper bunk. I tell her I'm happy either way—and that she can pick. I'm pretty sure I'll get little sleep regardless of which bed I'm in. So we leave our beds as assigned, and I set up my gear and head out the door, eager to explore the village.

At the first bar I pass, I see some Camino friends I've met previously and join them to chat for a few minutes. We make arrangements to meet for dinner later in the evening, in a restaurant between the church and the albergue. And then, at another table, I see Kim—she made it! She has a massive giant tankard of beer in front of her. I wave at her and smile as she holds up her beer with both hands and shouts, "Geonbae!!" "Yes, cheers! We did it!" I call back, smiling, and feel both happy and relieved to see that she has made it here safely, and that she is looking so much more cheerful. But I leave her to drink with her friends, while I set off to explore this pretty little mountain village that I have dreamt of for so long.

Later, at dinner, we have turned into a large group and are seated around a long refectory table, a fire blazing in the hearth. There is Shea from Ireland; David, a redheaded guy from New Zealand who is cycling the route; Cynthia from Washington, D.C.; Azaria from Australia; Will from England; Jeffrey from Singapore; and me, and then Kim arrives too, and pulls a chair up to the table. We sit in the restaurant for hours, talking, eating, and laughing. All of us are avoiding returning to the big busy albergue too early.

Our waitress, like so many Spanish servers, is completely unfazed by our inability to speak Spanish, our total lack of knowledge, and our general unruliness. She never once appears to be even remotely fed up, even when we stay on far too long.

I order the traditional Galician soup, caldo Gallego, and a basket of bread, and ask for a large glass of very good, local white wine: "Una copa grande de muy buen vino blanco local, por favor." It's probably the longest speech I've made yet in Spain. I have no idea if I've mangled it or got it right.

A few minutes later our remarkably efficient server is back. "For you, peregrina, an albariño, made here in Galicia," she says in English, smiling broadly, and puts down my wine. It's just ever so slightly effervescent, with the faintest scent of peaches. Then she's back again, juggling a load of plates and bowls and baskets of bread with staggering efficiency. She is the only one on duty, and yet she dishes up drinks and food with few words, remembering all our orders without any hesitation. My caldo Gallego is rustic, filling, and soothing—a simple, tasty stock full of beans, kale, onions, garlic, ham, and chorizo. Manners aside, I mop up every bit of the soup with the remains of my basket of bread. Then, reluctantly, given that we are the last table remaining, we pay our bills and fall out into the clear dark night, under a sky full of stars.

Back at the hostel it is as noisy as I'd feared. There's some sort of rowdy party going on in the kitchen, which is adjacent to the dorm room I'm in. There are people everywhere—going in all directions, raucous laughter, music, doors slamming. A large group of Koreans has joined the kitchen party. Though I know they happen, I have not had any truly rowdy nights on the Camino until now, and I'm really not looking forward to the night ahead.

I decide that rather than staying inside fretting and listening to the racket, it would be better to head outdoors for a bit longer. Earlier I noticed a long, broad stone wall on the sloping hill down below the albergue. I head there, bringing along my down jacket, my raincoat, and my phone to use as a flashlight. In the worst case, I figure perhaps I'll sleep a while outdoors. At the wall, I find some of my dinner companions, including Jeffrey and Azaria, sitting in a small group, talking quietly. A talented young Korean jazz singer arrives and starts to sing—his incredible, beautiful voice, his perfect pitch, fills the sky.

I head towards the group and wave at them but don't join in, happy just to be in their vicinity and away from the party raging inside the albergue. I spread out my gear atop the wide stone wall and lay myself down on it. Above me the Milky Way lights up the velveteen darkness of the sky with a trail of stars reaching from one side of the horizon to the other. I have never seen anything like this, not even on canoe trips in Canada's north. The band of light across the inky sky is magical. Incredible. I am transfixed. This is the *campus stellae*—the famous field of stars for which Santiago de Compostela is thought to be named. What a miracle to be here at this moment in time under this rare, dark, crystal-clear sky. Galicia is a place where rainfall, thick fogs, and heavy mists are the norm. O Cebreiro, at 1,330 metres, is frequently pummelled by some of the harshest weather in Spain. Tonight though, the sky is velvety dark and crystal clear—twinkling with starlight. A miracle. A gift from the universe. A glimpse into a distant galaxy.

The others soon join me. Eventually we are lined up in a long, low row of bodies atop the wall, directly under the band of stars, all of us still and silent under an absolutely cloudless sky, looking up at several hundred billion stars. The Milky Way is an incomprehensible hundred-thousand light years across and a thousand light years thick. But lying here on the stone wall, it seems as though I could simply reach up and put my hands amongst the stars. Even if I forget everything else I've ever known, I hope to remember this moment, this sky, this whole magical evening, for as long as I live.

Meanwhile, inside the albergue, the party rages on.

Caldo Gallego

Caldo Gallego, also known as caldo, is a very popular, traditional Spanish soup. It is often found on the menus of restaurants along the Camino. The basic ingredients are typically cabbage or turnip greens, potatoes, white beans, pork (bacon or chorizo), onions, garlic, and broth.

You can vary the amount of stock to make this a broth-based soup or more stew-like, according to your preferences. When I had the caldo in Spain, it was typically more broth based. When I make it at home, I make a thicker, more stew-like version. This is a very rustic and forgiving soup, and you can vary the quantities as you see fit. Serve the soup with a basket of good bread, some olive oil, and perhaps a wedge of Manchego cheese.

Serves 4

30 mL (2 tbsp) olive oil

2 medium onions, finely diced

4 cloves garlic, minced

300 g (10 oz) cured Spanish chorizo sausages, quartered lengthwise and then chopped into approx. 1 cm (½ inch) pieces

4 medium russet potatoes, peeled, and diced into 2 cm (¾ inch) chunks or according to your own preference

2 turnips, fist sized, peeled and diced (1 rutabaga would work in place of the turnips)

2 large carrots, peeled and chopped into 1 cm (½ inch) discs
  or according to your own preference

1 L (4 ¼ cups) well-seasoned stock (or more depending on
  how thick you like your soup)

540 mL (19 oz) can white cannellini beans, drained and
  rinsed

300–350 g (3–4 cups) chopped hearty greens such as kale,
  turnip greens, or broccoli rabe

½ tsp sweet or smoked Spanish paprika

¼ tsp chili pepper flakes

Salt and pepper to taste (this will depend on your stock)

In a large saucepan, gently heat the olive oil and add the diced onion. Cook at medium heat for about 5 to 8 minutes or until the onion is translucent and just starting to brown. Add the garlic and continue cooking for another 2 minutes.

Add the cured sliced chorizo and cook for another 2 to 3 minutes.

Add the cubed potatoes, turnips (or rutabaga), and carrots and toss together gently for a minute or two.

Add about 4 cups of the stock and bring soup to the boil, then reduce heat to medium, and cook until the vegetables are tender, approximately 25 minutes. Add more stock as needed/desired.

Add the cannellini beans and greens and cook over medium heat until the greens are fully wilted and tender, approximately 15 to 20 minutes.

Check seasonings and add paprika, chili pepper flakes, salt, and pepper as required. At this stage, you can reduce the heat and the leave the soup to cook on low heat until you are ready to serve it.

CHAPTER TWENTY-FOUR

O Cebreiro to Samos
October 30

"Let your soul stand cool and composed before a million universes."
—Walt Whitman, *Song of Myself*

I had no sooner returned from stargazing and climbed into my bed, when my very tall and imposing Spanish neighbour climbed out of his bunk. He went straight to the kitchen, where he bellowed at the top of his lungs, in perfect English, to the partying pilgrims from all over the world: *"Shut up and go to bed! This is a pilgrimage. Show some respect. Go now, or there will be consequences."*

I wondered what, exactly, the consequences might be. The truth is, there are not always overnight staff in all the albergues along the Camino. The lack of overnight supervision was not something I would ever have expected and is yet another reason to have the pan-European emergency number, 112, programmed into your phone while walking the Camino.

My Spanish bunkmate turned off the lights as he returned to the room and then climbed into his bed. Not a foot away from me in his bunk, he turned to look at me and said, "Koreans!" and then shook his head. To be fair though, there were more than just Koreans at the party.

"¡Buenas noches y duerme bien!" I whispered quietly, gently.

In the silence and darkness that ensued, I snuggled down into my sleeping bag, put in my wax earplugs, and fell soundly asleep.

When I awaken, hours later, it is pitch black, but my watch tells me that is early morning. With my earplugs out, I hear the first rustlings of people starting to wake up. That's it then, I'm out of my sleeping bag, quietly gathering my gear.

Moments later, I'm on the trail in the dark. The path leaves from behind the albergue and heads straight into a deep, dark forest. Above me, below me, all around me, everything is black. The forest, the sky, the ground below. The forest is so dense that even with the torch on my phone, I can only just make out the edge of the path on either side of me. I am seeing with my feet.

It occurs to me that I am completely and entirely alone, and that I have neither seen nor heard another person since I left the albergue. I stop and look behind me. Nothing but dense black. Same in front. The pilgrims I heard first thing must all be showering and making breakfast or waiting for first light. It's only then that I start remembering all the stories of wild dogs, Iberian wolves, and even brown bears in this mountainous region.

Fear is making me feel intensely alive. All my senses are on full alert, humming and vibrating. I keep walking deeper and deeper into the woods, scared and saying prayers to gods unknown. Why was I in such a rush to leave? Why am I so driven to this constant forward momentum? It's as though I am pulled on by unexplained forces, driven forward by the ghosts of my childhood. Here I am, soldiering on, solo. Forward march.

Suddenly, just ahead of me on the path, an owl hoots. This is not the first time an owl has appeared at a time of need—unbelievably, an owl has miraculously appeared at almost every critical juncture of my life. The owl hoots again. And then again. And again. It keeps flying on ahead of me, as though leading me onwards. We walk like this, together, for the better part of an hour. Eventually, as the sun starts to climb up behind me and light begins to creep into the day, I can see the owl perched overhead in the tree branches. Each time I see it, it hoots and then flies on ahead—perching, waiting, and hooting, before flying off. It can't possibly be keeping me company, but yet it is, intentionally or not. When I come to a clearing overlooking a steeply downward sloping green pasture, the owl is perched on a very visible branch, looking directly at me. The sun is beginning to light up swaths of the pasture below. Morning is upon us. For a few moments, I stand completely still, watching the owl steadily. Then it hoots one last time before disappearing down the mountain side, no doubt seeking cover before the sun is fully up.

Today's walk is a long descent. Everywhere I look it is mountainous and green, verdant, mossy, leafy, and heartachingly beautiful. The tiny villages along the way are mostly stone. Stone walls, stone homes, moss covered stones everywhere. German shepherds lurk in doorways, and skinny cats abound.

Between villages, cows graze on steeply sloping green pastures. Once again, there is cow dung everywhere. The trees are laden with chestnuts. The poplars are turning yellow. It is so rural, and peaceful and mountainous. So Galician. I am absolutely obsessed with all of it and how it resonates with me.

The further I walk, the more I find myself thinking about my paternal grandfather. It occurs to me that after a life lived in so many places, where I truly come from—the place that lives on inside me and still provides solace to me—my paternal grandfather's stone house on the banks of a river in Yorkshire. My grandfather was my first real love. He was the one who loved and accepted me unconditionally, utterly, completely, and without question—the patron saint of my childhood. This was the first and most constant truth of my life. I want to focus on this—it feels important.

I am busy thinking about my grandfather, and communing with rock and soil, owls and trees and the cool early morning mountain air, when suddenly Guy, the Frenchman who couldn't take a hint, strides up. I'd met him a couple of hundred kilometres back, when we ran into each other on the trail and then shared a twin room in a monastery. He'd asked for my email and sent me a note, saying that he wanted to meet me again. I deleted the email. Never answered. I had nothing to say and didn't feel that I owed him an answer. I hadn't really thought of him since.

"I've been watching for you," he says, in English. "I knew I'd find you! I am looking forward to spending some time together now that we have reunited." On he goes, switching to speaking French. He may mean well, but he's searching for something that I'm just not interested in. Not even one bit. And I can't keep up with his French. We walk together for the next couple of hours. And all the while, I feel happiness leaking away, feel myself deflating. Eventually there is a lull, and I tell him that I am sorry but that I really want to walk alone. "Guy, je suis désolé, mais je voudrais marcher seule," I say. "C'est important pour moi." I basically told Kim the same thing yesterday—I just want to walk alone. It's important for me.

Guy looks stunned. Crestfallen. He seems angry. I feel awful, but everything I have said is true. I'm walking to find my way back to myself—to find my centre again after years of cross-continental moves, of arrivals and departures, of turmoil and disappointments, of stops and starts and unbearable worry and sadness, of people and places and jobs left behind, and finally the grief over my difficult and dysfunctional family of origin. I am trying to put all of this and more behind me, one step at a time. I keep returning to the certainty of the path, the remarkable power of the brain-foot connection, the connection to the earth below my feet.

I haven't got the words in French to explain any of this to Guy, and nor do I want to. There is no point pretending otherwise. But now it's difficult. We are on the trail in the middle of nowhere, and so I suggest we walk to the next village and then find our own ways from there. I apologize again and tell him that I just want to be alone with my thoughts. But why, oh why, do I feel so horrible? Why is this so hard? Why is any version of no so difficult for me to say? And for others to hear.

Guy isn't waiting for the next village. He storms off, and I let him go. I walk deliberately slowly to let him get ahead. Then I remember that I have had neither breakfast nor coffee, and I have walked nearly twenty kilometres already since leaving O Cebreiro, and I decide to walk at whatever pace I please. I don't owe Guy a single thing. It is his own expectations and needs that are disappointing him.

It strikes me that we are both looking for the same thing, only I am looking within. He is still looking for completion from someone else. I feel my stance towards him melt and soften. He only wants what we all want, to be loved and understood. He deserves that, and I find myself hoping for him, really hoping, that he finds what he is looking for.

Half an hour later, I arrive in Tricastela and find an empty seat at a long outdoor table full of pilgrims, in front of a café. I order myself a large coffee and a sandwich. If Guy also happens to be here at this café, so be it. I've spoken my truth as honestly and kindly as I know how. I don't need to spare his feelings or mine any longer. I remind myself that honesty is always the best policy. There's no other way. But I also want to tell him that that I very much hope he finds the love and happiness that he is looking for soon.

While I'm eating my brunch, I learn from the other pilgrims that the clocks changed last night, the last Sunday in October. So even though I thought I'd left around the albergue in O Cebreiro at around 6:30 a.m, in actual fact it was 5:30. No wonder it was so terrifyingly dark in the forest when I set off earlier. Now here I am, twenty-one kilometres down the trail, and according to my guidebook, I'm at the end of today's walk, and yet it's not even ten o'clock in the morning.

Obviously there is no way I am stopping for the day any time soon. I reset my watch to the new time and haul out my guidebook, realizing how much I've come to appreciate it. Time to figure out a new plan. I decide to take the long route, which leaves the main trail and follows a secondary trail to Samos, home to one of the oldest and largest Benedictine monasteries in Spain. The only logic to my decision is that the monastery seems to be calling to me. If I were to walk the main route, there do not seem to be a lot of options for places big enough to stay in until I reach Sarria—which would once again mean walking two full day stages in one day. My decision is made.

Soon after I continue on my way, I run into Petra from Czechia, whom I'd met at the café in Tricastela. She is quiet and intelligent, and luckily for me, she speaks English well and wants to practise it at every opportunity. She's also heading towards Samos. We set off together. Before long we are deep in the Oribio river valley, in an impressive forest of chestnut, poplar and massive oak trees, and there we come across two women. The older of the two is from Alberta, Canada. She is eighty, and this is her third Camino. She's walking with another woman, much younger, and it seems as though they met on the Camino. I replay this in my head—this woman is eighty, and she has flown from Western Canada to Spain, where she is deep in the forest, walking her third Camino, and the woman with her has volunteered to accompany her. None of us stop to talk. Our conversation is a brief one, held while still walking. For days and even months afterward, I will think of this Canadian woman with wonder and wish we'd had a chance to talk further. I will wish I knew her name, had written down her address. I hope that I, too, might be capable and desirous of any such thing as walking the Camino when I am eighty.

Samos is home to the magnificent, sprawling, sixth-century Benedictine Monastery San Xulián de Samos. By the Middle Ages the monastery was both wealthy and powerful. Amongst other things, it provided shelter and hospice for pilgrims on their way to Santiago. Over the centuries the monastery was plundered repeatedly and also suffered from several fires. As a result, renovations began as early as the seventh century and seem to have continued on and off ever since. The monastery still offers accommodations for pilgrims in an albergue onsite, a donativo.

Finding the albergue is not completely straightforward, but after walking back and forth around the perimeter of the vast monastery and asking around,

Petra and I finally find the entrance. We pick a bunk bed along the wall well away from the bathrooms and set up our gear. Politely put, the place is very, very basic. At least we've got a bunk bed along the wall. I feel sorry for the others in the centre of the room, where the bunks are lined up chock-a-block.

After a quick shower, I head out to find a grocery store and find myself some consolation supplies that include a small bag of potato chips, a chocolate bar, and a banana, which I add only as an afterthought—because after all, a banana is a healthy, sensible thing to eat. I also pick up a tin of beer, a habit I have acquired on the Camino. I stash the supplies in my pack and find a seat on a bench in the sunshine, just outside the albergue. I am sitting there writing in my journal when I accidentally drop my favourite (and only) pen straight into the storm sewer below me. Just while I'm lamenting its loss, Dacia, one half of a young American couple comes along and tells me that she had seen me in the albergue earlier and thinks I should know that her bunk bed definitely had chinches (Spanish for bedbugs). She and her husband packed up their gear and left, and then found a reasonably priced and immaculate private second floor room at a small hotel just around the corner. She wonders if for the sake of twenty euros, I might not be more comfortable there.

"*Yes,* I would!" I say, thanking her profusely. I follow her around the corner to the hotel, where I promptly book myself a private room. That done, I scurry back to the albergue and surreptitiously pack up my sleeping bag and all my gear, but not before giving all it a good shake, hoping to leave any bedbugs behind. Then I sneak off without even mentioning my departure to anyone. There's no sign of either Petra or the hospitalero, so I can't even let them know where I've gone. I feel a bit like I've made a jailbreak.

Back at the hotel, I run into Dacia again in the small lobby. "We're meeting for dinner at the restaurant next door this evening, around seven, with anyone else we can find—would you like to join us?" she says.

"Hell, yes, I would!" I tell her again, both of us grinning wildly. Things are looking up.

I spend the rest of my afternoon doing laundry in my small bathroom sink and stringing it up around the room to dry. Unbelievably, there is a working radiator in my room. And when I inquire at the front desk about where to buy a new pen, the woman behind the counter reaches into a drawer and hands me one. There seem to be no end of small miracles happening here in Samos.

At dinner, there are eight of us, and we come from all over the world: Korea, the US, Japan, Singapore, Slovenia, Czechia, and Canada. We are immediately engaged in a lively exchange of names, and occupations, and Camino stories. The woman from Japan plans to stay and set up an ice-cream business right here in Samos—she has already started investigating premises. The guy from Slovenia is militantly right wing. The young Korean is the famous jazz singer who sang underneath the Milky Way at O Cebreiro.

I've ordered a glass of the local white wine, a zesty Albariño. My ensalada mixta is a beautiful mixture of colours and flavours—a bed of leafy greens topped with salty green and black olives, corn kernels, grated carrots, hearts of palm, pickled beets, little green cornichons, chopped tomatoes, and grated cheese, along with a basket of bread. The others are tucking into bowls of caldo Gallego, hamburguesas, potato croquettes, plates of mussels, pasta, chicken, and fries, along with draft beers and Mencía red wines.

My dinner and wine cost me about the equivalent of what I'd pay for the wine alone in Canada. I cannot believe how easy it is to find satisfying, delicious, wholesome, and reasonably priced food and drinks, even in the most rural villages, all the way along the Camino. Perhaps I've just been extraordinarily fortunate, but it strikes me over and over that food is something Spain does so remarkably well.

We are the most unimaginably varied, motley crew you could ever throw together, and yet we talk and laugh, staying way too late into the night, and are the last to leave the restaurant. And then it's back to my warm comfortable room in the small hotel, where I know by now not to bother with the sheets, and instead, I lay out my sleeping bag atop the bed and climb inside and promptly fall sound asleep.

ENSALADA MIXTA

Ensalada Mixta, or mixed salad, shows up on many Spanish menus. It can be a starter or a whole course, depending on the size of the salad and what you include. The ensalada mixta starts with a base of mixed greens and includes toppings according to whatever is available and in season. A Spanish ensalada mixta often includes some protein in the form of chickpeas, hardboiled eggs, shrimp, and other seafood, chopped chicken, tuna, or cheese.

There are savoury and fruity versions, and both versions are included here.

Savoury Ensalada

Serves 4 as a lunch or first course at dinner, along with a
rustic loaf of bread

454 g (1 lb or 8 cups) mixed salad greens, washed and well
   dried

chickpeas, marinated asparagus, hard-boiled eggs, etc.

tuna, chicken, chorizo, ham, etc.

finely sliced red onion, cubed carrots, cucumber, pickles,
   avocado, lemon juice, etc.

smoked salmon, cooked shrimp or prawns, cubed or grated
   cheese, etc.

Create a base of salad greens from any of the following: romaine, arugula, spinach, Boston, bibb, green or red leaf lettuce, chicory, mesclun, frisée, escarole, iceberg, and finely sliced cabbage.

Add any of the following, in any quantity, to enliven your ensalada: chickpeas, marinated green or white asparagus spears, chopped or sliced hard boiled eggs, cherry tomatoes or chopped tomatoes, olives, artichoke hearts, tuna or chopped chicken, sliced chorizo, serrano ham, prosciutto, baby corn or canned corn kernels, anchovies, chopped green onions, finely sliced red onion, raw or lightly steamed green beans, chopped carrot and/or cucumber, cubed or sliced cooked or pickled beets, gherkins or other pickles, chopped boiled potatoes, chopped avocado tossed in a little lemon juice, smoked salmon, cooked shrimp or prawns, cubed or grated cheese, etc.

Dressing

120 mL (½ cup) extra virgin olive oil

60 mL (¼ cup) sherry or wine vinegar

pinch white sugar

salt and pepper to taste

Add the ingredients to a jar with a lid and shake well. Add to the salad just before serving and toss gently.

Fruity Ensalada

Serves 4 as a lunch or first course at dinner, along with a
rustic loaf of bread
454 g (1 lb or 8 cups) mix of spinach and mild mixed salad
    greens, washed and well dried
3-4 mint leaves, finely chopped
berries, orange segments, stone fruit, etc.
finely sliced red onion
nuts
apple, avocado
lemon juice
feta, chèvre, blue cheese, or cubed Manchego

Start with the washed and well dried spinach and mild mixed greens, such
as iceberg, bibb lettuce, young arugula, green or red leaf lettuce, and a few
chopped mint leaves. Finely chop the mint leaves and toss with greens.

Add any of the following in any quantity: chopped grapes, raspberries, blueberries, sliced peaches or apricots, blackberries, mandarin orange segments,
pitted cherries, halved strawberries, a little red onion finely sliced, chopped
almonds, pecans, mixed nuts and seeds, chopped apple or avocado tossed in
a little lemon juice (add just prior to serving), and top with crumbled cheese.

Dressing
120 mL (½ cup) extra virgin olive oil
60 mL (¼ cup) white wine vinegar
2-3 tsp liquid honey
pinch salt

Add the ingredients to a jar with a lid and shake well. Add to the salad just
before serving and toss gently.

CHAPTER TWENTY-FIVE

Samos to Ferreiros

October 31

"We are all just walking each other home." —Ram Dass[22]

First thing in the morning I shower, dazzled by the luxury of my own bathroom and endless hot water. My clothes, all of them—two pairs of pants, two shirts, three pairs of underwear, and three pairs of socks—are clean and dry! I am giddy about so much cleanliness all at once. My pack has been thoroughly sorted out and carefully repacked. My phone is charged. I feel like a new person.

This small, warm, dry, quiet, solo room has been such a welcome reprieve from massive communal dorms; yet honestly, in this moment, I am so grateful to have experienced both. Each has taught me to appreciate the other. I would never have been so grateful for a room of my own, a bed to myself, quite so intensely as I am now, without having had the experience of sleeping (or at least trying to sleep) in massive dorm rooms stacked high with bunk beds and snoring pilgrims. Though, most of the people whom I've met on the Camino, I met in those very dorms.

I grab my backpack and head out the door into yet another sunny Spanish day. First stop is the café where we ate last night, this time for un grande café con leche and a buttery, warm croissant a la plancha con mermelada. I can order breakfast like a Spaniard now without even batting an eye.

Jeffrey from Singapore, who was at the table last night and also the night before in O Cebreiro, is also having breakfast in the café. He's headed to Sarria where he's meeting a friend and staying the night. I'm heading on past Sarria, but we agree to walk on together, at least for the first leg of my day. Jeffrey stayed in the monastery albergue, the same one I fled from, and says it was not a great night. In addition to bedbugs, he tells me that there was a lot of "noisy late-night behaviour," and that an elderly Canadian woman got up very late into the night and politely but firmly asked the noisemakers to pipe down, and reminded them that this was not some sort of party package expedition but a pilgrimage and to "please show some respect." I tell Jeffrey that I met that very woman walking to Samos yesterday, and that she is eighty years old and hiking the Camino for the third time. I am so sorry that she was subjected to this kind of behaviour. I wish I knew how to get a hold of her. I'd write and tell her what a hero she is to me.

Like my Chilean friend Sebastian, Jeffrey is an outstanding walking companion. He, too, is twenty-eight, exactly half my age. He's been living in Germany for the past few years, pursuing post graduate education. He is moving soon to Bangalore and is walking the Camino in a break between his studies and his new life in India.

His story brings back so many memories for me. I was twenty-eight when I boarded a plane in Northern Ontario headed for Melbourne, Australia, with a ten-month-old baby in my arms. We were moving to Australia, and all our worldly possessions were packed into four suitcases. We had booked the cheapest flights we could find—a complicated route from Northern Ontario to Toronto to Los Angeles to Tahiti to Auckland to Sydney and, finally, to Melbourne. We were thirty-three hours in transit, and when we finally arrived in Melbourne, bleary eyed and exhausted, we accidentally dropped our perfect beautiful baby on her head while we searched for our luggage. The baby was mercifully resilient, with nothing more than a bump on the head, but our luggage apparently had never left Toronto. The bigger headache. Our adventures were just beginning.

Jeffrey is softly and beautifully spoken and speaks several languages. He laughs easily. He is kind, has a huge heart, and is remarkably intelligent. And though he is not entirely sure what he wants to do with his life, he's busy figuring it out. Conversation with him is fascinating, and I could listen to his voice for hours.

In what seems like no time at all, we arrive in Sarria. I have a small errand to run here, as back in the village of Hospital de Órbigo I left behind a small kit containing my prescription medication, a tiny pocketknife, an equally small sewing kit, my nail clippers, my spare pen, and a gold necklace with a lovely gold St. Christopher pendant on it (St. Christopher being the patron saint of travellers). The owner of the albergue found the little kit after I'd left and kindly organized for a courier that runs backpacks and gear between stages on the Camino to deliver the kit to the municipal albergue in Sarria. I'd been able to replace my medications easily, with minimal effort and expense, by walking into a tiny farmacia and simply explaining to the pharmacist what happened. I'd expected to need to see a doctor, get a prescription, fill out forms, and call upon my travel insurance—but the pharmacist simply replaced my missing medications and sent me on my way. The fee seemed minimal. The lack of bureaucracy was astonishing. A tiny pharmacological miracle of sorts.

Jeffrey helps me find the municipal albergue. But alas, it isn't open and won't be until early afternoon. So, we head off up the steep streets of town to find a café and lunch while I wait for the albergue to open, and Jeffrey waits for his friend to arrive in town. We pick a restaurant with an outdoor table and order food. A few minutes later Petra walks up and joins us. Just after that David and Dacia arrive. Our lively conversation continues right on from where we left off last night. It's always interesting to hear what people experience on the Camino. All of us walking the same route, but each on their own path. Some people have had crazy experiences on the Camino, some have been horribly sick, and some, like me, seem mostly unscathed. A popular topic is which Camino route we might do next. Or what our best and worst experiences have been. And the food. We talk a lot about Spanish food and our favourite meals.

Sarria is quiet at noon today, but by all accounts, this is rarely the case. Sarria is the last possible place to join the Camino and still walk the minimum-required one hundred kilometres to qualify for the Compostela—the certificate granted to those who successfully walk the Camino de Santiago and have the necessary stamps in their pilgrim credencial to prove it. During peak season, Sarria can apparently be extremely busy, and I'd been forewarned that from Sarria on, the trail would be busy all the way to Santiago de Compostela. I pictured walking amid throngs of pilgrims. In the busiest months (June, July, and August) this might be the case. But now, almost November, things have been a lot slower and though the trail is not empty, the numbers of us walking have been pretty sparse.

After lunch, I leave my companions sitting in the sun while I trek back down the hill through town, to the municipal albergue. When I get there, the door is open, and I find Olga, the hospitalero. I tell her what I've come for, and she finds the package for me. Everything is exactly as it was when I left it behind. I am absolutely thrilled to have it back, but once again I lack the vocabulary for this exchange. "Gracias, mil gracias," I say, reaching out to shake Olga's hand. But she's having none of that and embraces me in a big motherly bear hug. "¡Buen Camino, peregrina!" she says. And then, like a grand Camino mama, she embraces me again and kisses me on both cheeks. The unexpected affection catches me completely off guard and makes me feel ridiculously emotional. I leave wiping tears from my face.

Back up the hill one last time, I bid farewell again to Jeffrey and burst into tears. Again. Perhaps it is because I don't think I'll ever see him again, or perhaps the Camino has opened up some great mysterious emotional chasm within me. But my feet need to move forward. I need to move forward. I strike off with Petra. Dacia and David have already hit the trail.

All afternoon we walk through forests and small villages, past fields of cows, chickens, roosters, occasional donkeys, and stands of chestnut trees. At one point, we see a small group of elderly Galicians gathering chestnuts. There's a long and noble history of chestnut use in Spain, dating back to Roman times. Chestnuts are gathered annually in the autumn and used all year long—finding their way into cakes, soups, vegetable dishes such as roasted chestnuts with Brussels sprouts, candied chestnuts known as marróns glacé, and a polenta-like porridge. Farina dolce, meaning sweet flour, is made from chestnuts, and is used in the preparation of many baked goods.

The Galician women are wearing cotton dresses with full-length cotton aprons, heavy leather shoes, and head scarves. They are collecting the chestnuts in their rolled-up aprons before placing them into baskets on the back of a small wooden cart pulled along by horses. When we catch up to them, the three women climb onto the back of the cart facing back, towards us, their serious faces wizened, sombre, as lined as apple dolls'. The cart bumps and jostles along the trail in front of us before pulling over at another stand of trees. The women jump off to gather more chestnuts, while the men stay with the horses and cart and talk between themselves. "¡Hola! ¡Buenas tardes!" I call out, and they all look over. One of the men says something that I cannot quite discern. I smile and nod, trying to work out the unfamiliar words. I want so badly to take a quick picture of them but refrain from taking this liberty and commit the moment to memory instead—these people from another land, another era.

Days later on the trail I hear the words, "Vaya con Dios" (Go with God), and I recognize them as the words that were spoken to me by the men on the wagon.

Later, sitting at my desk in Canada, I will wish I could study the scene again. What were they wearing, those women? Were they wearing simple cotton print dresses with battered old, heavy woollen cardigans and sturdy leather shoes, as they appear in my memory? And where do they live, I will wonder. What kind of homes do they live in? Do their grown children come home from jobs in the city to visit? What are their kitchens like? What do they do with the chestnuts? Or make of all the pilgrims? Mostly though, I will wonder, are they happy? Am I? It will occur to me again that I was deeply happy while walking in Spain.

A little further along the trail, we run into Dacia and David, who have stopped to admire a pair of fantastic donkeys. All four of them, peregrinos y burros, pilgrims and donkeys, are braying at each other loudly over the fence. They all seem to be enjoying this conversation immensely. We join in and fuss loudly over the donkeys, who are utterly delightful.

All afternoon we walk through forests interspersed with tiny villages — Barbadelo, Rente, Baxan, Cruce, Peruscallo, Cortiñas, Lavandeira, (Spanish for laundry), and A Brea, where a signpost tells us we are now one hundred kilometres shy of Santiago. A breeze, I think to myself. I'll be there easily, within four days.

Petra and I press on, arriving in the small village of Ferreiros (meaning blacksmiths), population twenty-seven, at around five o'clock. We inquire about albergues in the local bar, which seems to be the mainstay of the village, and are told there are two options: one private and very modern hostel and a small, older municipal one. Petra makes the call and chooses the older municipal albergue, just down the hill. The woman tending the bar makes a phone call and tells us that someone will meet us there in five minutes. When we arrive there is no one around.

Two minutes later the same woman who was working in the bar arrives and checks us in. There's one big room, and we appear to be alone here (hurray!) and have our choice of beds, so we pick two in a corner, away from the bathrooms — the usual strategy. While I'm setting up my gear, Petra checks out the sparsely equipped kitchen and rummages through her backpack, pulling out bread and cheese and an apple. She has cooked almost every single meal she has eaten on the Camino. Between the eclectic leftover supplies in the kitchen cabinets—some pasta, a small bag of short-grain rice, a quarter-full bottle of olive oil, a small tin of tomato paste, three onions, a package of dried soup, a couple of stock cubes, some garlic, salt and pepper, a few odds and ends of spices, and the supplies that we are both carrying—surely we have the makings of a meal. I've got my standard rations with me—chorizo, chocolate, and an orange. With a bit of imagination, we definitely have the ingredients for some sort of dinner. First we think we'll make pasta and use the tomato sauce, garlic, onion, and my chorizo. But then we open the fridge and find a small carton with two eggs in it and a small package of bacon with four, fat streaky rashers remaining. There's a note, dated from this morning. *Dear Pilgrim*, it reads. *Please feel free to use me up or throw me out. We bought more than we needed! ¡Buen Camino!*

Suddenly, I'm inspired. "Bacon and egg paella!" I call out to Petra. "We've got everything we need for bacon and egg paella!" We set to, frying the bacon and chorizo, and then removing it from the pan and throwing in the onion and garlic and olive oil, the spices, adding the ingredients in layers, caramelizing everything. Then comes the tomato paste. We're making sofrito—the underpinning to so many Spanish dishes. After we cook this down for several minutes, we season it all again, and add the rice and stock and turn the heat down. The aroma fills the kitchen, and we keep leaving just so we can walk back into the kitchen and smell it all over again.

With the paella nearly ready, we break the eggs over the rice and leave them to cook while we set the table in the dining room off to the side. Just as we've dished up our dinner and started to tuck in, the bartender arrives again, this time bringing us two young Spanish men. They sniff about appreciatively while we apologize for not having known that they were coming and offer them what remains in the pan. They are not worried and tell us that they are heading back to the bar to find food and drinks.

After we clean up our dinner dishes and tidy the kitchen, we also head back to the bar to use the free wi-fi and have a glass of wine. The Spanish guys are sitting at an outdoor table, drinking. I'm slightly nervous. They are young and seem kind of tough, and I'm worried that they plan to get drunk. After a bit they come indoors and order little green shots. Petra asks them what they're drinking, and they pass their glasses down to us, inviting us to try their drinks—orujo de hierbas, basically Spain's version of grappa, made from the residue of pressed grapes. It seems so intimate to drink from the same glasses. I'm not sure I should. What about the germs? Without a word, Petra takes her finger, dips it in the alcohol and swabs the rim of the glass all the way round. Then she takes a long, slow sip and puts the glass down, smiling broadly. I follow her lead, cautiously. "¡Wow, delicioso! Gracias," I say, passing the glass back.

"No, no, please, you enjoy!" says the taller, sterner looking of the two men, graciously and in English. They are clearly getting ready to go. "Enough for us now. Lock the door when you come in. Sleep well. ¡Buenas noches!"

Petra and I raise the glasses and finish the shots. The cold oruju goes down easily and feels surprisingly warm in my throat. It is sweet, slightly medicinal, and tastes herbal, a little floral, with hints of chamomile, mint, lemon, and honey. It seems familiar and yet not. Like drinking a sunlit autumn meadow. Like drinking Spain.

The dark closing in, we head back down the hill to our albergue, where the men have left the outside light on for us. We enter and find them already in their beds. Everything is quiet and calm and tidy. Shortly after, we turn the lights off and hit the sack ourselves. In bed, using the light of my phone, I make a quick note in my journal:

October 31—Halloween! Samos to Sarria to Ferreiros ~35.4 km
Breakfast with Jeffrey in Samos
Reunited with my kit of treasures and met Olga the loving hospitalero in Sarria
Some fabulous donkeys
Deeply lush, green, earthy, beautiful Galician landscape continues
Chestnut pickers
Petra
Bacon and egg paella
Two good Spanish men and some Orujo de Hierbas
Happy!

PAELLA

There were a number of dishes I didn't expect to try in Spain because of my allergy to peppers, especially bell peppers. Paella was one of them. Padrón peppers, the famous Spanish tapa, was another. I had to be careful with soups and stews, too. I knew the only way I could eat paella was if I made it myself, but even then, bell peppers seem to have become such an integral part of the dish that I wasn't sure if a paella made without them really qualified.

The origins of paella can be traced back to 330 BCE, when Alexander the Great first brought rice to Europe. It was sometime later, when Arab immigration to Spain brought the latest agricultural knowledge, including new cultivation and irrigation techniques, that rice dishes started to become more commonplace. But paella, as we know it now, is a much more recent dish, developed in Valencia in the mid-1800s.

In 2021, the government of Valencia—the region of Spain where paella originated—released an eight-page document eulogizing the history and virtues of paella. Incidentally, the name paella refers to the pan in which the dish is cooked and not the actual ingredients. The document declared paella "an item of cultural significance," on the grounds that a proper paella celebrates the "art of unity and sharing." This idea of sharing food—and not just any food, but food made with so much love, care, time, and attention to detail—strikes me as what makes Spanish cuisine so extraordinary.

Miguel Perez, of the Visit Valencia Tourism Board, announced that Valenica was not opposed to other paella recipes and invited chefs to create their own versions. Perez noted that an Irish chef had even created an exceptionally tasty paella with oysters and Guinness. Apparently, the Spanish tolerance for various forms of paella has moved on since Jamie Oliver's "Paella-Gate" incident in 2016. Oliver's version of paella combined chorizo and chicken thighs. It was the chorizo that caused all the issues—according to the Wikipaella website,[23] paella is made with white rice, green vegetables, rabbit, chicken, duck, snails, beans, and seasoning.

When I looked up the Irish chef's Guinness and oyster recipe, I noted there were no rabbits, chicken, duck, snails, or beans. It was all the licence I needed to go ahead and make paella from whatever I had on hand, and to be sure to do it slowly, lovingly, and with great care. Food, after all, like most everything else, evolves.

Bacon and Egg Paella

This recipe is easily doubled or tripled provided you have a big enough pan. When I make this at home, I double the recipe.

Serves 2

2 slices thick cut bacon, cut into 2.5 cm (approx. 1 inch) pieces

125 g (4 ½ oz) chorizo, chopped into bite size pieces

30 mL (2 tbsp) olive oil

1 small yellow onion, finely chopped

2-3 cloves garlic, minced

1 tsp paprika

½ tsp cayenne pepper

Salt and pepper

156 mL (5 ½ oz) can tomato paste

200 g (1 cup) short grain rice such as Spanish Bomba or Italian Arborio

475 mL (2 cups) stock (and more if needed)

Small pinch of saffron strands, crushed (optional)

2 eggs

Begin by cooking the bacon. As it browns, add the chopped chorizo and let it brown on both sides. Cook until the bacon is crispy. Remove the meats from the pan and set aside but leave any remaining fat in the pan. (Paella is a one-pan dish.)

Add a tablespoon or so of olive oil to the pan (more if the bacon fat is sparse) and make the sofrito base—add the onion and cook for a good 5 minutes, then add the garlic and cook for another couple of minutes, finally add the paprika, cayenne, and a couple of good grinds (or pinches) of salt and pepper. Give the spices a minute or two to release their flavours. Lastly, add the tomato paste and stir well.

Add the remaining tablespoon of olive oil and the rice, stirring until the rice is coated. Allow this mixture to cook for about 5 minutes on medium-low heat. In the meantime, if you're using saffron strands, add them to the stock and allow this to steep while the rice cooks undistributed for the full 5 minutes.

Stir in the stock. Check the seasonings, add more salt if needed. Turn the heat down another notch and allow the paella to cook, uncovered and undisturbed, for 12 to 15 minutes. Check to make sure the rice is not looking dried out. If it is, add more stock (or water) ¼ cup at a time. Don't stir the rice, just distribute the liquid evenly over the top of the paella. The rice should not be wet, but neither should it be dried out. A good paella forms a crispy, golden, caramelized crust on the bottom—this is called the socarrat.

Towards the end of the 12 to 15 minute cooking time, check to make sure the rice is tender. If not, continue cooking for another 5 minutes or so, adding more stock or water if necessary and checking the consistency of the rice before proceeding. Once the rice is tender, use a ladle or spoon to make two depressions in the surface of the rice. Break an egg into each depression. Cover the pan with a lid or foil and continue to cook until the eggs are sufficiently set—this may take longer than you expect, allow at least 8 to 10 minutes.

Once the eggs reach the desired stage, add the bacon and chorizo to the top of the paella and, if available, garnish with a little fresh parsley. For the full paella experience, bring the pan to the table and serve straight out of it.

A few olives and a little spicy mayo make excellent additions.

CHAPTER TWENTY-SIX

Ferreiros to Palas de Rei
November 1, All Saints' Day

"I am not afraid...I was born to do this." —Joan of Arc

As we sleep, October folds gently into November. Our new month begins in the bar, where we've come to find coffee and breakfast. The very idea of this feels so different from my everyday life, and yet at the same time, now it seems so normal. Our server is yesterday's bartender, the same woman who appears to run almost everything in this tiny village. I can't help but marvel at both her efficiency and her long hours.

Petra and I order strong coffee and slices of Torta de Santiago—the iconic and sublime Galician cake made from ground almonds, eggs, sugar, lemon zest, and sometimes a dash of brandy or sweet wine. It's a true European cake—a single layer, dense, packed with flavour, not overly sweet. Outside of Galicia, Torta de Santiago is usually known as Tarta de Santiago. The top of the cake is marked in icing sugar with the cruz de Santiago (cross of Saint James)—a hybrid between a sword and cross. The cake is easily one of the most delicious things I've ever eaten, anywhere, anytime. We contemplate asking for seconds, but our server is frantically busy, and we have a long day ahead of us, so reluctantly we take our leave. Our destination is Palas de Rei, thirty-five kilometres down the trail. Petra and I have a plan to walk together today, as she is an excellent walking companion, and we walk at a similar pace.

Even though Petra is walking with me today, I have taken to not committing to any plans for beyond a day. It is wonderful to have the right company, but a large part of my reason for walking the Camino still remains unresolved. I still want to forge a clearer vision of what I am trying to do with my life, where I am heading, what matters. All of this is so much harder to do when talking to someone else, no matter how fabulous they might be. It's a balancing act, and I feel as though I am constantly trying to find the intersection between loneliness and company.

Today is All Saints' Day, an important national public holiday, known in Spain as El Día de Todos los Santos. By all accounts, the entire population of the country is on the move as they return to their hometowns and villages to visit the gravesites of relatives. The day is marked by feasting, with a couple of dishes of particular importance being roasted chestnuts (castañas); small marzipan cakes known as pannellets; huesos de santo (saint's bones); and buñuelos de viento—light-as-air fritters often filled with custard, chocolate, and cream. According to folklore, the buñuelos de viento are so ethereal that eating them will release a soul from purgatory—deliverance by deliciousness.

Out on the trail, there's no discernible uptick in the number of pilgrims, despite the fact that we are now walking the most heavily travelled part of the Camino. I attribute the sparseness of pilgrims to the fact that we are walking so late in the season, and also due to having once again abandoned walking the traditional stages recommended by most of the major guidebooks. Either way, the path is mostly empty today and Petra and I are making excellent time and enjoying the woodlands, the hamlets, and the gently descending path.

By mid-morning, we're approaching the impressively long and elevated modern bridge suspended high above the river Miño. It leads into Portomarín, population 2,008, a place that has long been an important stop along the Camino. The history of Portomarín is a tale of two cities: the medieval city of Portomarín and the present day Portomarín. The old city once sat nestled on the riverbanks far below, at the foot of a Roman bridge, built in the second century. But in the 1960s, when the river was dammed in order to construct a new reservoir, the present-day city of Portomarín was moved to its new location, high upon a steep hill, well above its former site. Most of the old historically significant buildings were moved brick by brick and stone by stone to their new, elevated location. The husks of the medieval village—the old footings of the ancient buildings, and the old original bridge—live on below, sometimes but not always submerged, according to seasonal water levels.

As we approach Portomarín from atop the long, high bridge, the sky above is clear and blue. The sun is shining. But the entire vast river valley in front of us and below us, including the bank where the old city once was, is blanketed in thick, impenetrable, swirling white mist. Almost across the bridge, I pause briefly to take in the view. Below me, the mist parts briefly, and for one moment I have the shortest glance of the partially submerged crumbling ruins of the old city before everything disappears into the mist again. I stand still, momentarily stunned by the fleeting glance into the past—a swirling, slightly dizzying, watery window into a lost and distant time. Above the mist, high on the far side of the river, we see the new city, glinting, like Jerusalem—mystical and bathed in golden sunlight.

Portomarín is home to the twelfth-century church of San Xoán (Saint John), designed to be both a church and a castle. It's too soon to stop, so we skip visiting it, and also skip a snack of the town's traditional dishes of fried eels and eel empanadas. We are neither hungry nor ready to eat, and we still have twenty-five kilometres ahead of us, so we carry on past. ¡Ultreya! (Onwards!). "Next Camino," I say to myself, as if it's a refrain. I'll definitely try the eel empanadas next time!

All afternoon Petra and I walk, walk, and walk. Finally, we stop briefly at a café in Eirexe, a mere speck of a place that seems to consist only of a single building. We're hoping for a short break—a drink for Petra and a helado (ice cream) for me. I'd been longing for ice cream for days, possibly weeks. Fixated on the idea. But all my quests have turned up empty handed. I looked en route to O Cebreiro and was told, "No helado." I'm sure I was told much more, too, but all I heard was, "No ice cream." I came out with some chocolate instead, but I didn't actually want it. I stuffed it in my pack as part of my ongoing emergency rations. I've stopped elsewhere, too, once at a store with an A-frame metal ice cream sign placed right out front on the sidewalk. It showed images of a variety of packaged ice cream confections. I studied the sign for ages and selected something that looked like a salted caramel drumstick. But when I ventured into the store, they were all out of ice cream and had been since summer ended, months ago. I've inquired in grocery stores, too, but unless I wanted to buy an entire carton, I was out of luck.

Here in the café in tiny Eirexe, I finally find my fix in the form of a pre-fab ice-cream cornetto. Petra orders a beer. We sit in the sunshine at an outdoor table in the lovely and still leafy green garden, where we also find Will, from London. He's drinking red wine. Though I've only encountered him a few times, I've never seen him without a glass of red. He's his usual self-deprecating, cranky, funny, charming, and brutally honest self. He tells us he hates people. "All people? Even us?" I ask. "Not especially so," he answers, making me smile. He hates the Camino, too, he adds. Is sick to death of it, but won't give up. This makes me laugh out loud. "Good for you, Will, there's the spirit," I say. He tells us that when he finishes, he's moving to New York to join his girlfriend (or perhaps she's his fiancée or wife—the first we've heard of her), who has something to do with the movie or television industry. He was thinking of walking further this afternoon, but now he thinks he'll stop right here and order more wine and stay the night. "Why not?" he asks. "Why go on?" Oh yes, the sixty-four-million-dollar question. Why do any of us go on, ever? At least this is a beautiful spot. He can't really go far wrong whether he stays or continues on. We leave him with his wine, intent on our own journeys, delighted and strangely uplifted to have seen him again. Despite his gruff exterior, he's so utterly likeable.

We arrive in Palais de Rei at five in the afternoon, armed with a plan hatched by Petra: 1) Find a bank machine, 2) Get a quick glass of wine in a nice bar, 3) Book into an albergue for the night, 4) Make another dinner in the albergue kitchen. It's a fine plan. I'm all in.

In a small glass-fronted bar, with a bank machine close by, a pretty young Spanish woman serves me a large glass of perfect, smooth Godello—my new favourite white. Godello grapes originated in Northern Spain, in Galicia, and are also grown in Portugal. The wine has a lovely round, smooth feel to it and, according to the server, has hints of quince, pear, and peach, although what I notice most is that this wine is almost creamy—a silky smooth wine that slides too far too easily. Incredibly, my glass costs only a single euro.

We'd stay longer and drink another, but next is the all-important task of finding accommodation. Petra has her sights set on the modern, private albergue San Marcos, so we walk back through town, stopping on the way to buy a few groceries, and then head into the albergue, to inquire. The place is really busy. Packed in fact. But miraculously, they have two twin beds left, in a private room, up in the loft. Same price as the dorms. Will that work for us? "Si, claro!" Yes, yes, my goodness, of course it will! Please and thank you so very, very much. Our room is perfect. Light, bright, unexpectedly private, safe, quiet, and absolutely immaculate. We hit the showers and then unpack before heading to the communal kitchen, where Petra insists on making dinner for us—scrambled eggs, chorizo, and good Spanish bread.

Later, snug and comfortable in our nest in the loft, the lights dimmed, we listen to the happy ruckus of the pilgrims on the floors below us echoing through the building before all finally goes dark and quiet.

Just two more sleeps until Santiago de Compostela. I'm so close now that I'm like a child waiting for Christmas—the last days before are always the longest. I haven't been this excited for years.

Before drifting off, I write more cryptic notes in my journal:

November 1—All Saints Day Ferreiros to Palas de Rei 35 km

Breakfast of strong coffee and Torta de Santiago. Sublime!

Walking with Petra

Portomarin—the old and the new

Will, again, with a glass of red and gallons of attitude

Palas de Rei—and the most beautiful glass of Godello

A surprise private room in the loft

Dinner by Petra

Grateful and so excited!

Torta (or Tarta) de Santiago

Torta de Santiago is a Galician specialty. Elsewhere in Spain and around the world, it is typically known as Tarta de Santiago—a thin, European-style, gluten-free almond cake that has been made since the Middle Ages.

Spain is one of the world's biggest almond producers and exporters. Almond trees have flourished in Spain since as early as 600 CE, providing an invaluable, easily stored source of protein. Almond milk has been in existence since the Middle Ages, and there is compelling evidence that almond milk has been used as an alternative to dairy (especially during Lent) since then.[24]

This cake is typically served marked with the Cross of Saint James (find templates online). This beautiful, simple, intensely flavourful cake improves with age, so make it a day or two ahead if possible.

Serves 6–8

4 large eggs

200 g (1 cup) white sugar

150 g (1½ cups) finely ground almonds or almond flour
15 g (2 tbsp) regular all-purpose flour or rice flour
Grated zest of 1 lemon
15-24 g (2–3 tbsp) icing sugar to decorate

Preheat the oven to 175° C (350°F).

Liberally grease a 23 cm (9 inch) springform pan (in addition, you can line the pan with parchment paper although this step is not absolutely necessary).

Beat the eggs with an electric mixer for a minute or so, then add the sugar and beat until fluffy—another minute or so.

Using a spoon, stir in the finely ground almonds and flour, along with the lemon zest. Fold gently to combine the ingredients.

Using a spatula, scrape the batter evenly into the prepared pan.

Bake for about 30 minutes or until browned. Check to see if the cake is done by pressing the top of the cake gently. If it springs back, the cake it is done. If an indentation remains, return the cake to the oven for another 2 to 3 minutes. Repeat if necessary. It may need a further 5 minutes, but don't overcook the cake and dry it out. Place the cake on a cooling rack and leave to completely cool.

If using a Cross of Saint James template (found online), place the template in the centre of the cooled cake. Using a small sieve, sprinkle with icing sugar and carefully remove the template.

Slice the cake in thin wedges and serve it just as it is, or with whipped cream.

CHAPTER TWENTY-SEVEN

Palas de Rei to Arzúa

November 2

"How many loved your moments of glad grace.
And loved your beauty with love false or true;
But one man loved the pilgrim soul in you;
And loved the sorrows of your changing face."
—William Butler Yeats, *The Countess Kathleen and
Various Legends and Lyrics*

Several times during the night I wake myself up coughing again. I thought all this was behind me, but it seems to be back with a bit of an alarming vengeance. I'm worried I've kept Petra awake and feel bad. In the morning, she waves me off but says she's concerned for me. I'm a bit concerned, too, as I thought I'd managed to walk off this beast of a bug.

There's a large crowd of pilgrims and a lively breakfast scene going on in the basement of the albergue. For three euros each, we dine on croissants, orange juice, and coffee, and plan our day ahead. We both want to walk solo so that we can each spend the day sorting through our own thoughts, but plan to meet again at the end of the day, in Ribadiso, at a famous albergue along the banks of the river Iso. It is located in one of the oldest pilgrim hospitals along the route, and is, by all accounts, a wonderful spot to stop.

The walk today, if all goes according to plan, is a relatively easy twenty-six-and-a-half kilometres. For a good part of the morning, I'm walking on narrow dirt paths flanked by woodlands of oaks, poplars, and eucalyptus trees. By noon, I head into Melide, and I run into Donna, the American woman I met way back in Sahagún towards the end of the Meseta. I'm thrilled to see her again but wonder how she got ahead of me. It turns out that she suffered a leg injury and so has been walking bits and pieces but otherwise using public transportation, more or less keeping to the daily program with the help of taxis, buses, and trains. She is in remarkably good spirits—just as she was when I left her back in León.

Within minutes we're planning lunch together. Donna has found a highly rated restaurant, Casa Alongos, that serves both vegan food (for her), and pulpo (Galician for octopus), the local specialty, for me. I didn't want to miss trying pulpo, at least just this once. I'm worried about Donna's reaction to me eating pulpo. I'm also a bit worried about my own reaction to eating an animal as intelligent and evolved as an octopus.

I remember that my father drew the line at eating donkey meat. He'd worked on a farm as a young English boy and found the donkeys to be unbelievably intelligent. He'd felt that they understood language and emotions. And then, decades on, in France, he had eaten an unknown sausage, and when he found out later that it was donkey meat, he felt ill and heartbroken. I was touched that my gruff, very "stiff-upper-lip" English father turned out to have such a loyal heart. And yet, he had always been happy enough to eat pork sausages. In fact, he loved sausages. Especially blood sausage, which also happens to be tremendously popular in Spain.

I voice my concern about eating pulpo to Donna, who says, "You're here, you love food, maybe this is the only time you'll ever try it—go ahead!" So, I go ahead and order the pulpo and at the same time admit that vegetarianism and veganism are so much more ethical, and that even if I don't give up meat entirely, I'll move further in that direction. When it arrives though, the pulpo is sublime. Sweet, tender, and astonishingly delicious. And even though I'm worried about Donna's reaction to my eating it, she passes no judgement and never even flinches.

Donna isn't going any further today. She's staying put in town. While we're at lunch, she asks me when I expect to get to Santiago and where I'm staying, so I give her the name of my hotel, and she says she'll make a booking and see me there in a couple of days.

Before I leave the restaurant, I head to the bathroom. It's a huge, clean spacious, single-use facility. What a treat after so many less than pristine public bathrooms. I am only just a minute or so in the room when the lights go off, and the room is plunged into absolute darkness. I cannot see a single thing. I wait for my eyes to adjust to the dark, but it is absolutely pitch black and remains that way. I walk slowly and cautiously—arms outstretched like a zombie, taking baby steps across the room, hoping to find a light switch. Finally, I reach the wall and run my hands up and down, and back and forth, feeling in vain for a light switch. Then I try to find a door handle. For a few minutes, I struggle in the dark, not finding anything. Then I finally locate a bolt and manage to open the door. This reactivates the light, so I rush back to flush the toilet and quickly head to the sink to lather up my hands and arms, which have been all over the bathroom walls trying to find the door handle, before once again being plunged back in complete black. The lights are obviously on a timer, and the timer appears to last less than a minute. I ponder this. The incredible ridiculousness of the situation—of being caught with my pants down in the absolute pitch black in a completely unfamiliar space. I wonder how many others have been trapped in the dark and left groping the bathroom walls after being plunged into darkness. This isn't the first such experience I'd had of being trapped in a dark bathroom, either. I had a similar adventure in a bathroom back in Sarria, but at least there, the tiniest crack of light came in below the door, so that when my eyes finally adjusted, I could find my way without having to grope up and down walls.

Alone again on the path, all afternoon I walk through forests and small villages, cross bridges, and pass churches, arriving in Ribadiso around four o'clock. I walk into the grounds of the albergue and look around but see no one. Not a single person. I don't see any sign of Petra, nor of an office. I approach one of several small buildings, but the door is locked. I approach another and call out—but once again, there is absolutely no one around. Unless I am missing something, the place appears to be either closed or abandoned. In the end, I turn around, take my leave, and walk on another few kilometres, to the next village, Arzúa, regretting every step of the way. I should have stayed. I should have looked harder for Petra. I should have waited. Should have. Could have. Would have. Didn't. Serves me right, I think to myself.

This unexpected final stretch of the day feels longer than it should. I recognize that I am bearing down on the end of my walk, of my time in Spain. Suddenly, I feel quite sad, terribly alone, and surprisingly lonely. I'm so disappointed that I didn't find Petra as per our plan. We were such easy companions, and I loved the time we spent both walking and cooking meals together. For the very first time, I find myself starting to look forward to finishing the walk and going home.

In Arzúa, population 6,300, I head straight to the municipal albergue, pay my fee, and am assigned a bed number. When I find the bed, it is once again an upper bunk, in the middle of a long wall of bunks. The place is packed. No one says hello. No one says anything. No one is speaking English. I look at the bed and turn around. I walk straight back to the desk and tell the woman who checked me in that I would like my money back. Surprisingly enough, she says nothing, but reaches in her cash box and hands my money straight back over. I did not expect the transaction to be quite so easy. I expected a fuss, words I didn't understand. A rebuttal. But there is nothing except the cold hard cash in my hand.

I have no idea what to do next. I wander the streets for a bit, trying to find another possibility for a place to stay without any luck at all. I contemplate walking back to Ribadiso, but night is starting to draw in, and I've already walked thirty-plus kilometres, so backtracking just feels impossible. It seems there are so few options in this odd little town. Then I spy a tourism office, where I ask a woman behind the counter to help me find a private room for the night. She makes a call, and then holds her hand over the phone while she tells me there's a room at a pensión and tells me the price. It's nearly five times the cost of a bed in the albergue, but I cannot spend any more time wandering around Arzúa in the dark, looking for somewhere else to stay. I hand over my Visa and seal the deal. Minutes later, she sends me off with an address and an access code for entry. I have no idea where I'm going. When I finally find the place, it's a regular house with a couple of rooms allocated for guests. No one else appears to be staying here, not even the owners. Oddly, I am completely alone in someone else's house. It's frigidly cold and miserable and expensive. I pick a room and head back out to find a grocery store, where I buy myself a can of lemonade, a chorizo sandwich, a small bag of potato chips, some chocolate, and, for breakfast in the morning, an apple and a croissant. Just as I am about to check out, I notice cans of beer for thirty-five cents and add a can of beer to my meagre groceries. I return to the pensión and write in my journal and eat my dinner—the highlight of which is the shandy that I make with my beer and lemonade. What a mercy that I stopped for a proper meal in Melide. Lunchtime already seems so long ago, almost like a different era. And how strange it feels all alone, in this house, after weeks of dorms and shared rooms. I wonder who, if anyone, lives here and if so, where they are. Or who else might come through the door at any point.

All night long, a flickering red fluorescent exit sign flashes above my door. At one point, I move to another vacant room to get away from the light. But then I lie awake and worry that the owner might find me here in a room that I have not been assigned and charge me for both rooms, so I scurry back to my original room. The room is damper and colder than ever, and the flickering exit light pierces through my eyelids, through the sheet and blankets I pull over my head. Eventually I get up and find my fleece hat and pull it down over my eyes—but the light penetrates everything. It's been a day of lighting extremes—from pitch black bathrooms to bedrooms where the lights simply won't quit. Finally, at about three o'clock in the morning, having not slept at all, I start to cough. A deep, wracking, painful cough. I cough and cough and cough. And then, with the horrible fluorescent light still madly flashing and flickering above me, my body wracked and sore from coughing, cold and exhausted, my throat hoarse, I start to cry. And I cry and cry and cry, until like a baby, I cry myself to sleep.

UNA CLARA

I'd been in Spain for long enough that I was starting to be able to pick out more and more individual words, especially words that related to food and drinks. Several times, I'd been in restaurants and bars where groups of older men were drinking coffee or rounds of beer. I'd hear the term "clara" bandied around. When I looked it up, I was intrigued to learn it was the equivalent of an English shandy.

If you order "una Clara" in Spain, the bartender or waitstaff may ask, "de casera?" If you like the less sweet version, you might answer, "Si, de casera, por favor." And if you prefer your clara made with sweeter fizzy lemonade, you can answer, "No, una Clara con limón, por favor."

Clara

1 part beer to **1 part** gaseoso (soda, in Spain they use la
casera, which is similar to fizzy lemonade but less sweet)

Clara con Limón

1 part beer to **1 part** part lemon-flavoured soda (ginger ale
works too)

CHAPTER TWENTY-EIGHT

Arzúa to O Pedrouzo

November 3

"What makes night within us may leave stars."
—Victor Hugo, *Ninety-Three*

The day breaks clear, and I wake with a start, feeling determined not to have a repeat episode of last night. I give myself a little pep talk. "After all, there's meant to be suffering in pilgrimage," I say, aloud. I remind myself that whatever I've experienced has been so incredibly minor that it doesn't even count. And then I remember that so many of our greatest moments are preceded by helplessness or despair. And that sometimes going mad and finding sanity look the same. "Get up," I tell myself. *"Just get up.* Get up and start again. *Soldier on."* It's as though my tough-talking father has come along with me on this walk. I can imagine him saying, "You need to give yourself a *right good talking to."*

I pack my gear and walk back into the main strip of Arzúa, searching for a bar or café for a cup of coffee and possibly breakfast. Little is open so early, but I spy a bar and enter. I'm the only customer in the place and find a seat by the window, my back to anyone else who might come in. I'm too dishevelled and distraught for company. A young Spanish woman brings me my café con leche. Moments later she's back—with a large slice of cake. "Sin cargo," (no charge) she says, as she puts the cake down for me. "Mil gracias, muy amable" (a thousand thanks, very kind), I say, gratefully and vaguely tearful. She reaches out, touches my hand briefly, barely.

How could she know? How could she know how much I needed this bit of kindness, this small gesture of care that feels so huge? I fight a flood of tears, a total breakdown. I'm suddenly acutely lonely and homesick and exhausted. I'm simultaneously dreading finishing the Camino and at the same time desperate to be done. I'm also worried about my cough, which is back with a vengeance. Pull yourself together, I order myself again, silently, sternly. Shades of my father.

Over coffee and cake (which reminds me of Spanish Bar Cake, a childhood favourite sold long ago by a popular grocery store chain in Canada), I study the map, desperate to make some sort of plan. This is my final full day of walking. If I think it through, plan it properly, I should be able to walk into Santiago de Compostela by noon or early afternoon tomorrow, where I've booked what I hope is a lovely hotel, for four nights. And with any luck Donna will be there, too, with a room of her own.

I plan to stay the night just this side of Santiago. According to my guide-book, there are very few options after O Pedrouzo, and not wanting a repeat of last night, I decide I'll stop earlier rather than later. Plan as I might though, I know I'm only ever just stabbing in the dark. Hostels may be full. Or awful. I may have to walk on. And I may walk on even when it makes no sense. I seem prone to such behaviour. But the one thing I do not want to do is walk lonely and alone into Santiago de Compostela.

Though I've been fine by myself for the most part, last night was a miserable exception. Perhaps I am just ready for the end of my time on the trail. Ready to resume my life in Canada. See my family, my beautiful daughters, my friends, my home, my beloved dog.

I set off, leaving Arzúa behind, walking along a tree-lined trail that passes through forest of ancient oaks, across bridges, over small streams, through meadows and past villages of stone houses, stone walls, stone churches.

Along the way I notice a handsome couple whom I've seen before but not met. They are both tall, fit, and about my age. They have stopped to put on their rain gear when I walk up to them and introduce myself, uncertain if they speak English. They are not, as it turns out, a couple. They are friends. Joann is Canadian and lives a hop, skip, and jump from where I live. Gert is from South Africa but now lives in the United States. They met on their first day of the Camino and have walked more or less together ever since.

I'm sure they'd rather just walk on together, but when I tell them that I'm reluctant to walk into Santiago de Compostela alone and ask if they'd let me tag along with them at least for today, they graciously agree. They are headed to O Pedrouzo. My decision is cemented.

We stop for second breakfast at the Café Calzada. Rain is threatening, and we've had our rain gear on and off a few times, but it manages to hold off raining on us while we sit at an outdoor table with our coffees and sandwiches. I'm eating the leftover supermarket croissant that I stuffed into my pack before leaving my miserable, lonely pension early this morning.

It is not easy, I imagine, letting someone new barge in at this late stage of the game. And yet Gert and Joann are kind and accepting. I like them instinctively. They are well organized and know what they're doing. I appreciate that they're letting me join them, especially given that I'm a totally unknown quantity and that they are such a well-balanced team without me.

For most of the rest of the day we pass through forests of oaks, pines, and eucalyptus trees. Occasionally the sun breaks through, and shafts of light dance on the forest floor. I've noticed eucalyptus trees in various places along the Camino, but here in Galicia, they seem to be everywhere, fragrant and verdant. After all my years in Australia, I'm so familiar with these trees, but they seem strangely out of place here with their yellow gray or blue gray bark, amongst all the moss and rich shades of Galician green. Eucalyptus were introduced to Spain in 1863, and a century later, in the 1960s, with demand for paper and cardboard products increasing exponentially, great swathes of land were turned over to fast growing eucalyptus plantations. They are now the most planted hardwood trees in the world, but at great agricultural and ecological cost, depleting the soil, and deterring the growth of other native trees and plants.

By early afternoon we arrive in O Pedrouzo and book into the REM Hostel. Gert has done his research regarding accommodation, and apparently he's done it very well. The hostel is newish, clean, and incredibly well organized. Everything seems to be in perfect order. We pay, pick our beds (tucked in a corner, away from everything), and go through what are now well-rehearsed procedures: setting up our sleeping bags, unpacking, showering, washing clothes, etc. Later we head out to dinner at a local pizza bar just down the road. Again, Gert's research. Our two large pizzas—one seafood; one chorizo and olive—are fantastic. We order beer and wine, and it feels like a party—a fine and fitting final night on the Camino, a celebration of all that we have accomplished so far. We have done this. We have walked, trod, trundled, ambulated, coughed, snored, slept, and now we are nearly there, so close to the end.

By half past eight, we are back and tucked in our beds. There are all the usual albergue noises: people arriving, people setting up their beds, a group of Italians arriving with their bicycles, people showering, snoring, and moving around. The activities and noises no longer faze me. I'm safe and happy, grateful for the day's companionship and for the good food, and within seconds, I'm out like a light.

Tomorrow—Santiago de Compostela. Onwards!

Spanish Bar Cake with Burnt Butter Icing

This cake reminds me of a favourite cake from my childhood—a sweet, flavourful, and moist cinnamon and raisin cake with a glorious burnt butter icing.

For the cake
200 g (1 cup) raisins
118 mL (½ cup) boiling water
240 g (2 cups) all-purpose flour
290 g (1½ cups) white sugar
1½ tsp baking soda
1 tbsp cinnamon
1 tsp salt
125 mL (½ cup) oil (olive or canola)
2 large or extra-large eggs
375 g (1½ cups) unsweetened apple sauce

For the Burnt Butter Icing
85 g (6 tbsp) butter
195 g (1½ cups) icing sugar
45 mL (3 tbsp) cream or milk
2 tsp pure vanilla extract
¼ tsp salt

To make the cake: Preheat oven to 175°C (350°F).
Butter or grease a bundt cake or large tube cake pan, or a large loaf pan (21.6 × 11.4 × 6.35 cm or 8.5 × 4.5 × 2.5 in).

Place the raisins in a heat proof bowl and pour ½ cup boiling water over them. Set aside and let stand while you prep the rest of the cake.

In a large bowl, mix the flour, sugar, baking soda, cinnamon, and salt, making sure the cinnamon is thoroughly distributed evenly throughout the mixture.

Add the oil, eggs, and applesauce to the flour mixture, and mix well. Drain the raisins and stir them gently into the cake batter. Scrape the batter into the prepared cake pan.

Bake for 35–40 minutes or until the cake is done and the top bounces back slightly when pressed and a wooden skewer inserted in the cake comes out clean. Do not overcook this cake—it should be quite moist. Set the cooked cake aside to cool slightly while you prepare the icing.

To make the burnt butter icing: In a stainless-steel saucepan, melt the butter gently over medium heat, stirring constantly. Once the butter is melted, keep stirring, and set your timer for 8 minutes. The butter will foam slightly, this is normal. Keep stirring and eventually the butter will start to brown. Continue to stir until tiny brown flecks appear at the bottom of the pan and the butter has a caramelized, slightly nutty smell. The colour should be a deep golden-brown.

When it reaches this colour, remove the pan from the heat and allow the butter to cool for 5 minutes. Set the timer so that you don't lose track.

Once the timer goes off, stir in the icing sugar, milk or cream, vanilla, and salt. Whisk until thick and smooth, adjusting the consistency as necessary by either adding a little more cream or a little more icing sugar. Then pour the icing onto the cake and allow the icing to drizzle down the sides of the cake.

CHAPTER TWENTY-NINE

O Pedrouzo to Santiago de Compostela

November 4

"And to make an end is to make a beginning.
The end is where we start from." —T.S. Eliot, "Little Gidding"

The final day! Even after all these weeks of walking, and all the anticipation, it still seems impossible to be so close to the end. All I can think of is getting to Santiago de Compostela, about what it will be like to arrive at the end of this journey, and how fortunate I am to have made it this far. I am wondering how it will feel to finally land in this ancient, legendary city. A bit, I imagine, like Dorothy landing in Oz, like I might just wake up and discover that it was all just a dream.

It's raining, and then clearing briefly, and then pouring down again. A low, steel grey sky. All morning Gert, Joann, and I are taking our rain gear on and off as the sky clears momentarily, only then to put it back on again as the rain comes down in great theatrical deluges. I've had so little rain on my entire journey, so it only seems fitting that here, on my last day, in lush, verdant Galicia, I should experience the rain in Spain.

We walk, heads down through the rain. Through damp meadows and dense eucalyptus forests, before entering into suburban territory, some of the first we've seen along the Camino. We stop for breakfast in a small café and order tarta de manzana (apple tart) and coffees all round. Then onwards again, we tramp alongside busy roads, past road signs and graffiti, past the Santiago

Lavacolla airport, uphill to the Monte del Gozo (Hill of Joy). The Monte is so named because it is here, high on the hill, where pilgrims see for the first time the city of Santiago de Compostela and the spires of the famous cathedral. What we see, though, is impenetrable fog, intercepted only by rain.

On the final stretch into town the path travels alongside busy roads, over bridges, along sidewalks, and finally onto the city streets to the Plaza del Obradoiro—home of the magnificent, stunning Santiago de Compostela Archcathedral Basilica—the cathedral where the apostle Saint James the Great is reputed to be buried. We are here! We are actually here.

I have made it to the finish line.

Incredibly the sky clears, and a double rainbow hovers over the cathedral as we approach. A thousand cameras all around are snapping the miracle. I get out my phone, join the throngs, and take a picture or two, sheepishly, before putting my camera away. Gert, a seriously accomplished photographer, is busy taking photographs beside me.

The double rainbow lasts and lasts, lingering in the sky for what feels like hours. Groups of walkers keep arriving, and all of them take photographs—all of them delighting in the miracle in the sky. It seems like a symbol, but of what? Something divine? Something holy? I can't tear myself away. Looking at it all, and letting it sink in, I suddenly recall the words of Canadian poet and writer Bronwen Wallace: "If I had a god, I'd say we were holy and didn't know it."[25]

Perhaps I do. Perhaps I do have a god and faith. Perhaps in this moment, we are holy. Perhaps this feeling right here—this profound joy—is actually divine. Maybe it really is that simple.

Eventually we tear ourselves away from the rainbows over the cathedral and line up to get our Compostelas—the certificates that document our journeys. Afterwards we have a late lunch of bocadillo de calamares—Spain's brilliant sandwich stuffed to overflowing with fried calamari and garlic aioli, accompanied by beer. While we eat and drink, we make plans to find our accommodations. Gert will help us to find our hotel first, before setting off to find his own accommodation. Joann is going to share my double room for a couple of nights, and I'm grateful to have her quiet, thoughtful company.

Our room in the attic of a small boutique hotel is a soothing oasis with its huge windows in the slanted ceiling that open to look out across the terracotta rooftops of Santiago, and a huge, luxurious bathroom. But most of all, it is blissfully quiet and clean. And it is ours alone—after weeks and weeks of shared dorms and rickety bunk beds, the constant possible prospect and fear of bedbugs, not to mention dubious bathrooms shared with multitudes. By early evening, we've cleaned up as best we can given our limited array of clothes and footwear, and are heading back out under clear skies. Time to attend Mass at the cathedral before a celebratory dinner.

The three of us arrive in plenty of time to explore the cathedral. With its crypts and multiple facades, its libraries and archives, its chapels and towers and porticos and galleries, one could spend days exploring and still have more to learn about this place. The cathedral is massive and opulent and staggeringly beautiful. Construction began in 1075—the Romanesque era—and finished in 1211, though various renovations and reconstructions have been almost continuous ever since, and as a result the cathedral has elements of the Gothic and Baroque eras, amongst others. In 1985, UNESCO declared the Cathedral of Santiago de Compostela a World Heritage Site.

We've been forewarned not to expect the famous botafumeiro ceremony. The original purpose of the ceremony was quite literally to expunge the cathedral of the potent and undesirable stench of early pilgrims arriving in Santiago de Compostela. Many of them had walked for days or weeks without bathing. The function of the botafumeiro was to spread incense throughout the cathedral to disperse and eliminate the bad odours. This tradition arose in the eleventh century and has been in place ever since, despite the fact that most modern pilgrims don't arrive at the temple unclean or in need of fumigation. Now the ceremony is more a revered ritual, marking the long history of pilgrims making their way to Santiago de Compostela and to the cathedral.

The soaring costs make it far too expensive to offer the ceremony at every mass. There are the wages of the eight red-robed tiraboleiros—the men that are charged with swinging the massive incense censer—known as the botafumeiro (Galician for smoke-expeller). Plus, there's the incense itself, and the maintenance of the equipment, including the thurible—a massive man-sized, 1.6-metre tall censer said to be one of the biggest in the world—and the rope and pulley system, which was installed back in 1604, and no doubt there are also the insurance and electricity costs and more. So, unless someone is paying the five hundred euros required for the ceremony, we won't witness the theatrical spectacle. I'm not worried though; it's a thrilling enough finale to visit the grand cathedral—the finish line of the Camino—and attend a service in the huge and fabulously ornate cathedral.

We find seats amidst swirling rumours that a visiting delegation from overseas has paid for the botafumeiro ceremony. Our seats are directly under the trajectory of the massive swinging censer. I was completely unprepared for the powerful ceremony—the thundering organ music, the singing nuns, the eight red-robed handlers, the sheer staggering size of the censer, the botafumeiro itself flying above our heads dispensing clouds of incense, its incredible velocity, the massive arc it covers, the length of time involved, the grandeur, and the drama. A holy all-consuming spectacle that has been carried out here, in this cathedral, since the eleventh century. It is said that the great swinging censor symbolizes the true attitudes of believers. Most of us, myself included, seem awestruck. All of it takes me by thundering, fragrant storm.

Afterward, still reeling from the service in the cathedral and the flight of the botafumeiro, we head off to find a suitably celebratory place for dinner. Just near the cathedral we find a small, candlelit restaurant offering a special three-course pilgrims' menu, and we manage to get a table by the window. Outside, darkness is closing in, and the streetlights are slowly coming on, glinting like jewels in the dark. We order wine and the pilgrims' menu. Our first course is a Galician cod and raisin empanada. It's an interesting balance of strong sweet and savoury flavours, all intensified by being sealed and cooked in a soft pastry envelope. The main course is veal and braised vegetables. Much more subtle. The pacing of the menu both timewise and taste wise is a bit like the pacing of service in the cathedral—loud thundering crescendos followed by quiet contemplative moments—high drama followed by significant pauses.

Perhaps it's because I'm still thinking about the flight of the botafumeiro as it tore through the air just over our heads, and from the sound of the choir and thundering organ and the opulence of the cathedral, but I can't keep my focus entirely on the meal. I keep reliving the scene in the cathedral. It's not until our Torta de Santiago arrives that my attention is one hundred percent back and focused on the food. This dessert *is* Spain. It is the vast, beautiful, rugged landscape dished up on a plate, a taste I imagined back in my home kitchen in Canada. Even more specifically, it is Santiago de Compostela, named as it is for

Saint James the Apostle, or in Spanish, el apóstol Santiago. The main ingredients of the dessert are almonds, flour, sugar, eggs, lemon and sometimes sweet wine or brandy—all of which are grown and produced in Spain. The Torta de Santiago is outstandingly, unforgettably delicious.

I keep remembering that on top of everything else today—the food, the company, the swaths of swirling incense smoke that perfumed my clothes, the grandeur of the cathedral, the thundering music —tonight marks the culmination of the longest and greatest walk of my life. We lift our glasses, clink them together, congratulate each other. I give in to the sensory overload and just let the night wash over me. We are here, in beautiful Santiago de Compostela. We have done what we set out to do—walked one step at a time clear across Spain. Tonight we are celebrating the long walk. Nothing else matters.

Eventually we head out through the velvety dark night sky, back to our respective beds. On the way, we make plans to meet for breakfast after which we will head off to explore the famous, massive Saturday market—the Mercado de Abastos—where we will buy bread and cheese and pastries, and admire the incredible stands full of fresh fish and seafood, sausages, meat, flowers, and all of the wonderful produce of Spain.

I cannot imagine how I could ever be happier.

A TAPAS PARTY MENU

Tapas, also known as pintxos or pinchos—referring to festive bite-sized appetizers and snacks—are a way of life in Spain. The Spanish word pincho and Basque word pintxo both mean spike, used in this instance to refer to the wooden toothpick or skewer often used for serving and eating individual small portions of food usually accompanied by sangría, wine, or beer.

The terms pinxto (singular) or pintxos (plural) and pincho or pinchos are used in the northern region of Spain, especially in the Basque region, while elsewhere in Spain the terms tapa or tapas are commonly used.

Eating tapas is an important culinary and social activity in Spain. There is something wonderful about the diversity of delicious foods on offer, as well as the manageable bite-sized portions, that lends itself so well to socializing. Tapas need not be elaborate or complicated to be festive. Get creative with the presentation. Use small cupcake liners, small ramekins, ceramic Asian soup spoons, or small drinking glasses to serve items that require individual containers. Use wooden toothpicks or skewers for anything that can be speared.

Savoury Tapas

Empanadillas de la Reina (small empanadas) (p. 179)
Patatas Bravas (p. 203)
Chorizo al Vino Tinto (p. 90)
Espinacas con Garbanzos (p. 144)
Tortilla de Patatas served with aioli or spicy mayonnaise
    (p. 168)
Ensaladilla Ucraniana (p. 123)
Bocadillo de Chorizo y Queso, Tostado (p. 186)

Other easy additions to a tapas party

Skewered marinated artichokes with cubes of feta and small
    slices of sundried tomato
Gambas a la plancha
A variety of olives
Almonds, pistachios, roasted chestnuts

Sweets

Membrillo y Manchego Tapas (p. 153)
Natillas (p. 81)
Torta de Santiago (p. 247)
Spanish Bar Cake with Burnt Butter Icing (p. 258)
Turrón de Chocolate Blando (p. 60)

Drinks

Sangría or Tinto de Verano (p. 22)
Clara (Shandy) (p. 254)
A selection of juice, soft drinks, beer, and Spanish wines,
    including Cava (sparkling Spanish wine similar to
    Prosecco).

CHAPTER THIRTY

Homeward Bound

"There are a thousand ways to kneel and kiss the ground;
there are a thousand ways to go home again." —Rumi

I spent much of my time in Spain pounding down the Camino, walking back
in time through centuries, the sun rising behind me and setting before me. I
walked while I tried to figure out what I was doing with my life. It was a walk
I began in spirit years before I actually tackled it in person. I knew I needed to
walk, to navigate, to go forward, one foot in front of the other, because somehow
over the years, I'd lost my way. I'd lost any sense of belonging. I'd forgotten how
to be content, how to be happy and strong and grateful, how to navigate a life.

I never once expected to write about my experience. If I had, I might have
kept better, more systematic, and more strategic notes, taken more photographs, and maybe even have done interviews along the route. As it was, I kept
scant notes in the thinnest of Moleskine notebooks, where I recorded the barest
of details—where I'd walked from and to, the weather, what I ate, and sometimes the name of the wine I had with my dinner and the names of the people
I'd walked with. Those I remembered to ask wrote their names and addresses in
the back of my notebook. Sometimes I wrote cryptic notes about the gorgeous
landscape bathed in sunlight, or about the ancient churches and buildings. And
never once during my entire walk did I refer to the map on which, long before I
left for Spain, I'd painstakingly written in tiny letters all the details of things I
should not miss and the places I should stay.

As I walked, I kept thinking about both the outer physical journey and the
simultaneous inner journey—that expedition to the centre of the soul—no

matter how ridiculous or pretentious or contrived it sounded. The further I walked, the more I felt I was walking my way back to myself, reorganizing all the cells in my body, distilling myself to the barest bones, muscles, and nerves. And at the same time, I was internalizing the landscape, consuming it, committing it to memory.

When I finished the Camino, I had four glorious days in Santiago. Even though I had walked further than I ever had before to get to this city, I found myself walking as far in Santiago each day, as I had each day on the Camino itself. I didn't want to stop. I walked every street of the old city until I finally knew my way around it and could draw a map of the streets in my head. I toured the three-centuries-old Mercado de Abastos—Santiago's beautiful old food market. There I admired the aisles of stalls selling everything from chocolate to eels and octopus, long strings of sausages next to big baskets of chestnuts, beautifully elaborate and delicate pastries next to great hanging legs of Iberico ham, hundreds of varieties of cheese, including the local Galician specialty, Queso Tetilla—cheese formed in the shape of a female breast.

I ate in several glorious restaurants, attended services at the Cathedral every day but one, and witnessed three more botafumeiro ceremonies. I went back because of the service, and because I was in awe of the art, the architecture, the pomp, the history, the music, the language, the glory—all of it. It was powerful and beautiful and mesmerizing. I felt drawn there, compelled to go—a reverence for the reverent.

Later I ran into Guy, the Frenchman I had rebuffed along the way. I agreed to meet him for a breakfast of churros and hot chocolate. He'd met someone and was beaming with happiness. I was as happy for him as he was for himself. We parted as friends.

On my last full day in Spain, I took a bus trip to Finisterre, the dramatic, rock-bound peninsula on the west coast of Galicia—a place once thought to be the end of the earth. I walked through yet more ancient villages and scampered about on the dramatic rocks plunging steeply into the Atlantic Ocean. I watched as huge waves splashed and pounded as they made landfall.

As much as I was ready to go home, I never once wanted to leave the trail or Spain. I'd loved it all. Every wide open, heart-pounding moment; every single step of the route; every wind that ruffled my hair; every wildflower and spectacular mountain vista that made my spirits soar; every dinner with fellow pilgrims; every ancient village, and even, in hindsight, even the moments of anguish; the lost things, good and bad—a pair of Ray-Bans, three toenails, one eye shade for sleeping, a pen, a few pounds; the crowded and at times overwhelming albergues; the rickety bunk beds; the moments of feeling lost and scared and alone. All of it just served to reveal something better or make me stronger. I made peace with myself and with my past, I emerged fit and strong and happy, whole.

Then I tidied my beautiful hotel room, repacked my rucksack, and accidentally smashed my only souvenir, a lovely hand thrown pottery bowl I'd bought at the market in Santiago. I was uncharacteristically philosophical about its demise. One less thing to pack, I thought to myself.

I took the bus to the airport and flew from Santiago to Madrid and from Madrid to Paris, where I overnighted before flying home. On the final flight leg from Paris to Toronto, aboard the newest Dreamliner in Air Canada's fleet, I watched as Europe became smaller and smaller on the onscreen map. I landed in Toronto on a clear, cold, sunny November day. From Santiago de Compostela to Madrid to Paris and all the way back to Canada, I'd never had a smoother trip in all my life. From start to finish, all of it went like clockwork. Even in the chaotic Madrid airport, where the gates are not announced until just before boarding time, and all of the Spanish seem to be constantly running in all directions at once, I walked calmly to my gate and then watched out the window of the airplane as Madrid disappeared behind us. Oh Spain, I thought to myself, cómo te amo—how I love you.

Spain changed me. Opened up my heart, let me lay things to rest. I couldn't stop thinking about what made Spain so extraordinary, so special. It was too hard to name any one thing, because there is so much to Spain. It's a country that gives and gives and gives.

Spain is a monk, a monastery, a sunlit field of golden wheat stubble, an eleven-hundred-year-old church, a craggy mountain range, a Roman road, a lush, mossy, deeply green forest. It's a cobalt sky, a constant unexpected kindness, an old woman gathering chestnuts in her apron. A glorious ruin, a nun, a blessing, a cortado, an empanada, a donkey, an olive grove, a single, silken sip of white wine. And late at night high up in the mountains, lying atop an ancient stone wall under the Milky Way, it's a glimpse into a distant galaxy. Spain is a generous land of staggering contrasts, a country that is impossible to nail down.

It was only after I returned and thought deeply about how much the Camino and Spain had changed me that I wanted to write about my experience. I wanted to go back. I wanted to take better notes, delve into the reasons why so many people choose this particular journey, and explore all the many aspects and impacts of the long, slow walk.

I wanted to look more deeply into Camino culture and cuisine—stay in the places I'd missed the first time, learn more about the regional foods and wines along the route, eat the foods I hadn't had the chance to experience, and learn more about the incredibly rich, complex history of food in Spain. However, after walking twenty-five to thirty or more kilometres a day, I ate and drank whatever was readily available and in close proximity. I drank beautiful, inexpensive local wines. I mainlined chocolate daily, as though my life depended on it. And outside of developing pneumonia along the route (I was diagnosed after I arrived back in Canada)—I'd probably walked half the trail fighting it off—I'd rarely felt so well in my life. In all the many, many various places I ate, no one ever let me down—I always felt both heard and cared for and was never fed anything that made me even slightly uncomfortable. Quite simply, I loved the food of Spain.

And though I had been cooking my way through Spain before I left, I hadn't spent a lot of time researching the specific foods I'd find along the Camino Frances. Like most pilgrims, I learned as I went—probably the best way of all to learn. The more I learned, the more excited I became about Spanish cuisine. When I returned from the Camino, I started recreating the food I ate along the way, in my North American kitchen. Recipes, I believe, are tenacious living tributes to history and culture. They enhance our lives. But I also believe that recipes are like rivers; they flow, they change, they bend with the circumstances—according to the cook, the availability of ingredients, and even the ingredients themselves, which sometimes vary markedly between continents. That said, I was thrilled to discover good Spanish and Portuguese chorizo in my small Canadian town.

While I was walking, I thought a lot about the healing and deeply spiritual aspects of the Camino. Although the Camino has distinctly obvious religious origins and connotations, it was my understanding that most of the people I encountered along the Way were not walking the Camino for religious reasons.

And yet, I wondered, were the spiritual aspects a widespread and yet somehow unrecognized (almost covert) but fundamental aspect of the impact of the Camino for others, as they were for me? I wanted to know more about all of it. I spent a lot of time in churches while I was on the Camino and felt the presence of goodness and mercy far beyond the church walls. I stayed in convents and monasteries. Listened to endless church bells pealing. Watched nuns in full black habit picking up great cotton bags full of bread from the visiting bread vans in wonderful ancient villages. Saw priests walking about town and drinking coffee in bars. Read prayers posted at bus stops. Had my bar bill paid by a religious hospitalero in León. I ate bread and drank wine every day—a kind of perpetual eucharist. I thought hard about how the Spanish word for sky—cielo—was the same as their word for heaven and the simple, beautiful obvious connection between the two. And how, if we stop to think about it, the course of our lives on earth is just one long pilgrimage of one sort or another.

I am not particularly religious, but I did feel the presence of religion everywhere, not just in terms of the buildings, infrastructure, or actions of the faithful. This was not religion as dogma, but as a compass, one that points to goodness, kindness, and mercy. I felt reverence, faith, and a sense of the divine all around me. I felt the spiritual and healing aspects of the Camino most deeply when I was surrounded by mountains, but also on the wide open, sun shocked land of the Spanish Meseta—essentially anywhere where I was away from cities and villages, and often when I was alone.

Pilgrimage is about forward motion both in the physical self and also in the metaphysical self—about a communion of body, mind, place, and spirit. I found faith, too, not necessarily in the traditional religious sense, but faith in the universe, in humanity, in those I walked with, and an entirely new faith in myself. I began to see walking as a powerful form of prayer, a form of devotion that I could fully understand and appreciate.

Clocking up just over eight hundred kilometres walking across Spain, even taking into account the public transportation I'd resorted to on a couple of occasions, I felt something shift. A sense of strength, physical, mental, and spiritual, that I'd scarcely known before. A noticeable newfound belief in my own abilities, one that I could not simply ascribe to my body becoming stronger. I found a greater faith in myself and in humanity. I wondered how much all of that had to do with the physical strength I gained in walking every day, all day long, for so very many days. And how much, too, all the changes could be attributed to being outdoors; to being offline and away from the hypnotic whirlpool of mostly useless information on social media; instead, being physically connected to the earth. I also thought about all the care I'd received along the way, all the people who had helped me, the friends I'd made, and all the moments of grace and providence and generosity.

Ultimately, no matter the reason for walking, the walking itself is forward momentum, progression, medicine, meditation. I felt safer, calmer, more grounded. I found myself thinking at a steady five kilometres per hour. The idea excited me. It drove me onwards. After you walk far enough, there's a rhythm that forms, as though you've finally found your own natural frequency.

It was my connection with the ground, with the earth, with the very path itself that drew me on relentlessly, that I found so completely compelling. As Robert Macfarlane put it so beautifully, "For pilgrims walking the Camino, every footfall is doubled, landing at once on the actual road and also on the path of faith."[26] And what is faith, I reasoned with myself, if not belief in oneself, in others, in humanity in general?

I also found a sense of community that finally made my heart feel wide open. Even though I often elected to walk alone, I also walked in the presence of many others. I met countless wonderful people along my route—both other pilgrims and those tending to pilgrims.

There is a seriousness, sacredness, and sanctity to pilgrimage that I hadn't entirely reckoned on, though it became more and more obvious to me as I walked. By the time I finished my walk, I was inhabited by the path, wanted to start again, to know more, to learn more. To understand Spain, the Camino, others, and myself, more deeply. I wanted to go back—and do the things I'd skipped the first time, eat some of the dishes I'd missed. But then the global COVID-19 pandemic struck, and travel was no longer an option. Still, I couldn't leave the idea alone. The Camino had become so firmly cemented into my brain. I'd always been an incredibly keen walker, and this was not my first long-distance trek. But the changes in my life that began during the Camino seemed so deeply impactful and profound, and they continued on, long after I'd finished and returned home.

There is, I believe, nothing more conducive to clear thinking than long-distance walking. After the first couple of hundred kilometres, sola (alone), displaced, away from everything familiar—I was able to see more clearly, think more deeply, be more honest with myself.

I started to think of the Camino as not a solo trek but as a vast community of people coming together, over time. At least a thousand years. Probably much longer. Every footstep along the Camino lands on the footfall of the hundreds of thousands who went before, on centuries of history, and accumulated wisdom. And not just the people who went before, but the animals—the donkeys, horses, cattle, goats, dogs—all of us imprinting on the land, shaping the path for future pilgrims. I began to see walking as an act of faith, to see footfall as sight.

One cannot walk the Camino alone. As a pilgrim, you are dependent on thousands of people—other pilgrims, hospitaleros, volunteers, staff in albergues all along the route, priests and nuns, and an entire vast army of people who clean for, cook for, feed, and tend to pilgrims, day in and day out. Without them, no pilgrimage would be possible. And just as one pilgrimage ends, another begins—an endless infinite loop of walkers and seekers, carers, and providers.

The Camino changed me just as it changes almost everyone who ever does it. The long walk across Spain helped me climb off the ledge of a lifetime of high anxiety. I knew that my anxiety had helped nothing—served no useful purpose, and only made things worse, but I hadn't worked out a way to conquer it, and let it go.

There were other things that came about in my life as a result of walking the Camino. I felt less angry, less wronged, less judgmental, more forgiving, more appreciative, more thankful. It took me time to realize all the changes. I was home for months before I realized how utterly transformed I felt. Both the Camino and Spain lived on in me. They continue to do so. I was and am the living proof of Pliny the Elder's words, "From the end spring new beginnings."

Back home, I spent time cooking every Spanish dish I could think of, recreating the fare I'd eaten along the Way. All of it made me happy. I've included some of these recipes in this book. They are not meant to represent all of Spain or even all of the Camino, and they aren't necessarily absolutely authentic, since I experimented (by necessity) with ingredients I found locally. They are a few of my favourites—the simple recipes that I find myself turning to over and over again, keeping my connection with Spain and the Camino alive.

I fell deeply in love with Spain. I was so grateful for the experience. After I walked the Camino, love and happiness and gratitude started manifesting everywhere else in my life. I began to think of the importance of pilgrimage, not so much in religious, but in general, terms. After all, what is life if not one long pilgrimage? One long quest for meaning and connection and contribution. Words I barely thought of before my trek, let alone used, or hoped to embody.

After I returned from the Camino, and just before the global pandemic began, I went back to Australia with Chris, my ex. We'd moved there over and over, and yet somehow always ended up back in Canada. We left Canada with a baby when we first moved to Australia, and four years later, we returned to Canada with another new baby, our Australian-born daughter. In the years that followed, we moved back and forth between the two countries and eventually became Australian citizens. In many ways, we'd grown into our adulthoods in Australia. But we were always torn between the two nations and had come back to Canada in large part because that's where our aging parents were.

Chris and I spent the remainder of that (post-Camino) visit to Australia walking on wild empty beaches and through remote, dense forests, talking and dreaming about the possibility of a future together again. We were hiking in a forest of thousand-year-old myrtle beech and towering Australian mountain ash trees, as tall as California redwoods, when we first discussed the idea of reuniting. It was exhilarating and terrifying, but it also seemed like a natural progression. We'd back and forth-ed around the globe, why not in our marriage too? This is the geography we carry inside us—the maps and paths of our own beings. We knew each other like we knew nobody else and like nobody else knew us. We fit together. We loved each other. We had two beautiful daughters together. After a lifetime of moving homes and countries and continents, Chris was my home. What else mattered? Could we make it work? It was worth a try. Of course it was. Of course. Of course. Of course.

Later that year, after we returned home, we bought a house together. Our decades-long on-again-off-again relationship has never been better, happier, or stronger. And while I know that walking the Camino is not the sole reason for this, I also know that it played a huge role.

Somehow the long walk across Spain changed me, cured me, and most of all, opened me up again to all of the endless possibilities of love.

ACKNOWLEDGEMENTS

First, to Chris, with gratitude for a lifetime of love and support. For letting me go and taking me back. For being there, even when I wasn't. And to my beautiful, beloved daughters, Laura and Elly, and your partners, I cannot imagine a life without you.

Thank you to everyone at Goose Lane, including Susanne Alexander, publisher; Alan Sheppard, production editor; Julie Scriver, creative director; and also all the behind-the-scenes staff. A special shout-out to Simon Thibault, non-fiction acquisitions editor, for believing in this manuscript, providing editorial advice, and working patiently with me—my endless gratitude. And to Naomi K. Lewis and Jess Shulman for your diligent copy editing—thank you!

To Spain, and to all the hospitaleros and volunteers, and those who feed, house, and look after an endless stream of pilgrims, day after day, week after week, month after month, year after year—thank you for your kindness and for all your hard work. Bless your big, beautiful hearts.

To my fellow walkers: Sebastian, David and Camilla, Jeffrey, Gert, Joann, Sandra, Constance, Petra, Paul, Shell, Alistair, Kate, Kathy, Donna, Andrea, Uda, Cynthia, Will, Benedict, Leo, Silke, Guy, and all the others—thank you for your generosity and companionship. Eternal gratitude to Celine—for getting me to Spain in the first place.

To my friends — Joy McNevin, Elizabeth Greene, Wendy Frisch, Karen Rudie, Margi McKay, Carla Douglas, Susan Broad Kershaw (my first reader!), and Pamela Dillon — thank you all for your presence in my life.

To Don Gillmor, John MacIntyre, Susan Scott, Alex Strachan, Nicola Ross (my friend and mapmaker), Barbara Bell, Aara MacAuley, Isabel Huggan, and Tanis MacDonald—deepest gratitude for your support of my writing life.

To Michael Williams for my author photo, taken at the annual "Write on the French" Retreat at the Lodge at Pine Cove; and to Parnian Arjmand, for making me look presentable—my heartfelt appreciation.

And finally, profound gratitude to the Ontario Arts Council for various grants over the years, including the Writer's Works in Progress Grant that helped to support this work.

Packing List

Before You Leave Home

Consider programming the Pan European emergency number 112 into your cellphone and downloading this app, issued by the Spanish government: https://alertcops.ses.mir.es/mialertcops/info/info.xhtml

Basics

2 lightweight stuff sacks to keep your gear sorted

2 pairs pants (one of mine zipped off into shorts)

2 T-shirts, 1 long-sleeved shirt

2 water bottles—I used a pair of sturdy 500 mL recyclable water bottles

3 pairs underwear

3 pairs socks—Smartwool or Merino

eyeglasses/sunglasses

hat/gloves (lightweight) and a compact packable down jacket (for autumn/winter/spring walking)

hiking boots (lightweight) or sturdy hiking shoes

pillowcase with your name written or embroidered on it

raincoat and rain pants, or a rain poncho

sleeping bag (compact, compressible, lightweight: mine weighs 730 g)

sweater (Smartwool or polar fleece)

towel (Microfibre for quick drying)

Medical Kit and Valuables

acetaminophen/ibuprofen/antibiotic ointment/Pepto Bismol (travel size)

cross-body bag or fanny pack for valuables/personal items (cash, credit card, bank card)

passport, travel, and health insurance papers

prescription medications
travel documents and pilgrim
  credencial

medical tape/bandages/blister
  treatments

Miscellaneous

cellphone, adapter plug, charger
  (consider packing a two- or four-
  way USB charger)
clothes pegs (a few)
ear plugs (wax are more effective than
  foam; can be purchased in Spain)
eye shade
granola bars/power bars

guidebook (online versions also
  available for your smartphone)
knife, folding, with scissors (pack
  this with your stowed baggage)
laundry soap (in powder or bar)
notebook/pens
safety pins (large)
small sewing kit for repairs
Ziploc bags

Toiletries

brush/comb
multipurpose wet wipes, cut in half
  (useful for washing hands and
  face when bathroom and shower
  facilities are limited or unavailable)

nail clippers
sunscreen, deodorant (travel size will
  not last the whole Camino)
tissues (small package) or toilet paper
toothbrush/paste, soap/shampoo bar

Possible Additions

camera
backpack (small, nylon, ultra-
  lightweight for city outings, etc.)

guidebook (a maps-only version)
trekking pole(s) (I didn't bother)

Things I Wished I'd packed

book (I did not find an English
  bookstore in Spain)
leggings (can double as pyjamas and
  replace a pair of pants)
poncho (a good one, instead of a
  raincoat and rain pants)

shoes, lightweight compact (to wear
  out at night and travel in)
tunic, long lightweight

A Short Glossary
of Spanish Food and Beverage Terms

Basic Foods

apple—**manzana**

butter—**mantequilla**

cake—**la tarta or el pastel**

cheese—**queso**

ham—**jamón**

ice cream—**helado**

jam—**confitura** or **mermelada**

meat—**carne**

orange—**naranja**

salad—**ensalada**

sandwich—**sandwich** or **bocadillo** (a larger sandwich made on a baguette style loaf)

soup—**sopa**

without meat—**sin carne**

Coffee

black coffee—**Americano**

strong coffee with lots of hot, frothy milk—**café con leche**

single shot of espresso—**café solo**

espresso topped with frothy, hot milk—**cortado**

iced coffee—**café con hielo** (note the ice will come in a separate glass)

Water

carbonated water—**agua con gas**

water, a glass of—**un vaso de agua**

water, tap—**agua del grifo** or **agua natural**

Wine and Beer

beer—**una cerveza**

beer, bottled—**una botella de cerveza**

draft beer, double—**un doble**

draft beer, small—**una caña**

shandy—**una clara** (typically a beer mixed with a very slightly sweet mineral water) OR **una clara con limón** (a beer mixed with lemon-flavoured soft drink) OR **una clara muy clara** (higher ratio of soft drink to beer)

Cheers!—**¡Salud!**

wine, by the bottle—**una botella de vinto tinto/blanco**

wine, by the glass—**una copa de vinto tinto/blanco**

wine, red—**vino tinto**

wine, red with fruit and lemonade —**sangría**

wine, red with fizzy lemonade and a slice of lemon (less expensive than Sangría and very popular in Spain)—**tinto de verano**

wine, white—**vino blanco**

Useful Phrases and Food-related Terms

a menu, please—**la carta por favor/ un menú por favor**

a thousand thanks—**mil gracias**

how much is it?—**¿cuánto cuesta?**

I would like...please—**me gustaría... por favor** OR **me quisiera...por favor**

store—**la tienda**

supermarket/mini supermarket— **un supermercado** or **un mini supermercado**

thank you—**gracias**

the bill, please—**la cuenta, por favor**

Notes

1   John Noble Wilford, "When Humans Became Human," *New York Times*, February 26, 2002, https://www.nytimes.com/2002/02/26/science/when-humans-became-human.html.

2   A remarkable bonobo named Kanzi, living in the US, may be the exception that proves the rule about non-humans cooking their food. Raised amongst humans, Kanzi learned, among other things, both to build a fire and to cook marshmallows on a stick. See NBC News, "Marshmallow-Toasting Bonobo Charms Internet," April 14, 2014, https://www.nbcnews.com/science/science-news/marshmallow-toasting-bonobo-charms-internet-n82441.

3   It is widely believed that the word Compostela originates from the Latin, Campus Stellae (or field of stars). Others suggest that Compostela could derive from the Latin, Compositum or Composita Tella—meaning burial ground. See Wikipedia, "Santiago de Compostela," last modified June 10, 2013, accessed June 16, 2023, https://en.wikipedia.org/wiki/Santiago_de_Compostela.

4   Eric Blakemore, "Why Do We Know So Little About the Druids," *National Geographic*, November 15, 2019, https://www.nationalgeographic.com/history/article/why-know-little-druids.

5   Pliny the Elder, *The History of the World, Commonly Called the Naturall Historie of C. Plinius Secundus*, trans. Philemon Holland (London: A. Islip, 1634); Digitizing sponsor, Biodiversity Heritage Library, Smithsonian Libraries, accessed July 19, 2023, https://archive.org/details/historyofworldco21634plin/mode/2up.

6   Pliny the Elder, *The History of the World*, Book 19, 19, Section A, accessed July 21, 2023, https://archive.org/details/historyofworldco21634plin/page/18/mode/2up?view=theater&q=Pythagoras.

7   For my full packing list including the things I got wrong, see page 277.

8   World Population Review, "Olive Oil Productive by Country 2023," accessed June 16, 2023, https://worldpopulationreview.com/country-rankings/olive-oil-production-by-country.

9   World Population Review, "Wine Producing Countries 2023," accessed June 16, 2023, https://worldpopulationreview.com/country-rankings/wine-producing-countries.

10 Michael Eaude, *Catalonia: A Cultural History* (Oxford: Signal Books, 2007).

11 J. Robinson, ed., *The Oxford Companion to Wine*, 3rd ed., (Oxford: Oxford University Press, 2006), 652–65.

12 Torsten Günther et al, "Ancient genomes link early farmers from Atapuerca in Spain to modern-day Basques," *Anthropology* 112, no. 38, 119–22 (July 2015), https://www.pnas.org/doi/full/10.1073/pnas.1509851112.

13 All quotations from Rumi are from Shahram Shiva, *Rumi: The Beloved is You* (New York: Rumi Network, 2021).

14 John Brierley, *A Pilgrim's Guide to the Camino de Santiago*, 13th ed. (Camino Guides, 2016).

15 "Camping Out," by Ernest Hemingway, originally published in the *Toronto Daily Star* on June 26, 1920.

16 The Hemingway Soup recipe (also known as La Sopa de Navarra a la Burguete) is from: *The Hemingway Cookbook*, by Craig Boreth, Chicago Review Press, 1998. Copyright © 1998 by Craig Boreth. All rights reserved including the right of reproduction in whole or in part in any form. Any third-party use of this material, outside of this publication, is prohibited. This edition published by arrangement with Chicago Review Press c/o Susan Schulman Literary Agency.

17 The pan-European number for all emergency services is 112.

18 To see the wine fountain web cam, see "Fuente del vino," https://www.irache .com/es/fuente-del-vino.html.

19 Cotter, Adam, and Laura Savage, "Gender-based violence and unwanted sexual behaviour in Canada, 2018: Initial findings from the Survey of Safety in Public and Private Spaces," Statistics Canada, December 5, 2019, https://www150.statcan .gc.ca/n1/pub/85-002-x/2019001/article /00017-eng.htm.

20 Empanadas are thought to have first appeared in Medieval Iberia, during the Moorish Invasions. One of the earliest known references comes from a cookbook, *Libre del Coch*, by Robert de Nola, published in Catalan in 1520.

21 Gareth Thomas, "Foncebadón—Resurrection on the Margins," *Where Peter Is*, May 10, 2021, https://wherepeteris.com /postcard-5-foncebadon-resurrection-on -the-margins/#_ftn1.

22 This quotation is attributed to Ram Dass and is used with the permission of the Ram Dass Organization. For more information, please visit RamDass.org.

23 Wikipaella, "Where to Eat Authentic Paella?" accessed June 16, 2023, https:// wikipaella.org/.

24 Joshua Rapp Learn, "People Went Crazy for Almond Milk in the Middle Ages," *Discover Magazine*, February 9, 2021, https://www.discovermagazine.com /planet-earth/people-went-crazy-for -almond-milk-in-the-middle-ages.

25 Brownen Wallace, from the poem, "What it Comes to Mean," *Common Magic*, 78, Oberon Press, 1985.

26 Robert Macfarlane, *The Old Ways: A Journey on Foot* (New York: Penguin, 2012).

Index of Recipes

Bacon and Egg Paella 241

Basque Burnt Cheesecake 31

Bocadillo de Chorizo y Queso, Tostado 186

Bravas Sauce 204

Caldo Gallego 220

Clara 254

Clara con Limón 254

Chorizo al Vino Tinto 90

Empanadas de la Reina 179

Ensalada, Fruity 231

Ensalada, Savoury 230

Ensaladilla Ucraniana 123

Espinacas con Garbanzos 144

Fabada Asturiana 100

Flan 106

Hamburguesas de Cordero 114

Hemingway Soup 53

Lentejas 160

Membrillo y Manchego Tapas 153

Natillas 81

Pastel de Manzana 195

Patatas Bravas 203

Spanish Bar Cake with Burnt Butter Icing 258

Spanish Style Chorizo with Beans and Eggs a

  la Agés 130

Tapas Party Menu 266

Tex-Mex Chicken Tortillas in Spain 210

Tinto de Verano 22

Torta (or Tarta) de Santiago 247

Tortilla de Patatas/Tortilla Española 168

Trucha a la Navarra 45

Turrón de Chocolate Blando 60

Walk, Eat, Repeat combines Lindy Mechefske's passion for both food and hiking. One of Canada's foremost culinary writers, Mechefske is the author of four previous books on food and culture, including *Out of Old Ontario Kitchens* and *Sir John's Table: The Culinary Life and Times of Canada's First Prime Minister*, both of which won Taste Canada Gold Awards. A lifelong walker, her first experience of hiking was climbing peaks in the Adirondacks with her father as a five-year-old. Since then, Mechefske has hiked and climbed in the Alps, the Appalachians, and England's Lake District and Peak District. Mechefske lives in Kingston, Ontario.

Photo: Michael Willams